CONSIDERING THE RADIANCE

Books by A. R. Ammons

Ommateum, with Doxology (Dorrance, 1955)
Expressions of Sea Level (Ohio State University Press, 1963)
Corsons Inlet (Cornell University Press, 1965)
Tape for the Turn of the Year (Cornell University Press, 1965)
Northfield Poems (Cornell University Press, 1966)
Selected Poems (Cornell University Press, 1968)
Uplands (Norton, 1970)
Briefings: Poems Small and Easy (Norton, 1971)
Collected Poems 1951–1971 (Norton, 1972)
Sphere: The Form of a Motion (Norton, 1974)
Diversifications (Norton, 1975)
The Snow Poems (Norton, 1977)
The Selected Poems 1951–1977
(Norton, 1977; Expanded Edition, 1987)
Highgate Road (The Inkling X Press, 1977)
Six-Piece Suite (Palaemon Press Limited, 1978)
Selected Longer Poems (Norton, 1980)
A Coast of Trees (Norton, 1981)
Worldly Hopes (Norton, 1982)
Lake Effect Country (Norton, 1983)
Sumerian Vistas (Norton, 1987)
The Really Short Poems of A. R. Ammons (Norton, 1992)
Garbage (Norton, 1993)
The North Carolina Poems (North Carolina Wesleyan, 1994)
Set in Motion: Essays and Interviews
(University of Michigan Press, 1996)
Brink Road (Norton, 1996)
Glare (Norton, 1997)
Bosh and Flapdoodle (Norton, 2005)

CONSIDERING THE RADIANCE
Essays on the Poetry of
A. R. Ammons

EDITORS

David Burak and Roger Gilbert

ASSOCIATE EDITORS

Ingrid Arnesen, Alice Fulton,
Phyllis Janowitz, James McConkey

W. W. NORTON & COMPANY

NEW YORK • LONDON

For information about permission to reproduce selections from
this book, write to Permissions, W. W. Norton & Company, Inc.,
500 Fifth Avenue, New York, NY 10110

Manufacturing by The Courier Companies, Inc.
Book design by Brooke Koven
Production manager: Amanda Morrison

Library of Congress Cataloging-in-Publication Data

Considering the radiance : essays on the poetry of A.R. Ammons /
editors, David Burak and Roger Gilbert.—1st ed.
p. cm.
Includes bibliographical references.
ISBN 978-0-393-05999-1
1. Ammons, A. R., 1926—Criticism and interpretation. I. Burak,
David, 1945– II. Gilbert, Roger, 1960–
PS3501.M6Z73 2005
811'.54—dc22
2004027491

W. W. Norton & Company, Inc.
500 Fifth Avenue, New York, N.Y. 10110
www.wwnorton.com

W. W. Norton & Company Ltd.
Castle House, 75/76 Wells Street, London W1T 3QT

1 2 3 4 5 6 7 8 9 0

The City Limits

When you consider the radiance, that it does not withhold
itself but pours its abundance without selection into every
nook and cranny not overhung or hidden; when you consider

that bird's bones make no awful noise against the light but
lie low in the light as in a high testimony; when you consider
the radiance, that it will look into the guiltiest

swervings of the weaving heart and bear itself upon them,
not flinching into disguise or darkening; when you consider
the abundance of such resource as illuminates the glow-blue

bodies and gold-skeined wings of flies swarming the dumped
guts of a natural slaughter or the coil of shit and in no
way winces from its storms of generosity; when you consider

that air or vacuum, snow or shale, squid or wolf, rose or lichen,
each is accepted into as much light as it will take, then
the heart moves roomier, the man stands and looks about, the

leaf does not increase itself above the grass, and the dark
work of the deepest cells is of a tune with May bushes
and fear lit by the breadth of such calmly turns to praise.

A. R. AMMONS, 1926–2001

CONTENTS

PREFACE

David Burak

On the day after Valentine's Day in 1988, a particularly intriguing article appeared in *The New Yorker*. The invariably perceptive critic Helen Vendler speculated that after the publication of A. R. Ammons's definitive collected works, he would be considered one of the foremost poets of the twentieth century. In the years that followed, Ammons would, with a regularity which was often distressing even to Archie himself, find it necessary to refuse invitations to appear at a broad variety of institutions, including Notre Dame, the Smithsonian Institution, and Harvard, where Professor Vendler had hoped to have Archie read and make some comments to the Phi Beta Kappa students. Archie had wanted to honor the invitation to Harvard, and he'd been pleased when Vendler had told him that she felt that a reading of a selection from his work-in-progress, *Garbage*, would be quite appropriate for the occasion. However, as Professor Vendler noted, "Archie finally pleaded out of the Phi Beta Kappa appearance. His nerves got to him as they had on the occasion when he could not bear to come to [receive] the National Book Award." Despite Archie's difficulties with reading his work in public, he continued to create such a magnificent range and depth of poetic works that many of those individuals who believed his work merited widespread attention and respect continue to feel this is the case. Thus, we have brought together a volume of essays that provide illumination to a body of work that is, in turns, pragmatic and mystical, primitive and profound, steeped in a tradition that has deep roots in the rural South, and as sophisticated as that of any aesthete who cultivated his or her art while walking through New Haven, Boston, or New York.

Archie Ammons was also a true friend to many writers, young and/or aspiring. He would spend substantial amounts of time with us, focusing his attention on drafts of our poems and sharing drafts of his own works-in-progress. He was invariably careful not to critique our efforts in such a manner as to discourage us from continuing to improve our craft and pursue our aspirations. I can recall only a couple of occasions in approximately four decades when Archie became so vexed that his comments could be construed as lacerating, and these situations involved professorial peers who were strong enough to benefit from the criticism.

Thus, a few months after Archie's death, I was compelled to arrange a local-access television program in his honor. A group of colleagues and friends, including M. H. Abrams, James McConkey, Phyllis Janowitz, and Ingrid Arnesen, were all willing to venture downtown to Ithaca's Pegasus Studios to give tribute to the man who had been a close friend, colleague, mentor, and, in several cases, all three. Each participant read one of Archie's poems and commented briefly about why he or she selected the piece. A month later, then Cornell President Hunter Rawlings participated in a memorial service honoring Archie at the university's Sage Chapel, which was filled with approximately 500 people. A few days after that, I spoke with Mike Abrams and Jim McConkey about the idea of putting together a book comprised of some of the essays that most effectively elaborated upon Archie's unique poetic brilliance. Both of these gentlemen were quite encouraging about the potential merits of such a project and lent their support. Then Anna Geske joined the effort, bringing about three decades of wisdom as director of Cornell's Council for the Arts.

Shortly thereafter, we were fortunate to gain the involvement of Alice Fulton, the poet who has learned the most from Archie and managed to incorporate that often ineffable knowledge into her own modus operandi. Also, Phil Lewis, then dean of Cornell's College of Arts and Sciences, provided institutional and personal support that was crucial. In a similar vein, Roger Gilbert's willingness to become one of the editors and to take on the logistical responsibilities for expanding upon our extraordinary collection of essays and getting the material into presentable manuscript form, proved to be invaluable. Roger's intelligence and determination provided critical catalytic energy for bringing the project to a very high level of professional and aesthetic merit. In closing, I would like to express heartfelt gratitude for the involvement and support of Jill Bialosky, the Norton editor who has had oversight responsibility for bringing this volume to life. Also, we are appreciative of the efforts of Jill's assistant, Sarah Moriarty, for her close attention to the final preparation of the manuscript. Finally, we are most appreciative of the support of W. W. Norton & Company for its willingness to publish *Considering the Radiance* and, in so doing, provide an illuminating assessment of the work and life of one of America's most original and extraordinary poets.

INTRODUCTION

Roger Gilbert

Considering the Radiance: Essays on A. R. Ammons pays tribute to an American poet whom many consider one of the twentieth century's major figures. It also pays tribute to a teacher and conversationalist who left an indelible mark on the lives of countless students, friends, and colleagues. While several collections of essays on A. R. Ammons already exist, ours is the first to appear since the poet's death in 2001, and it therefore offers a more complete retrospect of his long and richly productive career than previous volumes have done. The critical essays in this book address every phase of Ammons's oeuvre, from his earliest beginnings in the 1950s to his late masterpieces, the long poems *Garbage* and *Glare*. But these essays also explore the more personal side of a poet some readers still see as forbiddingly abstract and intellectual. Many of the contributors to this volume were friends and students of the poet who knew him not as A. R. Ammons but as Archie, a warm, fragile man capable of painfully intense feelings as well as earthy humor.

This book is therefore intended not as a collection of scholarly articles, but as a gathering of appreciations, of both the poet and the man, addressed to the common reader rather than the specialist. Important scholarly work on Ammons has been compiled in two recent volumes, *Critical Essays on A. R. Ammons,* edited by Robert Kirschten (G. K. Hall, 1997) and *Complexities of Motion: New Essays on A. R. Ammons's Long Poems,* edited by Steven Schneider (Fairleigh Dickinson University Press, 1999), and future collections are sure to appear in coming years. Most of the essays we've chosen forgo the scholarly apparatus of footnotes and bibliography, offering more intimate accounts of Ammons's poetry and its pleasures. With one exception, we have also avoided reviews of the poet's books, since their occasional nature tends to occlude the larger perspective we've tried to present. For similar reasons we've excluded essays that focus on individual works by the poet. All of the critical essays included here offer a broad view of Ammons and his poetry, and we hope will be of special value to readers just beginning to discover the delights and complexities of his formidable body of work.

The collection begins with three crucial early essays that together helped consolidate Ammons's emerging reputation. Richard Howard's "The Spent Seer Consigns Order to the Vehicle of Change," originally published in 1966, offered the first extended consideration of the poet's work, and laid the ground for much subsequent discussion. This is followed by the longest piece in the collection, Harold Bloom's seminal 1971 essay "A. R. Ammons: 'When You Consider the Radiance,'" arguably the single most influential discussion of the poet. Bloom's essay powerfully situates Ammons in the Emersonian tradition, a view that subsequent critics have endorsed, questioned, or qualified, but seldom ignored. We've chosen to include John Ashbery's *New York Times* review of Ammons's *Collected Poems, 1951–1971,* "In the American Grain," both for its acuity and eloquence and because of Ashbery's frequent association with Ammons, who repeatedly cited him as the contemporary poet he most admired. (Ashbery's original review also dealt with John

Wheelwright's *Collected Poems*; we've excised most of that discussion for this book.)

The three essays that follow all appeared in 1973 in a special Ammons issue of the Cornell journal *Diacritics,* edited by Harold Bloom. The first two pieces are especially noteworthy as the work of two of Ammons's most important mentors in his early years, the poets Josephine Miles and Josephine Jacobsen; they are followed by a thoughtful discussion of Ammons's work by the late critic David Kalstone. In 1986 a special Ammons issue of *Pembroke* magazine appeared, edited by Shelby Stephenson, from which the next two essays are taken, by Daniel Mark Fogel and Frederick Buell. While a great deal of Ammons criticism was published in the nineties, most of it focused on individual poems, and can be sampled in the collections edited by Kirschten and Schneider mentioned above. We offer one piece from that decade, a 1998 essay by the poet and Nobel Prize–winning chemist Roald Hoffmann that was originally presented at a festival in honor of Ammons's retirement from teaching at Cornell. The remaining critical essays were published after Ammons's death in 2001. My own essay and those by Helen Vendler, David Lehman, Bonnie Costello, and James McConkey all take a valedictory look at the poet's long and varied career and try to describe the shape of its motion from its beginnings to its last phase.

These critical essays are followed by a group of more personal tributes to Ammons as a teacher and mentor. The longest of these, by the poet Alice Fulton, is also culled from the special Ammons issue of *Pembroke* magazine; the others all were written after the poet's death, several of them appearing in a special memorial issue of the Ithaca literary newspaper *The Bookpress.* Together these pieces offer moving testimony to the poet's dedication in working with younger writers. Bringing our selection of essays full circle, we conclude with an account by Zofia Burr of Ammons's decades-long correspondence with his own beloved teacher, Josephine Miles.

Many people have helped us to produce this tribute to Archie Ammons. Our thanks must go first to the authors of all the essays we have included, for their eloquence and insight. M. H. Abrams was a key supporter of this project from its inception, and offered much valuable advice. Kenneth McClane and Anna Geske also provided advice and encouragement along the way. We owe an enormous debt to the former Dean of the College of Arts and Sciences at Cornell, Philip Lewis, for his generous support of this project. Jill Bialosky and the staff of Norton have provided expert guidance at every stage. Finally, we would like to thank Phyllis Ammons for her support of this book.

CONSIDERING THE RADIANCE

"The Spent Seer Consigns Order to the Vehicle of Change"

Richard Howard

ALL OF A SUDDEN, with an unheralded and largely unacknowledged cumulus of books, a poet who accounts for himself with laconic diversity as the holder of the B.S. degree from Wake Forest College in North Carolina, as the principal of an elementary school in that state at the age of 26, as an executive, thereafter and inconsequently, in the biological glass industry:

> how you buy a factory:
> determine the lines of
> force
> leading in and out, origins, destinations of lines;
> determine how
> from the nexus of crossed and bundled lines
> the profit is
> obtained, the
> forces realized, the cheap made dear,
> and whether the incoming or outgoing forces are stronger
> (Collected Poems 119–120)

and currently as an English teacher:

> I'm waiting to hear if
> Cornell will give me
> a job: I need
>   to work &
>   maybe I write
>   too much:
>
> (Tape 62)

—suddenly, then, A. R. Ammons has exploded into the company of American poets which includes Whitman and Emerson and articulates the major impulse of the national expression: the paradox of poetry as process and yet impediment to process. More honestly than Whitman, acknowledging his doubts as the very source of his method ("teach me, father: behold one whose fears are the harnessed mares of his going!"), though without Whitman's dramatic surface, Ammons has traced out the abstractive tendency, the immaterialism that runs through all our *native strain,* in both acceptations of the phrase: to suffer or search out immersion in the stream of reality without surrendering all that is and makes one particularly oneself. The dialectic is rigorous in Ammons's version—the very senses which rehearse the nature of being for the self, the private instances of the sensuous world, must be surrendered to the experience of unity.

> we can approach
> unity only by the loss
>   of things—
> a loss we're unwilling
> to take—
> since the gain of unity
>   would be a vision
> of something in the
> continuum of nothingness:

> we already have things:
> why fool around?
>
> *(Tape 23)*

And how avoid the "humbling of reality to precept"? "Stake off no beginnings or ends, establish no walls," the poet urges, addressing that Unity: "I know if I find you I will have to leave the earth and go on out . . . farther than the loss of sight in the unseasonal, undifferentiated stark"—a region, a Death, to speak literally, where there is no poetry, no speech to one's kind, no correspondence perceived and maintained, but only the great soft whoosh of Being that has obsessed our literature from its classical figures, as Lawrence saw so clearly, down to Roethke, Wright Morris, Thornton Wilder.

In 1955, A. R. Ammons, a native and occasional resident of North Carolina, issued a wispy first book of poems and then held his peace, or rather his pugnacity, for ten years. When he next broke the silence, with a triad of voluble and original books at the age of forty, the development from that initial and inconclusive—certainly unconcluded—effort, the achievement in the terms of means and meaning reached so far that it is difficult, now, to see *Ommateum* for what it is, rather than an omen, a symptom.

The title means *compound eye,* as in an insect, and to the magnifying vision of such "iridescence of complex eyes" Ammons returns in the posterior books:

> I see how the bark cracks and winds like no other bark
> chasmal to my ant-soul running up and down
>
> *(Collected Poems 39)*

I suppose the thirty-some litanies in *Ommateum* are to be taken as so many various lenses, ways of looking at landscape, history and deity which together make up one of those strange bug-eyed views wherein the world is refracted into various but adjacent fragments. The book is dedicated to Josephine Miles, the distinguished poet and teacher Ammons had met during his studies (three semesters) at the University of California, and is prefaced by an arrogant, unsigned foreword which asserts that the poems "rather grow in the reader's mind than exhaust themselves in completed, external form." It is just such exhaustion, "the coercive charm of form" as Henry James called it, which the collection lacks, for all its nicely witnessed natural movements:

> and the snake shed himself in ripples
> across a lake of sand
>
> (*Collected Poems* 32)

or again, more wittily:

> The next morning I was dead
>   excepting a few peripheral cells
> and the buzzards
> waiting for a savoring age to come
> sat over me in mournful conversations
> that sounded excellent to my eternal ear
>
> (*Collected Poems* 13)

and despite its many fine passages, aspirations to share yet shed a nature regarded, throughout, as a goal and equally as a prison, the pitch is insistently wordy and too shrill:

> But the wind has sown loose dreams
> in my eyes
>   and telling unknown tongues
> drawn me out beyond the land's end
>   and rising in long
>   parabolas of bliss
> borne me safety
> from all those ungathered stones
>
> (*Collected Poems* 23–24)

After many such vociferations, one wonders whose voice it is that utters these hymns to—and against—Earth. The sapless lines, terminated only by the criterion of conversational or rhetorical sense, cannot beat against a stiffening rhythmic constant, and we are reminded of Miss Moore's prescription, taking her words in whatever pejorative sense they may bear: "ecstasy affords the occasion, and *expediency determines the form.*" Whose, then, is the voice that chants these prayers to the unstringing of all harps? The only aid the young poet affords is the assumption in several poems of the identity of the prophet Ezra. In a later book too, "I Ezra" returns, "the dying portage of these deathless thoughts," and we recall that this prophet is generally regarded as responsible for the revision and editing of the earlier books of Scripture and the determination of the canon. The persona appears in Ammons's poems, I think, when he is desperate for an authoritative voice; the nature of his enterprise is so extreme, and the risks he is willing to take with hysterical form and unguarded statement (unguarded by image, as Coleridge said that "a whole Essay might be writing on the Danger of *thinking* without Images") so parlous, that the need for such *authority* must be pretty constant:

> I am Ezra
> As a word too much repeated
> falls out of being
>
> (Collected Poems 1)

Yet even in this first book, especially as we tend to read it with the later work in mind, as a propaedeutic function of that work, it is evident that Ammons has discovered his tremendous theme: putting off the flesh and taking on the universe. Despite a wavering form, an uncertain voice, Ammons means to take on the universe the way Hemingway used to speak of taking on Guy de Maupassant—the odds, it is implied, more than a little in favor of the challenger. Here in *Ommateum*, then, is the first enunciation of the theme, in the crude form of a romantic pantheism:

Leaving myself on the shore
I went away
and when a heavy wind caught me I said
 My body lies south
 given over to vultures and flies
and wrung my hands
so the wind went on
· · · · · · · · · · · · · ·
The flies were gone
The vultures no longer searched
the ends of my hingeless bones
· ·
Breathing the clean air
I picked up a rib
 to draw figures in the sand
       (*Collected Poems* 9–10)

And more decisively, in one of the finest early pieces, with its
many echoes of Pound's diction and of course the metric of Dr.
Williams, properly assimilated to the poet's own requirements
which are speed, ease, and the carol of the separate phrase:

Peeling off my being I plunged into
the well
The fingers of the water splashed
  to grasp me up
  but finding only
  a few shafts
of light
  too quick to grasp
  became hysterical
  jumped up and down
  and wept copiously
So I said I'm sorry dear well but
went on deeper
finding patched innertubes beer cans

           and black roothairs along the way
           but went on deeper
           till darkness snuffed the shafts of light
               against the well's side
                  night kissing
               the last bubbles from my lips
                          (*Collected Poems* 10–11)

By the time, ten years later, of his second book, *Expressions
of Sea Level,* Ammons had extended and enriched this theme to
stunning effect—not only in versions of nature and the body, but
in terms of poetics as well, enforcing the substitution of the negative All for the single possibility of being.

            go back:
            how can I
         tell you what I have not said: you must look for it

         yourself: that

         side has weight, too, though words cannot bear it
         out: listen for the things I have left out:
               I am
               aware
         of them as you must be, or you will miss

         the non-song

         in my singing:
                          (*Collected Poems* 91)

Here Ammons has found, or fetched out, besides a functioning
arrangement of words on the page, the further device of the
colon, which he henceforth wields in its widest application as
almost his only mark of punctuation—a sign to indicate not
only equivalence, but the node or point of passage on each side
of which an existence hangs in the balance:

a tree, committed as a tree,
cannot in a flood
    turn fish,
sprout gills (leaves are
    a tree's gills) and fins:
    the molluscs
dug out of mountain peaks
are all dead:

(*Collected Poems* 83)

This observation, from a long poem called "Risks and Possibilities"—one of the penalties of his method, of course, is that Ammons requires length in order to indulge his effects, lacking that compression of substance which amounts to a "received form"—exhibits, too, a curious and rueful connivance with the universal doxology that to represent any one form of life is a limitation, a limitation that cannot be transcended beyond the mere consciousness of it. For only limited forms of life *matter,* and I intend the pun—are of *material consequence.* In one of his saddest poems, an astonishing meditation called "Guide," Ammons admits that it is not, really, worth "giving up everything to eternal being but direction," as the wind has done. With the humility of a man whose enormous ambitions have been chastened by a constatation of his restricted place in the world— and the chastening has been a religious experience, in the literal sense of religion: a linking, a binding, even a fettering—the poet returns to his body, his particular geography, and even his rather bleak sociology. Stretching his long legs on late-afternoon walks down the Jersey coast, he has learned that "when I got past relevance the singing shores told me to turn back":

What light there
no tongue turns to tell
to willow and calling shore

though willows weep and shores sing always
(*Collected Poems* 71–72)

In *Expressions of Sea Level* we are given a lot more to go
on, and consequently go a lot farther, than the persona of Ezra
and some rhapsodic landscapes of apocalypse. We are given,
with great attention to vegetable detail and meteorological con-
ditioning, the scenes of the poet's childhood in a North Carolina
backwoods, the doctrine and rationale of his metaphysical aspirations:

                              the precise and
            necessary worked out of random, reproducible,
          the handiwork redeemed from chance,
                              (*Collected Poems* 79)

              I will show you
        the underlying that takes no image to itself,
            cannot be shown or said,
      but weaves in and out of moons and bladderweeds,
              is all and
          beyond destruction
          because created fully in no
      particular form:
                              (*Collected Poems* 115)

and the resignation, the accommodation of himself to the tidal
marshes of New Jersey as the site of the poet's individual drama.
Here is a man obsessed by Pure Being who must put up with a
human incarnation when he would prefer to embody only the
wind, the *anima* of existence itself:

          So it came time
              for me to cede myself
          and I chose

    the wind
        to be delivered to

The wind was glad
      and said it needed all
the body
it could get
    to show its motions with . . .
                  (*Collected Poems* 75–76)

With the acknowledgment of these limitations has come an interest in other, equally limited, possibilities. One of Ammons's most interesting sidelines, a lagoon of his main drift, is a concern with archaic cultures whose aspect often reminds us, in its amalgam of the suggestive detail and the long loose line, in its own prose music, of Perse:

Returning silence unto silence,
the Sumerian between the rivers lies.
His skull crushed and molded into rock
    does not leak or peel.
The gold earring lies in the powder
of his silken, perished lobe.
The incantations, sheep trades, and night-gatherings
    with central leaping fires,
roar and glare still in the crow's-foot
walking of his stylus on clay.
                  (*Collected Poems* 47)

But not until a most recent book, *Corsons Inlet,* would the mode be brought into accord with the main burden of Ammons's song—the mad thing of his impulse. Song may seem an odd word for a verse in which I have described the music of prose, a verse which is as near as words can get us to our behavior, no more than a fairly cautious means of putting down phrases so that they will keep. Yet though the iambic cadence, and all it

implies and demands by way of traditional lilt, has been jetti-
soned as utterly as Dr. Williams ever decreed, there *is* a song in
Ammons's windy lines, a care for the motion of meaning in language which is the whole justice of prosody; consider the invocation to the wind, one more of many, and perhaps the loveliest:

> When the tree of my bones
> > rises from the skin I said
> come and whirlwinding
> stroll my dust
> > around the plain
>
> so I can see
> > how the ocotillo does
> and how saguaro-wren is
> and when you fall
> > with evening
>
> fall with me here
> > where we can watch
> the closing up of day
> and think how morning breaks
> > > > > (*Collected Poems* 76)

There is another strand of discourse in *Expressions of Sea
Level*, whose very title gives an idea of Ammons's use of new
vocabulary, one that Kenneth Burke would call "scientistic," I
guess, to mean the dramatic use of an exact nomenclature, in
Ammons's case a use quite properly managed:

> An individual spider web
> identifies a species:
>
> an order of instinct prevails
> > through all accidents of circumstances
> > though possibility is

high along the peripheries of
spider
        webs:
      you can go all
   around the fringing attachments

    and find
disorder ripe,
entropy rich, high levels of random,
    numerous occasions of accident:
                 (*Collected Poems* 114)

this poem concludes:

      if the web were perfectly pre-set
      the spider could
  never find
  a perfect place to set it in: and

      if the web were
perfectly adaptable,
if freedom and possibility were without limit,
      the web would
lose its special identity:
                 (*Collected Poems* 115)

The dangers of this kind of thing, the dangers of which Coleridge spoke, were evident, of course, to the author of "River," whose mastery of natural imagery and vocalic music is exact and generous, as in this example of what Hopkins called "vowelling off":

I shall
  go down
    to the deep river, to the moonwaters,

> where the silver
> willows are and the bay blossoms,
>
> to the songs
>   of dark birds,
>   to the great wooded silence
> of flowing
> forever down the dark river
>
> silvered at the moon-singing of hidden birds:
>   (*Collected Poems* 103)

The repetition of the short *i* and the variants on the sound of "river" in "forever" and "silvered" in the last two lines—not to sound too much like the late Dr. Sitwell—indicate and insure a consciousness of effects that become the living twist of things we call idiom.

Insurance is what we shall mostly need in dealing with Ammons's next book. Mooning around the house and waiting for *Expressions of Sea Level* to come off the press in December of 1964, the poet produced, in a two-month period, and with a determination to reach an end that became more than obsessive, became self-destructive, "a long thin poem" written on a huge roll of adding-machine tape run through the typewriter to its conclusion ("I am attracted to paper, visualize kitchen napkins scribbled with little masterpieces: so it was natural for me . . ."). The "serious novelty" of the enterprise is unquestionable, and there are many beautiful tropes in this long *Tape for the Turn of the Year,* chiefly in the form of pious assurances that the undertaking is or will be worthwhile:

> let this song
> make
> complex things salient,
> saliences clear, so

there can be some
understanding:

(*Tape* 4–5)

Enough to suggest that the text is not so much a poem as the
ground of a poem, the dark backing of a mirror out of which all
brightness may, as a condition, come. There are two moments of
confrontation, when Ammons links his 200-page transcribed
tape with the generality of his gift as a poet:

ecology is my word: tag
me with that: come
in there:
you will find yourself
in a firmless country:
centers & peripheries
in motion,
organic,
interrelations!

that's the door: here's
the key: come in,
celebrant,
to one meaning
that totals my meanings:

(*Tape* 112)

The other moment of address follows closely:

my other word is
provisional:
. . . .
you may guess
the meanings from *ecology*:

> don't establish the
>   boundaries
>   first,
>   . . . .
>   and then
>   pour
>   life into them, trimming
> off left-over edges,
> ending potential:
> . . . .
>   the center-arising
>   form
>   adapts, tests the
>   peripheries, draws in,
> finds a new factor,
> utilizes a new method,
>   gains a new foothold,
> responds to inner & outer
> change:
>
>   (*Tape* 116–117)

This is the poet arguing himself onward. His book arrives, the Muse ("a woman in us who gives no rest") reassures him (if not us), and in acknowledgment he turns, a moment, to address us before returning to his vocation in the most luscious of his books so far, *Corsons Inlet*:

> I've given you the
> interstices: the
>   space between
>   . . . .
>   I've given you
>   the dull days
> when turning & turning
> revealed nothing:

. . . .
    I've given
you long
uninteresting walks
so you could experience
vacancy:
. . . .
our journey is done:
thank you
for coming:
. . . .
the sun's bright:
the wind rocks the
   naked trees:

                        (Tape 204–205)

Published almost simultaneously with the indiscreet, revelatory *Tape, Corsons Inlet,* from the title poem with its sure grasp of site ("the 'field' of action with moving, incalculable center") to the farewell to the reader, to poetry, and to the spirit of place given at the end ("surrendered self among unwelcoming forms: stranger, hoist your burdens, get on down the road"), stands as the farthest and still the most representative reach into, upon, and against Being which the poet has yet made. It opens with a poem that nicely illustrates the perfected diction Ammons has now achieved, a rhythmical certainty which does not depend on syllable-counting or even accentual measure, but on the speed and retard of words as they move together in the mind, on the shape of stanzas as they follow the intention of the discourse, and on the *rests* which not so much imitate as create the soft action of speech itself. There is a formality in these gentle lines which is new to American poetry, as we say that there is a draughtmanship in the "drop-drawings" of Pollock which is new to American painting: each must be approached with a modulated set of expectations if we are able to realize what the poet, the painter is about. Consider the close of this first poem, "Visit," in Ammons's fourth book, and compare its resonance—reserved but not evasive, convinced but not assertive—with the heartier music of a similar passage, too famous to quote, in Frost:

> or you can come by the shore:
>
> choose the right: there the rocks
> cascade less frequently, the grade more gradual:
> treat yourself gently: the ascent thins both
>   mind and blood and you must
>   keep still a dense reserve
>
> of silence we can poise against
> conversation: there is little news:
> I found last month a root with shape and
>   have heard a new sound among
>   the insects: come.
>
> *(Collected Poems* 130)

The device of the colon helps keep a dense reserve of silence to poise against the "conversation" here, and the reason for the visit—finding a root with shape and hearing a new sound—is a kind of compressed *ars poetica* of Ammons's enterprise, that understanding of natural process which will include the negative moment: "what destruction am I blessed by" the poet asks in "the moment's height," but his prosody asks the question in a firmer, more axiological *set,* the resources of imagism that are generally employed to accommodate a natural movement here made over to a powerful abstraction:

> exhilaration
> sucking him up,
>
> shuddering and
> lifting

him
jaw and bone

and he said
what

destruction am I
blessed by?

(*Collected Poems* 160–161)

Then comes the book's title poem, like so many of Ammons's largest statements that account of "a walk over the dunes" which is also a natural history of the poem itself:

the walk liberating, I was released from forms,
from the perpendiculars,
     straight lines, blocks, boxes, binds
of thought
into the hues, shadings, rises, flowing bends and blends
     of sight:

(*Collected Poems* 148)

The interrelations of *making* and of a beneficent destruction are here followed out ("I was released from forms"), the actions of sea and land serving as the just emblem of the mind's resources, so that the poet can discuss his undertaking precisely in the terms of his locus, and indeed acknowledges his inability to wield any terms *except* those afforded him by what Kenneth Burke calls the scene-agent ratio:

          I allow myself eddies of meaning:
yield to a direction of significance
running
like a stream through the geography of my work:
   you can find

in my sayings
>
>>swerves of action
>>like the inlet's cutting edge:
>there are dunes of motion,
organizations of grass, white sandy paths of remembrance
in the overall wandering of mirroring mind:

but Overall is beyond me: is the sum of these events
I cannot draw, the ledger I cannot keep, the accounting
beyond the account:
>>>>>>(*Collected Poems* 148)

It is characteristic that so many of these poems—and in the previous book as in the one to come—take up their burden from
the shore, the place where it is most clearly seen that "every living thing is in siege: the demand is life, to keep life"; whether he
investigates the small white blacklegged egret, the fiddler crab,
the black shoals of mussels, the reeds, grass, bayberry, yarrow,
or "pulsations of order in the bellies of minnows," Ammons is
concerned to enunciate a dialectic, "the working in and out,
together and against, of millions of events," and *event* is precisely his word—

>>>>>no finality of vision,
>that I have perceived nothing completely,
>>that tomorrow a new walk is a new walk.
>>>>>(*Collected Poems* 151)

he insists: Ammons rehearses a marginal, a transitional experience, he is a littoralist of the imagination because the shore, the
beach, or the coastal creek is not a *place* but an *event*, a transaction where land and water create and destroy each other, where
life and death are exchanged, where shape and chaos are won and
lost. It is here, examining "order tight with shape: blue tiny flowers on a leafless weed: carapace of crab: snail shell" that Ammons

finds his rhythms, "fastening into order enlarging grasps of disorder," and as he makes his way down the dunes, rhythms are "reaching through seasons, motions weaving in and out!"

The rebellion against Being and into eternity is put down by the body itself on those expeditions the poet makes, safaris into mortality which convince him that "the eternal will not lie down on any temporal hill," and that he must "face piecemeal the sordid reacceptance of my world." It is not acceptance, but *reacceptance* which must be faced, the world which must be learned *again* as the poet, borrowing Shelley's beautiful image, "kindles his thoughts, blowing the coals of his day's bright conscious" in order "to make green religion in winter bones." In *Corsons Inlet* doctrine has been assimilated into "one song, an overreach from which all possibilities, like filaments, depend: killing, nesting, dying, sun or cloud, figure up and become song—simple, hard: removed." That is Ammons's definition of his aspiration—a long way from the breezy expostulations in *Ommateum*—and, I believe, of his achievement as well: his awareness and his imagination have coincided. Not that the poet has lost his initial impulse—for example, the close of the finest poem in that first volume, quoted earlier—"night kissing / the last bubbles from my lips"—finds itself enlarged and suited to the poet's wider utterance here, so that the poem called "Libation" in *Corsons Inlet* ends: "Now keep me virile and long at love: / let submission kiss off / the asking words from lips." There is a loyalty to finite being, "losing the self to the victory / of stones and trees, / of bending sandpit lakes, crescent / round groves to dwarf pine," Ammons says in the last poem of the book, "Gravelly Run," a central impulse that "extends the form, leads us on," and if there is also a freedom to explore an eccentric impulse, as in the brilliant poem "The Strait," it is a freedom granted because the divergent "filaments" have been braided back into the main strand, a rope of sand indeed. The poem concerns a worshipper at the phythoness' cave, questioning the ways of receiving the oracle, and ends with the kind of "simple, hard: removed" words which so often suggest, in the poet, the pre-Socratic impulse:

go

to your fate:
if you succeed, praise the
    god:
if you fail,
discover your flaw."
                    (*Collected Poems* 109)

Yet such terrors of self-knowledge are generally, by this climax of submissive response in the poet's work, abated by his more habitual reference to the design, the order, the form of the natural world: "for it is not so much to know the self," Ammons admits,

as to know it as it is known
    by galaxy and cedar cone,
as if birth had never found it
and death could never end it:
                    (*Collected Poems* 55–56)

In 1966 Ammons published his fifth book, in which again "events of sense alter old dunes of mind, release new channels of flow, free materials to new forms": *Northfield Poems* enacts Ammons's now familiar insurgence against finitude, and his resignation, once the impossibilities of both macrocosm and molecule are confessed, to the demands of form as *the vehicle of change*:

            unlike wind
        that dies and
    never dies I said
        I must go on
                consigned to
        form that will not
    let me loose

except to death
till some
syllable's rain
anoints my tongue
and makes it sing
to strangers:

(*Collected Poems* 59)

"some syllable's rain" intimates this poet's trust in language, when any confidence in the body's identity, as in that of bog and bay, is lost; in all these "riding movements" the transformation finally relied on is the transformation of process into words; as Valéry said in the canonical utterance about such littoral metamorphoses, the poet comes to learn *le changement des rives en rumeur,* the change of shores to sound. For Ammons, there is a liberation as well as an acknowledgment of inadequacy about his failure to reduce himself to singleness or to swell to a "savage" chaos:

when I tried to think by what
millions of grains of events
    the tidal creek had altered course,
        when I considered alone
a record
of the waves on the running blue creek,
    I was released into a power beyond my easy failures,

(*Collected Poems* 139)

The power is the strength, the wit, the *balance* of mind which enables him to fall back on his verbal nature, acknowledging that "the dissolved reorganizes to resilience" in his language, that reflexive tool of his specific incarnation:

only the book of laws founded
against itself,

founded on freedom of each event to occur as itself,
lasts into the inevitable balance events will take.

(Collected Poems 140)

Ammons's poems are that book of laws founded against itself, perpetually questioning not only the finality, but the very finitude of the world, deploring in an almost Catharist way the "fact" that "coming into matter, spirit fallen trades eternity for temporal form," asserting that it is their part to consummate— by the "gist of 'concrete observations,' plaint to the drift"—the world's body which, as in "February Beach," is in constant modification:

> creation may not be complete,
> that the land may not have been
> given
> permanently,
> that something remains
> to be agreed on,
> a lofty burn of sound, a clamoring and
> coming on:

(Collected Poems 159)

In this metaphysical breviary, the self is forever giving itself instructions about its own disembodied aspirations—"if you must leave the shores of mind," Ammons adjures his "Discoverer," reverting to his familiar accommodation of the Sea of Being in the salt marshes of Northfield,

> if to gather darkness
> into light, evil into good,
> you must leave the shores of mind,
> remember us, return and rediscover us.

(Collected Poems 137)

The dissident Ezra, who reappears in one or another of these poems, is said to listen from terraces of mind "wind cannot reach or weedroots"—and at once we know this is not the Way: for Ammons, only what comes back into being by an eternal yet secular reversion—remembered, returned to, rediscovered—is viable:

> The world is bright after rain
> for rain washes death out of the land and hides it far
> beneath the soil and it returns again cleansed with life
>   and so all is a circle
> and nothing is separable
>   (*Collected Poems* 36)

Indeed, the prophetic lurch to the edges of being—into the "scientific" area of "cytoplasm's grains and vacuoles" on the one hand, and the pulsing, shooting abstractions of "matter and energy" on the other—is repudiated in the final statement of *Northfield Poems,* though there are no final statements in the world of Ammons, of course, only articles of belief, only a mastered credulity:

> energy's invisible
> swirls confused, surpassed
> me: from that edge
> I turned back,
> strict with limitation,
> to my world's
> bitter acorns
> and sweet branch water.
>   (*Collected Poems* 183)

A. R. Ammons:
"When You Consider the Radiance"

Harold Bloom

> *Nature centers into balls,*
> *And her proud ephemerals,*
> *Fast to surface and outside,*
> *Scan the profile of the sphere;*
> *Knew they what that signified,*
> *A new genesis were here.*
>
> Emerson, "Circles"

I N 1955, A. R. AMMONS, in his thirtieth year, published his first book of poems, *Ommateum, with Doxology*. *Ommateum* consists of thirty Whitmanian chants, strongly influenced by the metric of Ezra Pound (though by nothing else in Pound). *Doxology* is an intricate religious hymn, in three parts, more ironic in tone than in direction. In the lengthening perspective of American poetry, the year 1955 will be remembered as the end of Wallace Stevens's career, and the beginning of Ammons's, himself not Stevens's heir but like Stevens a descendant of the great originals of American Romantic tradition, Emerson and Whitman. Beyond its experimentation with Poundian cadences, *Ommateum* shows no trace of the verse fashions of the fifties; I cannot detect in it the voice of William Carlos Williams, which indeed I do not hear anywhere in

Ammons's work, despite the judgments of several reviewers. This line of descent from Emerson and Whitman to the early poetry of Ammons is direct, and even the Poundian elements in *Ommateum* derive from that part of Pound that is itself Whitmanian.

Ommateum's subject is poetic incarnation, in the mode of Whitman's *Sea-Drift* pieces, Emerson's "Seashore," and Pound's "Canto II." The Whitman of "As I Ebb'd with the Ocean of Life" is closest, suggesting that poetic disincarnation is Ammons's true subject, his vitalizing fear. In the "Foreword" to *Ommateum* he begins his list of themes with "the fear of the loss of identity." The first poem of the volume, the chosen beginning of this poet's outrageously and wonderfully prolific canon, is an assumption of another's identity. This other, "Ezra," is neither Pound nor the biblical scribe of the Return, but a suddenly remembered hunchback playmate from childhood, brought back to the poet's consciousness by a report of his death in war. The whole of Ammons is in the first poem, but half a lifetime's imaginings will be necessary to transfigure this shore-burst into the radiance already implicit here:

> So I said I am Ezra
> and the wind whipped my throat
> gaming for the sounds of my voice
>   I listened to the wind
> go over my head and up into the night
> Turning to the sea I said
>   I am Ezra
> but there were no echoes from the waves
> The words were swallowed up
>   in the voice of the surf
> or leaping over swells
> lost themselves oceanward
>   Over the bleached and broken fields
> I moved my feet and turning from the wind

>   that ripped sheets of sand
>   from the beach and threw them
>   like seamists across the dunes
>   swayed as if the wind were taking me away
>   and said
>   I am Ezra
>   As a word too much repeated
>   falls out of being
>   so I Ezra went out into the night
>   like a drift of sand
>   and splashed among the windy oats
>   that clutch the dunes
>   of unremembered seas

>   (*Collected Poems* 1)

As in the "Ode to the West Wind" and "As I Ebb'd with the Oceans of Life," so here the poet's consciousness is assaulted by the elements he seeks to address, reproved by what he hopes to meet in a relationship that will make him or keep him a poet. The motto of Ammons's first poem might be Whitman's:

Nature here in sight of the sea taking advantage of me to dart
    upon me and sting me,
Because I have dared to open my mouth to sing at all.

Later in *Ommateum*, Ammons echoes "As I Ebb'd" more directly, recalling its terrifying contraction of the self:

>   Me and mine, loose windrows, little corpses,
>   Froth, snowy white, and bubbles,
>   (See, from my dead lips the ooze exuding at last,
>   See, the prismatic colors glistening and rolling,)
>   Tufts of straw, sands, fragments . . .

This becomes, in his ninth chant, Ammons's emblems of the last stage of "peeling off my being":

but went on deeper
till darkness snuffed the shafts of light
    against the well's side
        night kissing
    the last bubbles from my lips
                            (*Collected Poems* 11)

The Emersonian ambition to be possessed fully by the Transcendental Self is Ammons's early theme as it was Whitman's, and is still pervasive in Ammons's latest lyrics, but turned now in a direction avoided by his precursors:

When you consider the radiance, that it does not withhold
itself but pours its abundance without selection into every
nook and cranny not overhung or hidden; when you consider

that bird's bones make no awful noise against the light but
lie low in the light as in a high testimony; when you consider
the radiance, that it will look into the guiltiest

swervings of the weaving heart and bear itself upon them,
not flinching into disguise or darkening; when you consider
the abundance of such resource as illuminates the glow-blue

bodies and gold-skeined wings of flies swarming the dumped
guts of a natural slaughter or the coil of shit and in no
way winces from its storms of generosity; when you consider

that air or vacuum, snow or shale, squid or wolf, rose or lichen,
each is accepted into as much light as it will take, then
the heart moves roomier, the man stands and looks about, the

leaf does not increase itself above the grass, and the dark
work of the deepest cells is of a tune with May bushes
and fear lit by the breadth of such calmly turns to praise.
                            (*Collected Poems* 320)

This extraordinary poem, "The City Limits," marks one of the limits of Ammons's art, and almost releases him from the burden of his main tradition. "The guiltiest swervings of the weaving heart," for a poet as poet, are those that swerve him away from his poetic fathers into an angle of fall that is also his angle of vision. For an Emersonian poet, an American Romantic, the angle of vision becomes the whole of life, and measures him as man. Sherman Paul, acutely measuring Emerson's own angle, provides the necessary gloss for this Emersonian poem, "The City Limits":

> The eye brought him two perceptions of nature—nature ensphered and nature atomized—which corresponded to the distant and proximate visual power of the eye. These powers, in turn, he could have called the reasoning and understanding modes of the eye. And to each he could have assigned its appropriate field of performance: the country and the city.

We can surmise that the sorrow of all Emersonian poets, from Whitman to Ammons and beyond, comes from the great central declaration: "I become a transparent eyeball; I am nothing; I see all; the currents of the Universal Being circulate through me; I am part or particle of God." But if "Thought is nothing but the circulations made luminous," then what happens when the circulations are darkening? The currents of the Universal Being do not cease to circulate, ever, and the "mathematic ebb and flow" of Emerson's "Seashore" is no consolation to temperaments less rocky than Emerson's own (one thinks not of Whitman, but of middle Stevens, and late Roethke). To a grim consciousness like Frost in "Directive," the wisdom of the Emerson of *The Conduct of Life* is acceptable, admirable, even inevitable, and this late Emersonian strain may never be so worked out in our poetry as to vanish. But Ammons has none of it, and the toughness of his own consolations and celebrations comes out of another tradition, one that I do not understand, for everything that is Southern in American culture is necessarily a darkness to me. Ammons is a poet of the Carolina as well as the Jersey shore, and his relation to Whitman is severely modified by rival spirits of place. The Ezra-poet is as obsessed with sandstorms as any Near Easterner; for him the wind makes sheets of sand into sea mists. In "The City Limits" the radiance, despite its generosity, cannot reach what is overhung or hidden, and what is wholly hidden cannot be accepted into the light it will not take. There is for Ammons a recalcitrance or unwilling dross in everything given, and this "loneliness" (to use one of his words for it) marks his verse from *Ommateum* on as more than a little distinct from its great precursors.

I am writing of Ammons as though he had rounded his first circle in the eye of his readers, and there is no other way to write about him, even if my essay actually introduces him to some of its readers. The fundamental postulates for reading Ammons have been set down well before me, by Richard Howard and Marius Bewley in particular, but every critic of a still emergent poet has his own obsessions to work through, and makes his own confession of the radiance. Ammons's poetry does for me what Stevens's did earlier, and the High Romantics before that: it helps me to live my life. If Ammons is, as I think, the central poet of my generation, because he alone has made a heterocosm, a second nature in his poetry, I deprecate no other poet by this naming. It is, surprisingly, a rich generation, with ten or a dozen poets who seem at least capable of making a major canon, granting fortune and persistence. Ammons, much more than others, has made such a canon already. A solitary artist, nurtured by the strength available for him only in extreme isolation, carrying on the Emersonian tradition with a quietness directly contrary to nearly all its other current avatars, he has emerged in his most recent poems as an extraordinary master, comparable to the Stevens of *Ideas of Order* and *The Man with the Blue Guitar*. To track him persistently, from his origins in *Ommateum* through his maturing in *Corsons Inlet* and its companion volumes on to his new phase in *Uplands* and *Briefings,* is to be found by not only a complete possibility of imaginative experience, but by a renewed sense of the whole line of Emerson, the vitalizing and much maligned tradition that has accounted for most that matters in American poetry.

Emerson, like Stevens and Ammons after him, had a fondness for talking mountains. One thinks of Wordsworth's old men, perhaps of the Virgilian Mount Atlas, of Blake's Los at the opening of Night V, *The Four Zoas,* of Shelley's Mont Blanc, which obstinately refuses however to take on human form, and affronts the human revolutionary with its hard, its menacing otherness. Emerson's Monadnoc is genial and gnomic:

> "Monadnoc is a mountain strong,
> Tall and good my kind among;
> But well I know, no mountain can,
> Zion or Meru, measure with man.
> For it is on zodiacs writ,
> Adamant is soft to wit:
> And when the greater comes again
> With my secret in his brain,
> I shall pass, as glides my shadow
> Daily over hill and meadow.
> . . . .
> Anchored fast for many an age,
> I await the bard and sage,
> Who, in large thoughts, like fair pearl-seed,
> Shall string Monadnoc like a bead."

Emerson is not providing the golden string to be wound into a ball, but one of a series of golden entities to be beaded on a string. Monadnoc awaits the Central Man, the redemptive poet of "Bacchus." Thoreau, in his fine poems on the mountains, characteristically avoids Emerson's humanizing of an otherness, and more forcefully mountainizes himself:

But special I remember thee,
Wachusett, who like me
Standest alone without society.
Thy far blue eye,
A remnant of the sky,
Seen through the clearing or the gorge,
Or from the windows of the forge,
Doth leaven all it passes by.
. . . .
Upholding heaven, holding down earth,
Thy pastime from thy birth;
Nor steadied by the one, nor leaning on the other,
May I approve myself thy worthy brother!

Wachusett is not to be strung like a bead, however strong the bard and sage. Thoreau is a more Wordsworthian poet than Emerson, and so meets a nature ruggedly recalcitrant to visionary transformations. Ammons, who has a relation to both, meets Emerson's kind of mountains, meets a nature that awaits its bard, even if sometimes in ambush. In *Ommateum*, there is not much transformation, and some ambuscade, and so the neglect encountered by the volume can be understood. Yet these chants, setting aside advantages in retrospect, are remarkable poems, alive at every point in movement and in vision. They live in their oddly negative exuberance, as the new poet goes out into his bleak lands as though he marched only into another man's phantasmagoria. One chant, beginning "In the wind my rescue is," to be found but mutilated in the *Selected Poems* (1968), states the poet's task as a gathering of the stones of earth into one place. The wind, by sowing a phantasmagoria in the poet's eyes, draws him "out beyond the land's end," thus saving him "from all those ungathered stones." The shore, Whitman's emblem for the state in which poets are made and unmade, becomes the theater for the first phase of Ammons's poetic maturity, the lyrics written in the decade after *Ommateum*.

These are gathered in three volumes: *Expressions of Sea Level*
(1964), *Corsons Inlet* (1965), and *Northfield Poems* (1966),
which need to be read as a unit, since the inclusion of a poem in
one or another volume seems to be a matter of whim. A reader
of Ammons is likeliest to be able to read this phase of him in the
Collected Poems, whose arrangement in chronological order of
composition shows how chronologically scrambled the three
volumes are.

Ammons's second start as a poet, after the transcendental
waste places of *Ommateum*, is in this "Hymn":

I know if I find you I will have to leave the earth
and go on out
    over the sea marshes and the brant in bays
and over the hills of tall hickory
and over the crater lakes and canyons
and on up through the spheres of diminishing air
past the blackset noctilucent clouds
        where one wants to stop and look
way past all the light diffusions and bombardments
up farther than the loss of sight
    into the unseasonal undifferentiated empty stark

And I know if I find you I will have to stay with the earth
inspecting with thin tools and ground eyes
trusting the microvilli sporangia and simplest
    coelenterates
and praying for a nerve cell
with all the soul of my chemical reactions
and going right on down where the eye sees only traces

You are everywhere partial and entire
You are on the inside of everything and on the outside

I walk down the path down the hill where the sweetgum
has begun to ooze spring sap at the cut

and I see how the bark cracks and winds like no other bark
chasmal to my ant-soul running up and down
and if I find you I must go out deep into your
    far resolutions
and if I find you I must stay here with the separate leaves
                                            (*Collected Poems* 39)

The chants of *Ommateum* were composed mostly in a single
year from the spring of 1951 to the spring of 1952. In 1956,
Ammons fully claims his Transcendental heritage in his
"Hymn," a work of poetic annunciation in which the "you" is
Emerson's "Nature," all that is separate from "the Soul." The
difficult strength of "Hymn" depends on a reader's recognition
that the found "you" is: "the NOT ME, that is, both nature and
art, all other men and my own body." Juxtapose a crucial passage of Emerson, and the *clinamen* that governs the course of
Ammons's maturity is determined:

> The world proceeds from the same spirit as the body of man.
> It is a remoter and inferior incarnation of God, a projection
> of God in the unconscious. But it differs from the body in
> one important respect. It is not, like that, now subjected to
> the human will. Its serene order is inviolable by us. It is,
> therefore, to us, the present expositor of the divine mind. It is
> a fixed point whereby we may measure our departure.

Emerson's fixed point oscillates dialectically in Ammons's
"Hymn." Where Emerson's mode hovers always around
metonymy, parts of a world taken as the whole, Ammons's sense
of the universe takes it for a symptom. No American poet, not
Whitman or Stevens, shows us so fully something otherwise
unknown in the structures of the national consciousness as
Ammons does. It cannot be said so far that Ammons has developed as fluent and individual a version of the language of the self
as they did, but he has time and persistence enough before he

borrows his last authority from death. His first authority is the height touched in this "Hymn," where everything depends upon a precision of consequences "if I find you." "The unassimilable fact leads us on," a later poem begins, the leading on being Ammons's notion of quest. If all that is separate from him, the "you," is found, the finding will be assimilated at the final cost of going on out "into the unseasonal undifferentiated empty stark," a resolution so far as to annihilate selfhood. One part of the self will be yielded to an apprehension beyond sight, while the other will stay here with the earth, to be yielded to sight's reductiveness, separated with each leaf.

This is the enterprise of a consciousness extreme enough to begin another central poem, "Gravelly Run," with a quiet terrifying sense of what will suffice:

> I don't know somehow it seems sufficient
> to see and hear whatever coming and going is,
> losing the self to the victory
>   of stones and trees,
> of bending sandpit lakes, crescent
> round groves of dwarf pine:
>
> for it is not so much to know the self
> as to know it as it is known
>   by galaxy and cedar cone,
>
> (*Collected Poems* 55)

But as it is known, it is only a "surrendered self among / unwelcoming forms." The true analogue to his surrender is the curious implicit threat of Emerson's Orphic poet:

We distrust and deny inwardly our sympathy with nature. We own and disown our relation to it, by turns. We are like Nebuchadnezzer, dethroned, bereft of reason, and eating grass like an ox. But who can set limits to the remedial force of spirit?

The remedial force of spirit, in this sense, is closest to being that terriblest force in the world, of which Stevens's Back-ache complains. Ammons, who knows he cannot set limits to such force, warns himself perpetually "to turn back," before he comes to a unity apparently equal to his whole desire. For his desire is only a metonymy, and unity (if found) compels another self-defeating question.

> You cannot come to unity and remain material:
> in that perception is no perceiver:
>   when you arrive
> you have gone too far:
>   at the Source you are in the mouth of Death:
>
> you cannot
>   turn around in
> the Absolute: there are no entrances or exits
>   no precipitations of forms
> to use like tongs against the formless:
>   no freedom to choose:
>
> to be
>   you have to stop not-being and break
> off from *is* to *flowing* and
>   this is the sin you weep and praise:
> origin is your original sin:
>   the return you long for will ease your guilt
> and you will have your longing:
>
>   the wind that is my guide said this: it
> should know having
>   given up everything to eternal being but
> direction:
>
> how I said can I be glad and sad: but a man goes
>   from one foot to the other:

wisdom wisdom:
> to be glad and sad at once is also unity
and death:
> wisdom wisdom: a peachblossom blooms on a particular
tree on a particular day:
> > unity cannot do anything in particular:

are these the thoughts you want me to think I said but
> the wind was gone and there was no more knowledge then.
> > > > (*Collected Poems* 79–80)

The wind's origin is its original sin also; were it to give up
even direction, it would cease to be "Guide," as this poem is
entitled. If the wind is Ammons's Virgil, an Interior Paramour or
Whitmanian Fancy remains his Beatrice, guiding him whenever
wind ceases to lead. The poetic strength of "Guide" is in its
dialectical renunciation of even this daimonic paramour. For the
wind speaks against what is deepest and most self-destructive in
Ammons. "Break off from *is* to *flowing*" is a classic phrasing of
the terrible dream that incessantly afflicts most of our central
poetic imaginations in America. "Unity cannot do anything in
particular"; least of all can it write a poem.

The wind, Ammons's way to knowledge, is certainly the most
active wind in American poetry. In *Ommateum*, the wind is a
desperate whip, doubting its own efficacy in a dry land. It moves
"like wisdom," but its poet is not so sure of the likeness. In the
mature volumes, it is more a blade than a whip, and its desperation has rendered it apologetic:

> Having split up the chaparral
> blasting my sight
> the wind said
> > You know I'm
> > the result of
> forces beyond my control

I don't hold it against you
I said
It's all right I understand

(*Collected Poems* 48–49)

For the wind "dies and never dies," but the poet goes on:

consigned to
form that will not
let me loose
except to death
till some
syllable's rain
anoints my tongue
and makes it sing
to strangers:

(*Collected Poems* 59)

To be released from form into unity one dies or writes a poem; this appalling motive for metaphor is as desperate as any wind. Wind, which is "not air or motion / but the motion of air," speaks to a consciousness that is not spirit or making, but the spirit of making, the Ezra-incarnation in this poet:

I coughed
and the wind said
Ezra will live
to see your last
sun come up again

I turned (as I will) to weeds and
the wind went off
carving
monuments through a field of stone
monuments whose shape

> wind cannot arrest but
> taking hold on
>   changes
>
> while Ezra
>   listens from terraces of mind
> wind cannot reach or
> weedroots of my low-feeding shiver
>   (*Collected Poems* 61–62)

When the poet falls (as he must) from this Ezra-eminence, the terraces of mind dissolve:

> the mind whirls, short of the unifying
> reach, short of the heat
>   to carry that forging:
>   after the visions of these losses, the spent
> seer, delivered to wastage, risen
>   into ribs, consigns knowledge to
>   approximation, order to the vehicle
> of change,
>   (*Collected Poems* 77)

He is never so spent a seer as he says, even if the price of his ascensions keeps rising. If from moment to moment the mode of motion is loss, there is always the privileged *Moment* itself:

> He turned and
> stood
>
> in the moment's
> height,
>
> exhilaration
> sucking him up,

shuddering and
lifting

him
jaw and bone

and he said
what

destruction am I
blessed by?

(*Collected Poems* 160–161)

The burden of Ammons's poetry is to answer, to name that enlargement of life that is also a destruction. When the naming came most complete, in the late summer of 1962, it gave Ammons his two most ambitious single poems, "Corsons Inlet" and "Saliences." Though both poems depend upon the context of Ammons's canon, they show the field of his enterprise more fully and freely than could have been expected of any single works. "Corsons Inlet" is likely to be Ammons's most famous poem, his "Sunday Morning," a successfully universalizing expression of a personal thematic conflict and its apparent (or provisional) resolution. But "Saliences," a harder, less open, more abstract fury of averted destructions, is the better poem. "Corsons Inlet" comforts itself (and us) with the perpetually renewed hope of a fresh walk over the dunes to the sea. "Saliences" rises past hope to what in the mind is "beyond loss or gain / beyond concern for the separate reach." Both the hope and the ascension beyond hope return us to origins, and can be apprehended with keener aptitude after an excursus taking us deeper into Ammons's tradition. Ammons compels that backward vision of our poetry that only major achievement exacts, and illuminates Emerson and all his progeny as much as he needs them for illumination. Reading Ammons, I brood on all

American poetry in the Romantic tradition, which means I yield
to Emerson, who is to our modern poetry what Wordsworth has
been to all British poetry after him; the starting-point, the defining element, the vexatious father, the shadow and the despair,
liberating angel and blocking-agent, perpetual irritant and solac-
ing glory.

John Jay Chapman, in what is still the best introductory
essay on Emerson, condensed his estimate of the seer into a great
and famous sentence: "If a soul be taken and crushed by democracy till it utter a cry, that cry will be Emerson." In the year
1846, when he beheld "the famous States / Harrying Mexico /
With rifle and with knife!," Emerson raised the cry of himself
most intensely and permanently:

> Though loath to grieve
> The evil time's sole patriot,
> I cannot leave
> My honied thought
> For the priest's cant,
> Or statesman's rant.
>
> If I refuse
> My study for their politique,
> Which at the best is trick,
> The angry Muse
> Puts confusion in my brain.

The astonished Muse found Emerson at her side all through
1846, the year not only of the Channing "Ode," but of "Bacchus" and "Merlin," his finest and most representative poems,
that between them establish a dialectic central to subsequent
American poetry. In "Bacchus," the poet is not his own master,
but yields to daimonic possession. In "Merlin," the daimonic
itself is mastered, as the poet becomes first the Bard, and then
Nemesis:

Who with even matches odd,
Who athwart space redresses
The partial wrong,
Fills the just period,
And finishes the song.

The poet of "Bacchus" is genuinely possessed, and yet falls (savingly) victim to Ananke—he is still *human*. The poet of "Merlin" is himself absorbed into Ananke and ceases to be human, leaving "Bacchus" much the better poem. To venture a desolate formula about American poetry: our greater poets attain the splendor of Bacchus, and then attempt to become Merlin, and so cease to be wholly human and begin to fail as poets. Emerson and his descendants dwindle, not when they build altars to the Beautiful Necessity, but when they richly confuse themselves with the Necessity. Poetry, Emerson splendidly observed, must be as new as foam and as old as the rock; he might also have observed that it had better not itself try to be foam or rock.

A strain in Ammons, ecological and almost geological, impels him towards identification with the American version of Ananke, and is his largest flaw as a poet. Robert Bly brilliantly parodied this strain by printing a passage from *The Mushroom Hunter's Field Guide* under the title, "A. R. Ammons Discusses the Lacaria Trullisata":

The somewhat distant,
broad, purplish
to violaceous gills,
white spore

Deposit, and
habitat
on sand distingu-
ish it. No
part of the fruit-

Ing body is ever
glutinous.
Edibility. The question
is academic: It is

Impossible to get
rid of
all the sand.

And so on. The Ammonsian literalness, allied to a similar destructive impulse in Wordsworth and Thoreau, attempts to summon outward continuities to shield the poet from his mind's own force. "A Poem Is a Walk" is the title of a dark, short prose piece by Ammons that tries "to establish a reasonably secure identity between a poem and a walk and to ask how a walk occurs, what it is, and what it is for," but establishes only that a walk by Ammons is a sublime kind of Pythagorean enterprise or Behmenite picnic. Emerson, who spoke as much wisdom as any American, alas spoke darkly also, and Ammons is infuriatingly Emersonian when he tells us a poem "is a motion to no-motion, to the still point of contemplation and deep realization. Its knowledges are all negatives and, therefore, more positive than any knowledge." "Corsons Inlet," "Saliences," and nearly a hundred other poems by Ammons are nothing of the kind, his imagination be thanked, rather than this spooky, pure-product-of-America mysticism. Unlike Emerson, who crossed triumphantly into prose, Ammons belongs to that company of poets that *thinks* most powerfully and naturally in verse, and sometimes descends to obscure quietudes when verse subsides.

"Corsons Inlet" first verges on, and then veers magnificently away from worshipping the Beautiful Necessity, from celebrating the way things are. "Life will be images, but cannot be divided nor doubled," might be the poem's motto; so might: "Ask the fact for the form," both maxims being Emerson's.

Ammons's long poem *Tape for the Turn of the Year* contains the self-admonishment: "get out of boxes, hard / forms of mind: / go deep: / penetrate / to the true spring," which is the initial impulse of "Corsons Inlet." The poet, having walked in the morning over the dunes to the sea, recollects later in the day the release granted him by the walk, from thought to sight, from conceptual forms to the flowings and blendings of the Coleridgean Secondary Imagination. Released into the composition of "Corsons Inlet," he addresses his reader directly (consciously in Whitman's mode) to state both the nature of his whole body of poetry, and his sense of its largest limitation:

> I allow myself eddies of meaning:
> yield to a direction of significance
> running
> like a stream through the geography of my work:
>   you can find
> in my sayings
>   swerves of action
>   like the inlet's cutting edge:
>   there are dunes of motion,
> organizations of grass, white sandy paths of remembrance
> in the overall wandering of mirroring mind:
>
> but Overall is beyond me: is the sum of these events
> I cannot draw, the ledger I cannot keep, the accounting
> beyond the account:
>   (*Collected Poems* 148)

Within this spaced restraint, there is immense anguish, and the anguish is not just metaphysical. Though this anguish be an acquired wisdom, such wisdom proffers no consolation for the loss of quest. The anguish that goes through "Corsons Inlet," subdued but ever salient, is more akin to a quality of mind in Thoreau than to anything in Emerson or Whitman. What Tran-

scendentalists wanted of natural history is generally a darkness
to me, and I resort to the late Perry Miller for some light on "the
Transcendental methodology for coping with the multifarious
concreteness of nature. That method is to see the particular as a
particular, and yet at the same time so to perceive it as to make
it, or itself, yield up the general and the universal." But that is
too broad, being a Romantic procedure in general, with neither
the American impatience nor the American obsession of particularity clearly distinguished from Wordsworthianism. Wordsworth was wonderfully patient with preparations for vision, and
was more than content to see particulars flow together and fade
out in the great moments of vision. Emerson scanted preparations, and held on to the particulars even in ecstasy. In Thoreau,
whatever his final differences with his master, the Emersonian
precipitateness and clarity of the privileged moment are sharp-
ened. When I read in his *Journals,* I drown in particulars and
cannot find the moments of release, but *The Natural History of
Massachusetts,* his first true work, seems all release, and very
close to the terrible nostalgias "Corsons Inlet" reluctantly abandons. William Ellery Channing, memorializing Thoreau clumsily
though with love, deluges us with evidences of those walks and
talks in which Overall was never beyond Thoreau, but came
confidently with each natural observation. But Ammons, who
would want to emulate Thoreau, cannot keep the account; his
natural observations bring him wholly other evidences:

> in nature there are few sharp lines: there are areas of
> primrose
>   more or less dispersed;
> disorderly orders of bayberry; between the rows
> of dunes,
> irregular swamps of reeds,
> though not reeds alone, but grass, bayberry, yarrow, all . . .
> predominantly reeds:
>
> (*Collected Poems* 148–149)

All through the poem beats its hidden refrain: "I was released from . . . straight lines," "few sharp lines," "I have drawn no lines," "but there are no lines," "a wider range / than mental lines can keep," "the waterline, waterline inexact," "but in the large views, no / lines or changeless shapes." A wild earlier poem, called "Lines," startlingly exposes Ammons's obsession, for there nature bombards him, all but destroys him with lines, nothing but lines:

Lines flying in, out: logarithmic
    curves coiling
toward an infinitely inward center: lines
    weaving in, threads lost in clustral scrawl,
        weaving out into loose ends,
wandering beyond the border of gray background,
    going out of vision,
        not returning;
or, returning, breaking across the boundary
    as new lines, discontinuous,
        come into sight:
fiddleheads of ferns, croziers of violins,
    convoluted spherical masses, breaking through
        ditchbanks where briar
stem-dull will
    leave and bloom:
        haunch line, sickle-like, turning down, bulging, nuzzling
under, closing into
    the hidden, sweet, dark meeting of lips:
        the spiralling out
or in
    of galaxies:
        the free-running wavy line, swirling
configuration, halting into a knot
    of curve and density: the broken,
        irreparable filament: tree-winding vines, branching,

falling off or back, free,
   the adventitious preparation for possibility, from
      branch to branch, ash to gum:
the breaker
   hurling into reach for shape, crashing
      out of order, the inner hollow sizzling flat:
the longnecked, uteral gourd, bass line
   continuous in curve,
      melodic line filling and thinning:
concentrations,
   whirling masses,
      thin leaders, disordered ends and risks:
explosions of clusters, expansions from the
   full radial sphere, return's longest chance:
      lines exploring, intersecting, paralleling, twisting,
noding: deranging, clustering.

                   (*Collected Poems* 104–105)

This is Ammons's Mad Song, his equivalent of Stevens's "A Rabbit as King of the Ghosts," another poem of the mind's mercilessness, its refusal to defend itself against itself. "Deranging, clustering" is the fear and the horror, from which "Corsons Inlet" battles for release, mostly through embracing "a congregation / rich with entropy," a constancy of change. The poet who insists he has drawn no lines draws instead his poem out of the "dunes of motion," loving them desperately as his only (but inadequate) salvation, all that is left when his true heaven of Overall is clearly beyond him. Yet this remains merely a being "willing to go along" in the recognition not of the Beautiful but the Terrible Necessity:

the moon was full last night: today, low tide was low:
black shoals of mussels exposed to the risk
of air
and, earlier, of sun,

waved in and out with the waterline, waterline inexact,
caught always in the event of change:
   a young mottled gull stood free on the shoals
   and ate
to vomiting: another gull, squawking possession, cracked a crab,
picked out the entrails, swallowed the soft-shelled legs, a ruddy
turnstone running in to snatch leftover bits:

risk is full: every living thing in
siege: the demand is life, to keep life: the small
white blacklegged egret, how beautiful, quietly stalks and spears
         the shallows, darts to shore
            to stab—what? I couldn't
see against the black mudflats—a frightened
fiddler crab?

(Collected Poems 149–150)

This great and very American passage, kin to a darker tradition than Ammons's own, and to certain poems of Melville and
Hart Crane, is "Corsons Inlet's" center, the consequence of the
spent seer's consignment of order to the vehicle of change. I
remember, each time I read it, that Ammons is a Southerner, heir
to a darker Protestantism than was the immediate heritage of
the New England visionaries or of Whitman. But our best
Southern poets, from Poe and Timrod through Ransom, Tate,
Warren, have not affected his art, and a comparison to a Southern contemporary like James Dickey indicates sharply how
much Ammons is the conscious heir of nineteenth-century
Northern poetry, including a surprising affinity to Dickinson in
his later phase of *Uplands* and *Briefings*. But, to a North Car-
olinian one hundred years after, Transcendentalism comes hard
and emerges bitterly, with the Oversoul reduced from Overall to
"the overall wandering of mirroring mind," confronting the
dunes and swamps as a last resource, the final form of Nature or
the Not-Me.

From the nadir of "every living thing in / siege," "Corsons Inlet" slowly rises to a sense of the ongoing, "not chaos: preparations for / fight." In a difficult transitional passage, the poet associates the phrasal fields of his metric with the "field" of action on every side of him, open to his perception "with moving incalculable center." Looking close, he can see "order tight with shape"; standing back, he confronts a formlessness that suddenly, in an extraordinary epiphany, is revealed as his consolation:

> orders as summaries, as outcomes of actions override
> or in some way result, not predictably (seeing me gain
> the top of a dune,
> the swallows
> could take flight—some other fields of bayberry
>   could enter fall
>   berryless) and there is serenity:
>
>   no arranged terror: no forcing of image, plan,
> or thought:
> no propaganda, no humbling of reality to precept:
>
> terror pervades but is not arranged, all possibilities
> of escape open: no route shut, except in
>   the sudden loss of all routes:
>   (*Collected Poems* 150–151)

"No arranged terror" is the crucial insight, and if we wish to inquire who would arrange terror except a masochist, the wish will not sustain itself. The poem's final passage, this poet's defense, abandons the really necessary "pulsation of order," the reliable particulars, for what cannot suffice, the continued bafflement of perceiving nothing completely. For Ammons, the seer of *Ommateum* and the still-confident quester of the "Hymn," this bafflement is defeat, and enjoying the freedom that results from scope eluding his grasp is hardly an enjoying in any ordinary sense. The poem ends bravely, but not wholly persuasively:

> I see narrow orders, limited tightness, but will
> not run to that easy victory:
>   still around the looser, wider forces work:
>   I will try
>   to fasten into order enlarging grasps of disorder, widening
> scope, but enjoying the freedom that
> Scope eludes my grasp, that there is no finality of vision,
> that I have perceived nothing completely,
>   that tomorrow a new walk is a new walk.
>   (*Collected Poems* 151)

Origin is still his original sin; what his deepest nature longs for, to come to unity and yet remain material, is no part of "Corsons Inlet," which grants him freedom to choose, but no access to that unity that alone satisfies choice. The major poem written immediately after "Corsons Inlet" emerges from stoic acceptance of bafflement into an imaginative reassurance that prompts Ammons's major phase, the lyrics of *Uplands, Briefings,* and the work-in-progress:

> Consistencies rise
> and ride
> the mind down
> hard routes
>   walled
> with no outlet and so
> to open a variable geography,
>   proliferate
> possibility, here
> is this dune fest
>   releasing

mind feeding out,
gathering clusters,
fields of order in disorder,
where choice
can make beginnings,
  turns,
  reversals,
where straight line
and air-hard thought
can meet
unarranged disorder,
  dissolve
before the one event that
creates present time
in the multi-variable
  scope:

                          (*Collected Poems* 151–152)

"Saliences" thus returns to "Corsons Inlet's" field of action, driven by that poet's need not to abide in a necessity, however beautiful. Saliences etymologically are out-leapings, "mind feeding out," not taking in perceptions but turning its violent energies out into the field of action. If "Corsons Inlet" is Ammons's version of "The Idea of Order at Key West" (not that he had Stevens's poem in mind, but that the attentive reader learns to compare the two), then "Saliences" is his *The Man with the Blue Guitar,* a discovery of how to begin again after a large and noble acknowledgment of dark limitations. "Saliences" is a difficult, abstract poem, but it punches itself along with an overwhelming vigor, showing its exuberance by ramming through every blocking particular, until it can insist that "where not a single single thing endures, / the overall reassures." Overall remains beyond Ammons, but is replaced by "a round / quiet turning, / beyond loss or gain, / beyond concern for the separate reach." "Saliences" emphasizes the transformation of Ammons's obsessive theme, from the long-ing for unity to the assertion of the mind's power over the par-ticulars of being, the universe of death. The Emersonianism of Ammons is constant; as did Whitman, so his final judgment of his relation to that great precursor will be: "loyal at last." But "Saliences" marks the *clinamen*; the swerve away from Emer-son is now clarified, and Ammons will write no poem more crucial to his own unfolding. Before "Saliences," the common reader must struggle with the temptation of naming Ammons a nature poet; after this, the struggle would be otiose. The quest that was surrendered in "Guide," and whose loss was accepted in "Corsons Inlet," is internalized in "Saliences" and afterward.

"Saliences" approximates (indeliberately) the subtle proce-dure of a subtradition within Romantic poetry that goes from Shelley's "Mont Blanc" to Stevens's "The Auroras of Autumn." The poet begins in an austere, even a terrifying scene of natural confrontation, but he does not describe the scene or name the terror until he has presented fully the mind's initial defense against scene and terror, its implicit assertion of its own force. So "Saliences" begins with a vision of the mind in action "in the multi-variable / scope." A second movement starts with the wind's entrance ("a variable of wind / among the dunes, / mak-ing variables / of position and direction and sound") and cli-maxes at the poem's halfway point, which returns to the image of the opening ("come out of the hard / routes and ruts, / pour over the walls / of previous assessments: turn to / the open, / the unexpected, to new saliences of feature"). After this come sev-enty magical lines of Ammons upon his heights (starting with: "The reassurance is / that through change / continuities sinu-ously work"), lines that constitute one of a convincing handful of contemporary assurances that the imagination is capable always of a renovative fresh start.

The dune fest, which in the poem's opening movement is termed a provocation for the mind's release from "consisten-

cies" (in the sense of Blake's Devourer), is seen in the second
movement as "Corsons Inlet's" baffled field of action:

> wind, a variable, soft wind, hard
> steady wind, wind
> shaped and kept in the
> bent of trees,
> the prevailing dipping seaward
> of reeds,
> the kept and erased sandcrab trails:
> wind, the variable to the gull's flight,
> how and where he drops the clam
> and the way he heads in, running to the loft:
> wind, from the sea, high surf
> and cool weather;
> from the land, a lessened breakage
> and the land's heat:
> wind alone as a variable,
> as a factor in millions of events,
> leaves no two moments
> on the dunes the same:
>   keep
> free to these events,
> bend to these
> changing weathers:
>
>   (*Collected Poems* 152–153)

This wind has gone beyond the wind of "Guide," for it has
given up everything to eternal being, even direction, even veloc-
ity, and contents itself to be shaped and kept by each particular
it encounters. Knowing he cannot be one with or even like this
wind, knowing too he must be more than a transparency, an Eye
among the blind particulars, the poet moves to a kind of upper
level of Purgatory, where the wind ceases to be his guide, and he
sees as he has not seen before:

when I went back to the dunes today,
    saliences,
congruent to memory,
spread firmingly across my sight:
the narrow white path
rose and dropped over
grassy rises toward the sea:
sheets of reeds,
tasseling now near fall,
filled the hollows
with shapes of ponds or lakes:
bayberry, darker, made wandering
chains of clumps, sometimes pouring
into heads, like stopped water:
    much seemed
constant, to be looked
forward to, expected:

(*Collected Poems* 153–154)

It is the saliences, the outleapings, that "spread *firmingly* across my sight," and give him assurances, "summations of permanence." The whole passage, down through the poem's close, has a firm beauty unlike anything previous in Ammons. Holding himself as he must, firmly apart from still-longed-for unity, he finds himself now in an astonishing equilibrium with the particulars, containing them in his own mind by reimagining them there:

                                    in
    the hollow,
where a runlet
    makes in
at full tide and fills a bowl,
extravagance of pink periwinkle
along the grassy edge,
and a blue, bunchy weed, deep blue,

> deep into the mind the dark blue
> constant:
>> (*Collected Poems* 154)

The change here, as subtle as it is precarious, only just bears description, though the poet of *Uplands* and *Briefing* relies upon it as though it were palpable, something he could touch every way. The weed and the mind's imaginative constancy are in the relation given by the little poem "Reflective," written just afterward:

> I found a
> weed
> that had a
>
> mirror in it
> and that
> mirror
>
> looked in at
> a mirror
> in
>
> me that
> had a
> weed in it
>> (*Collected Poems* 170)

In itself this is slight; in the context provided by "Saliences" it is exact and finely wrought. The whole meaning of it is in "I *found*," for "Saliences" records a finding, and a being found. Because of this mutual finding, the magnificent close of the poem is possible, is even necessary:

> where not a single single thing endures,
> the overall reassures,

deaths and flights,
shifts and sudden assaults claiming
limited orders,
the separate particles:
earth brings to grief
much in an hour that sang, leaped, swirled,
yet keeps a round
   quiet turning,
beyond loss or gain,
beyond concern for the separate reach.

                       (*Collected Poems* 155)

I think, when I read this passage, of the final lines of Wordsworth's great Ode, of the end of Browning's "Love Among the Ruins," of the deep peace Whitman gives as he concludes "Crossing Brooklyn Ferry," and of Stevens closing "As You Leave the Room":

An appreciation of a reality

And thus an elevation, as if I left
With something I could touch, touch every way.

And yet nothing has been changed except what is
Unreal, as if nothing had been changed at all.

This is not to play at touchstones, in the manner of Arnold or of Blackmur, but only to record my experience as a reader, which is that "Saliences" suggests and is worthy of such company. Firm and radiant as the poem is, its importance for Ammons (if I surmise rightly) transcends its intrinsic worth, for it made possible his finest poems. I pass to them with some regret for the splendors in *Selected Poems* I have not discussed: "Silver," "Terrain," "Bridge," "Jungle Knot," "Nelly Myers," "Expressions of Sea Level," and for the long poem, *Tape for the*

Turn of the Year, a heroic failure that is Ammons's most original and surprising invention.

Uplands, published in the autumn of 1970, begins with a difficult, almost ineluctable lyric, "Snow Log," which searches for intentions where they evidently cannot be found, in the particulars of fallen tree, snow, shrubs, the special light of winter landscapes; "I take it on myself," the poet ends by saying, and repeats the opening triad:

> Especially the fallen tree
> the snow picks
> out in the woods to show:
>   (*Collected Poems* 272)

Stevens, in the final finding of the ear, returned to the snow he had forgotten, to behold again "nothing that is not there and the nothing that is." "Snow Log" seems to find something that is not there, but the reader is left uncertain whether there is a consciousness in the scene that belongs neither to him nor to the poet. With the next poem, "Upland," which gives the volume both its tonality and title, the uncertainty vanishes:

> Certain presuppositions are altered
> by height: the inversion to
> sky-well a peak
> in a desert makes: the welling
>
> from clouds down the boulder fountains:
> it is always a
> surprise out west there—
> the blue ranges loose and aglide
>
> with heat and then come close
> on slopes leaning up into green:

a number of other phenomena might
be summoned—

take the Alleghenies for example,
some quality in the air
of summit stones lying free and loose
out among the shrub trees: every

exigency seems prepared for that might
roll, bound, or give flight
to stone: that is, the stones are
prepared: they are round and ready.
                    (*Collected Poems* 276–277)

A poem like this is henceforth Ammons's characteristic work: shorter and more totally self-enclosed than earlier ventures, and less reliant on larger contexts. He has become an absolute master of his art, and a maker of individual tones as only the greater poets can accomplish:

the stones are
prepared: they are round and ready.

"Upland" does not attempt to define "some quality in the air" that alters presuppositions and makes its stones prepared for anything at any time. The poem disturbs because it compels us to accept the conflicting notions (for us) of surprise and preparation as being no conflict for the intentionality held by those summit stones. It satisfies as much as disturbs because something in us is not wholly apart from the summit stone's state-of-being; a natural apocalypticism is in the air, and pervades our rare ascensions to the mind's heights. Ammons, who is increasingly wary of finalities, praises hesitation in the next lyric, "Periphery":

One day I complained about the periphery
that it was thickets hard to get around in
   or get around for
an older man: it's like keeping charts

of symptoms, every reality a symptom
where the ailment's not nailed down:
   much knowledge, precise enough,
but so multiple it says this man is alive

or isn't: it's like all of a body answering
all of pharmacopoeia, a too
   adequate relationship:
so I complained and said maybe I'd brush

deeper and see what was pushing all this
periphery, so difficult to make any sense
   out of, out:
with me, decision brings its own

hesitation: a symptom, no doubt, but open
and meaningless enough without paradigm:
   but hesitation
can be all right, too: I came on a spruce

thicket full of elk, gushy snow-weed,
nine species of lichen, four pure white
   rocks and
several swatches of verbena near bloom.

                  (*Collected Poems* 274–275)

    All the poems in *Uplands* have this new ease, but the conscious mastery of instrument may obscure for us the prevalence of the old concerns, lightened by the poet's revelation that a search for saliences is a more possible quest than the more primordial romancing after unity. The concerns locate themselves still in Emerson's mental universe; Ammons's "Periphery," like Dickinson's "Circumference," goes back to the astonishing "Circles" of 1840 with its insistence that "the only sin is limitation" and its repeated image of concentricity. The appropriate gloss for Ammons's "Periphery" (and for much else in *Uplands*) is: "The natural world may be conceived as a system of concentric circles, and we now and then detect in nature slight dislocations which apprise us that this surface on which we now stand is not fixed, but sliding." Ammons calls so being apprised "hesitation," and his slight dislocation is the radiant burst of elk, snow-weed, lichen, white rocks, and verbena that ends "Periphery" so beautifully.

In *Uplands* and the extraordinary conceptions of the recent volume, *Briefings,* the motions of water have replaced the earlier guiding movements of wind. "If Anything Will Level with You Water Will," the title of one fine poem, is the credo of many. "I / mean the telling is unmediated," Ammons says of a rocky stream, and his ambition here, enormous as always, is an unmediated telling, a purely visionary poetry. It is not a poetry that discourses of itself or of the outward particulars, or of the processes of the poet's mind so much as it deals in a purer representation than even Wordsworth could have wanted. The bodily eye is not a despotic sense for Ammons (as it became for Thoreau), who has not passed through a crisis in perception, but rather has trained himself to sense those out-leapings later available to the seer (like Emerson) who had wisdom enough to turn back from Unity. For pure representations in the later Ammons, I give "Laser" (from *Uplands*) as a supreme example:

> An image comes
> and the mind's light, confused
> as that on surf
> or ocean shelves,
> gathers up,

parallelizes, focuses
and in a rigid beam illuminates the image:

the head seeks in itself
fragments of left-over light
to cast a new
direction,
any direction,
to strike and fix
a random, contradicting image:

but any found image falls
back to darkness or
the lesser beams splinter and
go out:
the mind tries to
dream of diversity, of mountain
rapids shattered with sound and light,

of wind fracturing brush or
bursting out of order against a mountain
range: but the focused beam
folds all energy in:
the image glares filling all space:
the head falls and
hangs and cannot wake itself.

(*Collected Poems* 187–188)

I risk sounding mystical by insisting that "an image" here is neither the poetic trope nor a natural particular, but what Ammons inveterately calls a "salience"; "the image glares filling all space." Not that in this perception there is no perceiver; rather the perceiving is detached, disinterested, attentive without anxiety or nostalgia. Perhaps this is only Ammons's equivalent of the difficult "half create" of "Tintern Abbey" or Emerson's "I

am nothing; I see all," but it seems to ensue from the darker
strain in him, that goes back to the twenty-sixth poem in
Ommateum, "In the wind my rescue is," which stated a hope-
less poetic question: "I set in my task / to gather the stones of
earth / into one place." In *Uplands*, a profound poem, "Apolo-
gia pro Vita Sua," makes a definitive revision of the earlier
ambition:

> I started picking up the stones
> throwing them into one place
> and by sunrise I was going far away
> for the large ones
> always turning to see never lost
> the cairn's height
> lengthening my radial reach:
>
> the sun watched with deep concentration
> and the heap through the hours grew
> and became by nightfall
> distinguishable from all the miles around
> of slate and sand:
>
> during the night the wind falling
> turned earthward its lofty freedom and speed
> and the sharp blistering sound muffled
> toward dawn and the blanket was
> drawn up over a breathless face:
>
> even so you can see in full dawn
> the ground there lifts
> a foreign thing desertless in origin.
>
> (*Collected Poems* 38)

"Distinguishable" is the desperate and revelatory word. To
ask, after death, the one thing, to have left behind "a foreign

thing desertless in origin," the cairn of a lifetime's poems, is to
have reduced rescue into primordial pathos. Yet the poem, by its
virtue, renders more than pathos, as the lyric following, on the
same theme, renders more also:

> Losing information he
> rose gaining
> view
> till at total
> loss gain was
> extreme:
> extreme & invisible:
> the eye
> seeing nothing
> lost its
> separation:
> self-song
> (that is a mere motion)
> fanned out
> into failing swirls
> slowed &
> became continuum.

> (*Collected Poems* 216)

"Offset" is the appropriate title; this is power purchased by
the loss of knowledge, and unity at the expense of being material. *Uplands,* as a volume, culminates in its last lyric, "Cascadilla
Falls," placed just before the playful and brilliant long poem,
"Summer Session 1968," in which Ammons finds at last some
rest from these intensities. Despite its extraordinary formal control and its continuous sense of a vision attained, *Uplands* is a
majestically sad book, for Ammons does not let himself forget
that his vision, while uncompromised, is a compromise necessarily, a constant knowing why and how "unity cannot do anything
in particular." The poet, going down by Cascadilla Falls in the

evening, picks up a stone and "thought all its motions into it,"
and then drops the stone from galactic wanderings to dead rest:

> the stream from other motions
> broke
> rushing over it:
> shelterless,
> I turned
>
> to the sky and stood still:
> Oh
> I do
> not know where I am going
> that I can live my life
> by this single creek.
>
> (*Collected Poems* 206–207)

From this self-imposed pathos Ammons wins as yet no
release. Release comes in the ninety delightful lyrics gathered
together in *Briefings* (first entitled, gracefully, but misleadingly,
Poems Small and Easy), this poet's finest book. Though the
themes of *Briefings* are familiar Ammonsian, the mode is not.
Laconic though transfigured speech has been transformed into
"wasteful song." The first poem, "Center," places us in a freer
world than Ammons would give us before:

> A bird fills up the
> streamside bush
> with wasteful song,
> capsizes waterfall,
> mill run, and
> superhighway
> to
> song's improvident
> center
> lost in the green

bush green
answering bush:
wind varies:
the noon sun casts
mesh refractions
on the stream's amber
bottom
and nothing at all gets,
nothing gets
caught at all.

(*Collected Poems* 162–163)

The given is mesh that cannot catch because the particulars have been capsized, and so are unavailable for capture. The center is improvident because it stands at the midmost point of mind, not of nature. *Briefings* marks an end to the oldest conflict in Ammons; the imagination has learned to avoid apocalyptic pitch, but it has learned also its own painful autonomy in regard to the universe it cannot join in unity. With the confidence of this autonomy attained, the mind yet remains wary of what lurks without, as in "Attention":

Down by the bay I
kept in mind
at once
the tips of all the rushleaves
and so
came to know
balance's cost and true:
somewhere though in the whole field
is the one
tip
I will someday lose out of mind
and fall through.

(*Collected Poems* 169)

The one particular of dying remains; every unmastered particular is a little death, giving tension to the most triumphant even among these short poems. "Hymn IV," returning to the great "Hymn" and two related poems of the same title, seals up the quest forever:

> You have enriched us with
> fear and contrariety
> providing the searcher
> confusion for his search
>
> teaching by your snickering
> wisdom an autonomy
> for man
> Bear it all
>
> and keep me from my enemies'
> wafered concision and zeal
> I give you back to yourself
> whole and undivided
>
> *(Collected Poems* 42)

I do not hear bitterness in this, or even defiance, but any late Emersonian worship of the Beautiful Necessity is gone. With the going there comes a deep uncertainty in regard to poetic subject, as "Looking Over the Acreage" and other poems show so poignantly. The ironically moving penultimate poem of *Briefings* still locates the poet's field of contemplation "where the ideas of permanence / and transience fuse in a single body, ice for example, / or a leaf," but does not suggest that the fusion yields any information. The whole of *Briefings* manifests a surrender of the will-to-knowledge, not only relational knowledge between poetic consciousness and natural objects, but of all knowledge that is too easy, that is not also loss. Amid astonishing abundance in this richest of his volumes, I must pick out one lyric as representative of all the others, for in it Ammons gives full measure of a unique gift:

> He held radical light
> as music in his skull: music
> turned, as
> over ridges immanences of evening light
> rise, turned
> back over the furrows of his brain
> into the dark, shuddered,
> shot out again
> in long swaying swirls of sound:
>
> reality had little weight in his transcendence
> so he
> had trouble keeping
> his feet on the ground, was
> terrified by that
> and liked himself, and others, mostly
> under roofs:
> nevertheless, when the
> light churned and changed
>
> his head to music, nothing could keep him
> off the mountains, his
> head back, mouth working,
> wrestling to say, to cut loose
> from the high, unimaginable hook:
> released, hidden from stars, he ate,
> burped, said he was like any one
> of us: demanded he
> was like any one of us.
>
> (*Collected Poems* 192–193)

It is the seer's horror of radical light, his obduracy to transcendence, that moves the seer himself, moves him so that he cannot know what he should know, which is that he cannot be like ourselves. The poem's power is that we are moved also, not by the horror, which cannot be our own, but by the transcendence, the sublime sense we long to share. Transcendent experience, but with Emerson's kind of Higher Utilitarianism ascetically cut off by a mind made too scrupulous for a new hope, remains the *materia poetica* of Ammons's enterprise. A majestic recent poem like "The City Limits" suggests how much celebration is still possible even when the transcendent moment is cruelly isolated, too harshly purified, totally compelled to be its own value. Somewhere upon the higher ridges of his Purgatory, Ammons remains stalled, unable for now to break through to the Condition of Fire promised by *Ommateum,* where instead of invoking Emerson's Uriel or Poe's Israfel he found near identity with "a crippled angel bent in a scythe of grief" yet witnessed a fiery ascent of the angel, fought against it, and only later gained the knowledge that "The eternal will not lie / down on any temporal hill."

In the American Grain

John Ashbery

T HE PURE PRODUCTS of America don't always go crazy:
Dr. Williams himself is a demonstration of this. But the
effort of remaining both pure and American can make
them look odd and harassed—a lopsided appearance characteristic of much major American poetry, whose fructifying main-
stream sometimes seems to be peopled mostly by cranks
(Emerson, Whitman, Pound, Stevens), while certified major
poets (Frost, Eliot) somehow end up on the sidelines. This is suggested again by the unexpected appearance of two voluminous
Collected Poems by two poets who now seem destined to pass
abruptly from the status of minor to major cranks.

Both John Wheelwright and A. R. Ammons are full of tics
and quirks; both frequently write as though poetry could not be
a vehicle of major utterance, as though it were itself a refutation
of any such mythic nonsense; in both the poem is not so much a
chronicle of its own making as of its unmaking. Often, as in
Ammons's "Working Still" or Wheelwright's "North Atlantic
Passage," the final product looks like a mess of disjointed notes
for a poem. Yet each poet finishes by stretching our recognition
of what a poem can be and in so doing carries the notion of

poetry a little higher and further. Each seems destined to end up, albeit kicking and struggling, as classic American. . . .

A. R. Ammons's *Collected Poems* comes almost as unheralded as Wheelwright's sudden belated materialization. Ammons's first book, *Ommateum*, published in 1955, seems not to have attracted much attention; his second appeared nine years later. Recently he has been more prolific, and critics, particularly Harold Bloom and Richard Howard, have considered his work seriously and at length, but few had probably anticipated a *Collected Poems* of such dimensions (almost 400 pages, to which must be added the recent Norton reissue in a separate volume of his 200-page poem *Tape for the Turn of the Year*). If his importance was suspected before, it is now, as so often happens, confirmed merely by the joining of several volumes in one—not only because the solidity and brilliance are at last fully apparent but because, as also often happens, the occasionally weaker early poems somehow illuminate and give access to the big, difficult later ones.

Without wishing to fall into the trap of comparing Wheelwright and Ammons merely because of the hazards of publication, one cannot help being struck by certain resemblances. Both are American originals (in the French sense of *un original* as someone who is also quite eccentric), and they are products as much of the American landscape as of its poetic tradition, in devious ways. Wheelwright's relation to New England is as tenuous but as real as Ives's cacophonous *The Housatonic at Stockbridge* is to the bucolic scene which prompted it. The relation lies deeper than resemblance. Ammons's landscape is American sidereal; a descendant of Emerson, as Bloom has pointed out, he is always on the brink of being "whirled / Beyond the circuit of the shuddering Bear" from the safe confines of backyard or living room. But the fascination of his poetry is not the transcendental but his struggle with it, which tends to turn each poem into a battleground strewn with scattered testimony to the history of its making in the teeth of its creator's reluctance and distrust of "all this fiddle."

Reading the poems in sequence one soon absorbs this rhythm of making-unmaking, of speech facing up to the improbability of speech, so that ultimately Ammons's landscape—yard, riverbed, ocean, mountain, desert, and soon "the unseasonal undifferentiated empty stark"—releases the reader to the clash of word against word, to what Harold Bloom calls his "oddly negative exuberance." The movement is the same, from the visible if only half-real flotsam of daily living to the uncertainties beyond, but one forgets this from one poem to the next; each is as different as a wave is from the one that follows and obliterates it. One is left, like the author at the end of his best-known poem, "Corsons Inlet," "enjoying the freedom that / Scope eludes my grasp, that there is no finality of vision, / that I have perceived nothing completely, / that tomorrow a new walk is a new walk."

The poet's work is like that of Penelope ripping up her web into a varicolored heap that tells the story more accurately than the picture did. And meanwhile the "regional" has become universal, at an enormous but unavoidable cost, the destructiveness of the creative act in Ammons ("what / destruction am I / blessed by?") permits him to escape, each time, the temptations of the *paysage moralisé*. Much has been written about the relation of the so-called "New York School" of poets to the painting of men like Pollock, but in a curious way Ammons's poetry seems a much closer and more successful approximation of "Action Painting" or art as process. ("The problem is / how to keep shape and flow.")

Marianne Moore pointed out that "inns are not residences" and a basic corrective impulse runs throughout Ammons, giving rise to a vocabulary of pivotal words. "Saliences" (the title of one of his best poems), "suasion," "loft," "scary," "motion," and "extreme" are a few which assume their new meaning only after a number of encounters, a meaning whose sharpness corrects a previous one whose vagueness was more dangerous than we knew. A "loft" (also frequently used as a verb) is not a summit, but a way station and possibly the last one; saliences are pertinent and outstanding but not necessarily to be confused with meaning; suasion is neither persuasion nor dissuasion. The corrective impulse proceeds as much from prudence as from modesty; in any case it can coexist with occasional outbursts of pure egotism: "I want a squirrel-foil for my martin pole / I want to perturb some laws of balance / I want to create unnatural conditions" (but the poem of which this is the beginning is entitled "The Imagined Land"), just as Ammons's frugality and his relentless understatement are countered by the swarming profusion of the poems.

This austerity could lose its point in the course of such a long volume: the restricted palette; the limited cast of characters (bluejays, and other backyard denizens figure prominently, along with the poet's wife, child, and car, not to forget the wind with whom he has dialogues frequently in a continuing love-hate relationship); the sparse iconography of plant, pebble, sand, leaf, twig, bone, end by turning the reader back from the creature comforts he might have expected from "nature" poetry to the dazzlingly self-sufficient logic which illuminates Ammons's poetry and in turn restores these samples from nature to something of their Wordsworthian splendor—but Wordsworth recollected in the tranquillity of midcentury mindless America, and after the ironic refractions of Emerson, Stevens, and Williams. For despite Ammons's misgivings, his permanent awareness of "a void that is all being, a being that is void," his "negative exuberance" is of a kind that could exist only after the trials of so much negation.

> I can't think of a thing to uphold:
> the carborundum plant snows
> sift-scum on the slick, outgoing river
> and along the avenues car wheels

float in a small powder: my made-up
mind idles like a pyramid:
("Working Still," *Collected Poems* 276)

But if he is unable to find a saving word for the polluted (in
so many ways) American scene, his speech elevates it even as it
refuses to transform it. "No American poet," writes Harold
Bloom in an essay on Ammons, "When You Consider the Radiance," in his book *The Ringers in the Tower*, "not Whitman or
Stevens, shows us so fully something otherwise unknown in the
structures of the national consciousness as Ammons does." And
for Americans who feel that America is the last truly foreign
country, this something comes startlingly alive in poem after
poem, as in the magnificent "One: Many":

> and on and on through the villages,
> along dirt roads, ditchbanks, by gravel pits and on
>   to the homes, to the citizens and their histories,
> inventions, longings:
> I think how enriching, though unassimilable as a whole
> into art, are the differences: the small-business
> man in
>   Kansas City declares an extra-dividend
> and his daughter
>   who teaches school in Duquesne
> buys a Volkswagen, a second car for the family:
> out of many, one:
> from variety an over-riding unity, the expression of
> variety:
>
> (*Collected Poems* 140)

How perfect and how funny in its Whitmanesque nod to the
automotive industry is that "buys a Volkswagen, a second car
for the family": it seems as much by its music as by its sense to
sum up everything that is beautiful and wrong in our vast,

monotonous, but very much alive landscape. And Ammons knows this well; he ends the poem with an unemotional summation that, in its reluctant acceptance of the "opaque" world that is still "world enough to take my time, stretch my reason, hinder / and free me," can also stand for the work:

> no book of laws, short of unattainable reality itself,
> can anticipate every event,
> control every event: only the book of laws founded
>   against itself,
> founded on freedom of each event to occur as itself,
> lasts into the inevitable balances events will take.
>
> (Collected Poems 140)

Light, Wind, Motion

Josephine Miles

T HE LOCATION OF A. R. AMMONS in craggy Ithaca, in a
New Jersey salt-marsh, even in the heart of California
(northern), gives some sense of his place in poetry. His are
the particulars of the modern American natural world, those
corners of intensity, wild or domestic, where leaf-shoot, bud,
and seed follow the courses of natural day and season, he with
them. The long Protestant progression from sixteenth century
Sylvester's translation of the *Seven Days* to Blackmore's cosmic
setting and Miltonic America's fields and streams brings to
Ammons the berries harsh and crude of a poetry charged with a
natural world, itself charged with messages of spirit divine and
human.

This is not verbal, thinking, reasoning, complex poetry; seldom does a writer make do with so few subordinate clauses, so
few *whichs, whos,* and *therefores.* Nor is it a poetry of revelation in the shape of sublime forms larger than life and in sweep-
ingly assumed modifications and qualities. Rather, it is a search,
a seeking, a running, turning, looking, finally a saying, of small
truths implying large, turning the protestant into the acceptor
and celebrator of classic norms.

Ammons's early "Hymn" is an example of the range, reaching for, returning always to, fine detail, beyond a Wordsworth in his declarative strength, closest to the scope of an Emerson in the vitality of his physical world. When I read Ammons's poetry, I think I am there, and then I feel curiosity both about the place where he is and the special quality of the poetry which puts him there.

Coming to a pinywoods
    where a stream darted across the path
like a squirrel or frightened blacksnake
I sat down on a sunny hillock
    and leaned back against a pine
and picked up some dry pineneedle bundles from the ground
and tore each bundle apart a needle at a time
    It was not Coulter's pine
    for *coulteri* is funnier looking
    and not Monterey either
and I thought God must have had Linnaeus in mind
orders of trees correspond so well between them
and I dropped to sleep wondering what design God
had meant the human mind to fit
    and looked up and saw a great bird
warming in the sun high on a pine limb
tearing from his breast golden feathers
            ("Interval," *Collected Poems* 36)

The visionary golden bird is perfect Blake or Spenser, but the detailed actions are of a different narrative specificity: I sat down . . . and leaned back . . . and picked up . . . and tore apart . . . and thought . . . and dropped to sleep . . . and looked up and saw. At the center is the concern for *kind*; Linnaeus is in God's mind. What kind of pine is Ammons? Not Coulter's pine, and not Monterey either. Let Linnaeus consider him.

His sentence structure is paratactic, biblical, portentous in its *and—and—and* and its many participial suspensions like those of Milton and Blake. Yet it is active rather than descriptive in its direct verb structures. So we see a paradox of combination. Is he declaring or assuming? Is he proposing or qualifying? Does he challenge or accept? The very first poem in the collected volume of his work suggests the combination:

> Over the bleached and broken fields
> I moved my feet and turning from the wind
> that ripped sheets of sand
> from the beach and threw them
> like seamists across the dunes
> swayed as if the wind were taking me away
> and said
> I am Ezra
> As a word too much repeated
> falls out of being
> so I Ezra went out into the night
> like a drift of sand
> and splashed among the windy oats
> that clutch the dunes
> of unremembered seas
> ("So I Said I Am Ezra," *Collected Poems* 1)

The natural world is qualified in *broken, windy, unremembered,* while Ammons restlessly moves into it and says, though doubtful of his own words, a name, *I am Ezra.* Like prophets of old, Ezra, Nehemiah, Esther, he moves in the world seeking to understand, and seeing golden birds, but like new prophets he searches in the minute details of a Huxley or a Darwin, in language technical yet subjective:

> Though the sound of my voice
> is a firmamental flaw, my self, in the rockheart,

in southern oakmoss blown tangled,
its supple pincers snaring
new forks of life, braiding thin limbs
of the wateroak on gooseberry hills
beside swamps where the raccoon runs
and dips his paw in the run-of-the-swamp
musky branchwater for darting crawfish
scuttling a mudwake before them; my self,
voluble in the dark side of hills
and placid bays, while the sun grows
increasing atmosphere to the sea,
correcting the fault of dawn; my self,
the drought of unforested plains,
the trilobite's voice,
the loquacity of an alien room troubled
by a blowfly, requires my entertainment
while we learn the vowels of silence.

         ("Doxology," *Collected Poems* 16–17)

This very emphasis on sight, saying, and silence is part of the seer's role, the resort to forces beyond language, the unutterable. So Ammons's structure can blend his own restless role with that of the resourceful universe in that poise which may characterize the transcendent.

The sound of the lines supports this structure both by coinciding with it and by pulling against it. Ammons's usual short lines present the short details of his perception; then a swinging loop of suspended grammar from line to line allows the speaker to move on from one to the next. The relation of line to line is not that of Charles Olson's tension, breaking at charged points, but rather of tenuous connection which is strengthened whenever Ammons moves. In the brief "Round," for example, the chief noncorrespondent line is "from too much / spinning & spun / the big spin's calm:" where the shift from passive to active is countered and thus softened by the line; "their / windbreak" on the other hand reflects the meaning; at the end, "out of the still into" again blurs the return of getting up. After his *Tape for the Turn of the Year* in which he made an effective exercise of narrow units of sound, Ammons widened to many larger and smoother lines, much like Wallace Stevens's; but they do not seem to differ in principle from the early short ones; breaks and swings are part of his plan; details and scopes, part of his vision, and "Round" is characteristic.

> I sat down
> from too much
> spinning & spun
> the big spin's calm:
> I said
> this is
> like it is:
>
> bluebirds
> stripped my shoelaces
> for nesting:
> pill bugs took the cool
> under my shoesoles
> and weeds, sprung up,
> made me their
>
> windbreak:
> I said
> this is
> like it is
> and got up turning
> out of the still into
> the spinning dance.
>
> (*Collected Poems* 228–229)

In "Round" we can see a center for his vocabulary as well as for sound and structure; his motions among small living entities, his outward turn, his poised central statement of accepting norm in *this is / like it is.* If we look at words he uses most in poems both early and late (specifically the first 500 lines of the 1951 and the first 900 lines of the 1966 poems in the *Collected Poems,* 3,000 words each), we recognize singular items in the traditional, his own specific ecology. To traditional bodily terms like *body, eye, hand, head, voice,* he adds from his interest in saying and silence, *lip* and *throat*; to traditional earthly terms like *air, day, earth, light, night, sun,* he adds the strongly nineteenth and twentieth century specifics of *evening, morning, field, hill, leaf, rain, rock, tree, water, wing, wind,* and his even more particular *oak* and *willow,* which we may take to represent all those pill bugs and their ilk of which he is so fond. So far, the materials of a Wordsworth, but then no more; there are no major terms of emotion in his work, no statements of feeling in reaction. Rather, the work of meaning is done partly by his own characterizing abstractions, like *mind, motion, nothing, self, silence*; partly his characteristically participial adjectives, *coming, saying, turning,* along with reserved *cool* and *dry,* and partly by his involving verbs *become, break, drop, fall, hold, keep, look, mean, need, run,* along with other more traditional ones like *see, say, tell, think, turn.* In other words, Ammons moves among but thinks apart, cool in the motion, meaning, and need of silence, aware over and over of details of body and natural objects far past tradition, but drawing from tradition to his time. He looks more closely at a world we know. He reports exactitudes of light, sound, and motion. He is not content to flee beyond exactitudes, because as he says in "Crevice," "Seeing into myth is / knowledge myth can't sanctify: / separating symbol and / translucence / disembodies belief." So the fine scrutiny of "The Quince Bush":

> The flowering quince bush
> on the back hedge has been

run through by a morning
glory vine

and this morning three blooms
are open as if for all light,
sound, and motion: their adjustment
to light is

pink, though they reach for
stellar reds and core violets:
they listen as if for racket's
inner silence

and focus, as if to starve, all motion:
patterns of escaped sea
they tip the defeated, hostile,
oceanic wind:

elsewhere young men scratch and fire:
a troubled child shudders to a freeze:
an old man bursts finally and
rattles down

clacking slats: the caterpillar pierced
by a wasp egg blooms inside with
the tender worm: wailing
walls float

luminous with the charge of grief:
a day pours through a morning glory
dayblossom's adequate, poised,
available center.

(*Collected Poems* 217–218)

This is / like it is, bringing sense and mind together at a center here stable but ever precarious; "my empty-headed / contem-

plation is still where the ideas of permanence / and transience fuse in a single body, ice, for example, / or a leaf" ("The Put-Down Come On").

Ammons inherits the *dry rock* and *silence* of Eliot and Pound; he does little with Stevens's kind of abstractions like *real* and *being* and *human*, little with Eberhart's *truth* and *reason*, little with Roethke's *dirt* and *root* and *weed*, despite his similar love of detail, little with the modern emphasis on *colors* and *memory*, as in W. T. Scott; little with Rukeyser's *pain* and *animal*; little with Lowell's *glass* and *ice*, though much with *break*; little with the *street, room, door, window* tendencies of the young; with his younger contemporaries of the 1930s and 1940s he shares, in addition to the many chief traditional terms of *day* and *night*, *life* and *death*, the more special *voice* and *silence* and *cry*, the *turn* and *rain* of Rothenberg, the *field, grass, morning* of Kelly, and Matthews's *body* and *bone*. His proportioning of two adjectives to four nouns to two verbs to three connectives is closest to Emerson, the balance of adjective and verb quite different from the relative scarcity of adjectives in younger poets. In sum, his words follow in the Yeats, Muir, Eliot, Thomas, Lawrence milieu of body in motion, running, crying, in rock, wind, and silence, as this milieu is shared also by the younger Snyder, Rothenberg, Kelly, Matthews, Tate; while his structures of sound and proportion sustain the poise of an earlier American tradition in Emerson's balanced forms and specificities of *rose* and *morning*.

The peopled world and the constructed world are not his chief substance. This is not to say they do not inform his work, but they do so, like his feelings, by implication. Ammons is not a part of a whole new tendency in the language of modern poetry, that tendency toward a world of human making, of rooms, doors, windows, streets, mirrors. He worked at a glass factory in New Jersey, yet the marshes make his substance; the mirror has a weed in it.

On the other hand, one modern tendency he is strongly a part of, the increased particularization of substance. For him, traditional *cold* becomes *cool*, as for others, *fall* becomes *drop* and *break*, *move* becomes *run* and *turn*, *day* and *night* become *morning* and *evening*, *earth* becomes *field* and *hill* and *grass* and *rock*, *tree* becomes *leaf*, even for him *oak* and *willow* in many repetitions; *air* becomes *wind*; *water, rain*; *body, head, hand* become *bone, lip, throat*. Much of the future of the language of poetry may lie in these directions as he and others discern them, toward cell, fibre, and grain.

As Ammons's work has developed over the years it has more and more established a sense of the general in the particular, *the* weed in *a* weed, *the* leaf in *a* leaf, in the generalities of nature which persist and the generalities of meaning and need which mind sees persisting. In the very recent 112 meditative sections of "Hibernaculum," the search and worry toward generalization work strongly. As in 59 and 77, 78:

59

  what if we're not seeking the light at all,
the transfixion (stare to stare in a bereft learning)
but worrying the corners of our confined, held

suasions for the exit we could, from the starved light,
choose: why has the dark taken so much if darkness is
not the satisfaction: and how have we found the will

to thrive through the light from sway to sway: O
Plotinus (Emerson, even) I'm just as scared as comforted
by the continuity, one sun spelling in our sun-made heads:
(Collected Poems 370)

. . . .

77

believe all is fire why then everything is, including
the stones' dull music, solid, slow, and
cold: and the weatherless moon less is nevertheless

singing blips of meteoric bits, the flash
smirching to glistening moon-tears of solar effusions,
the wind, the solar wind, that pours out coronal lacings

into a great space: and then the mud by the swamp
ponds with cloud trails of crawdads scurrying is working
with little cellular thrivings: and the cool fire of

78

ferns climbing tree-footings from the deep freshets:
allow, allow for the cryogenic event even, low down
nearly where the atoms give up relation and drift in slow

falls, incredible, spaceless beads: that is an extreme
form of burning, say, but of the fire: I can't
help thinking that what we have is right enough, the

core of the galaxy, for example, a high condition,
ample, but here, though, on the surface at least,
toads, picnics tables, morning glories, firs afire:

(*Collected Poems* 376–377)

We bring the universe of fire back again, to picnic tables, right
enough.

Two poems, both moving out of nature into human structure, "The City Limits" and "The Eternal City," suggest the
development Ezra has been making, from a lessening of first

lines beginning with *I*: I broke a sheaf . . . I called the wind . . . I came . . . , to a persistence of first lines beginning with *The*: The blackbird . . . The blast . . . The burdens of the world. . . . "The Eternal City" is a beauty of this kind.

> After the explosion or cataclysm, that big
> display that does its work but then fails
> out with destructions, one is left with the
>
> pieces: at first, they don't look very valuable,
> but nothing sizable remnant around for
> gathering the senses on, one begins to take
>
> an interest, to sort out, to consider closely
> what will do and won't, matters having become
> not only small but critical: bulbs may have been
>
> uprooted: they should be eaten, if edible, or
> got back in the ground: what used to be garages,
> even the splinters, should be collected for
>
> fires: some unusually deep holes or cleared
> woods may be turned to water supplies or
> sudden fields: ruinage is hardly ever a
>
> pretty sight but it must when splendor goes
> accept into itself piece by piece all the old
> perfect human visions, all the old perfect loves.
>
> (*Collected Poems* 348–349)

Ammons celebrates; he is less restless, or Ithaca winters are longer. The lines lengthen, the generalizations provide more texture than action does. At the end of the *Collected Poems*, he's reading Xenophon. But look, then, in "Eyesight":

It was May before my
attention came
to spring and

my word I said
to the southern slopes
I've

missed it,

He's in motion again. And the proportions hold.

The Talk of Giants

Josephine Jacobsen

THE PUBLICATION OF A. R. Ammons's *Collected Poems,
1951–1971* (New York: W. W. Norton, 1973), has focused
attention on a poet who has quietly risen to the top rank of
American poets. Actually, it was obvious in his first book
(*Ommateum,* 1955), that his work was strong and original, and
formidable in its promise. Belonging to no clique, identifiable by
no gimmicks, he continued to publish increasingly commanding
books, while still having a relatively narrow contact with the
poetry-reading public. In the past ten years his poetry began to
come into its own, with the publication of *Expressions of Sea
Level* in 1964, and the rapid appearance of three other books,
Corsons Inlet and *Tape for the Turn of the Year* in 1965, and
Northfield Poems in 1966. By the time *Selected Poems* arrived in
1968, his stature had been fully recognized by a number of critics. From that period to the recent publication of his collected
poems, his reputation has widened and deepened, and he is now
being recognized for what he is—one of the finest American
poets of his generation.

Ammons's poetry is a poetry which is profoundly American,
without being in any way limited by this characteristic. His use

of language, his vocabulary and phrasing are utterly and flexibly American. The universal terms of science emerge accurately and naturally from the poems' roots.

The poetry can now be read in its bulk and ripeness. It is science-minded, passionately absorbed with the processes around the poet, the constant, complex, fascinating processes of water, wind, season and genus. But if Ammons's poetry is in the tradition of "nature poets," its essence is far different from the lyric, limpid joy of John Clare, or the *paysage moralisé* of Wordsworth, or the somber farmer-wisdom of Robert Frost, or the myth-ridden marvels of D. H. Lawrence's tortoises, serpents and gentians. Ammons sees the datum of nature as *evidence*; intricate, interlocking fragments of a whole which cannot be totally understood, but which draws him deeper and deeper into its identity. No poet now writing in English has so thoroughly created on the page the huge suggestion of the whole through its most minute components.

One major aspect of the work is its concern with choices:limitation. There are choices for the root, the bird, the insect, the poet; and there are the limitations within which these choices operate. There are alternatives, but these are affected constantly by all the other alternatives chosen by contingent forms of life. The poet chooses between silence and words, and the proportion of each. Silence takes the forms of deliberate omission, understatement, statement in a lower or offbeat tone, abbreviation, refusal to be governed by the reader's satisfaction. "Coon Song" (*Collected Poems*) is a perfect example of the last. The coon, in actuality, has no alternatives, but the poet arbitrarily creates an alternative for him, without affirming it:

> you want to know what happened,
> you want to hear me describe it,
> to placate the hound's-mouth
> slobbering in your own heart:
> . . . .

I am no slave that I
should entertain you, say what you want
to hear, let you wallow in
your silt: one two three four five:
one two three four five six seven eight nine ten:
(*Collected Poems* 88)

The poem is moving underground, in silence, as the count goes on. In *Tape for the Turn of the Year* the process shows itself clearly: the thread of the poem, the authentic connection with the invoked Muse, is followed through the diversions of eating, getting the mail, shovelling snow, carting groceries, as the poem shows itself, dives into the ordinary detail which is part of its crucial silence, surfaces again.

Choices are limited, but vital. Does one love enough, and rightly? At what point does compassion rot into sentimentality, pessimism become ingratitude? At what point does optimism corrupt the attention to truth?

The choices:limitation duality becomes more important as the work progresses. Often the choice is more illusory than actual; usually something, somewhere else, is invisibly interacting to limit that choice. Nevertheless, the element of choice exists. In the case of the poet, it is brilliantly evident and utilized. He chooses the large, or the small, though inevitably, at their extremes and beyond his control, they will merge into the indefinable. He chooses speech, or that defining shadow of speech which is silence, attempting to employ just so much of silence as communication will allow. He chooses irregularities, within the limiting tone of the poem; the respites of colloquialisms, abbreviations, clowning, which are the poem's own kinds of varied silences. He chooses, above all, not to make a choice final:

my other word is
provisional:
we'll talk about that

> someday,
> tho you may guess
> the meanings from *ecology*:
>
> don't establish the
>   boundaries
>   first,
>   the squares, triangles,
>   boxes
>   of preconceived
>   possibility
>   and then
>   pour
>   life into them, trimming
> off left-over edges,
> ending potential:
>   let centers
>   proliferate
>   from
> self-justifying motions!
>
> (Tape 116)

Over and over we are warned that the closed conclusion, like the attempt to distort evidence for the salvation of our hopes, is death. We are allowed only the constant tension between the defined and the indefinable, between the need to be identified and the need to be lost, between hope and reality:

> have I prettified the
>   tragedies,
>   the irrecoverable
>   losses: have I
> glossed over the
> unmistakable evils:
> has panic

tried to make a flower:

then, hope distorts
me:
    turns wishes into lies:

I care about the statement
of fact:
    the true picture
    has a beauty higher
    than Beauty:

                    (*Tape* 153)

A second vital aspect of the poems is the concern with utility:waste. When Ammons writes in "Catalyst" (*Collected Poems*),

    Honor the maggot,
      supreme catalyst:
he spurs the rate of change:
(all scavengers are honorable: I love them
all,
will scribble as hard as I can for them)
              (*Collected Poems* 110)

his is not a merely ecological admiration for maximum efficiency. It is the admiration of the poet, this particular poet; the belief that the Muse is as formidably economical as the natural system of waste and replenishment. Poetry has no accidental lapses; instead, it continues to define, by its underground presence, by its saliences and invisibilities, by those surrounding silences which define its metaphors, as a plain sets forth a solitary tree.

    but betimes & at times
    let me out of here:

I will penetrate into the
void
& bring back
nothingness
to surround all these
       shapes with!

                              (*Tape* 63)

In Ammons's poetry there are differing silences—all useful,
all used. There is the silence which ensues when the thing con-
templated becomes too large or too small for speech, when the
particular disappears into sizelessness, the sizelessness of the
unimaginably small, the unimaginably great. In neither direction
does the imagination cease to function, but silence takes over as
its expression. Often one has very clearly this sense of a speech
just beyond the imagination's speech: a minute, insect-like voice
drilling at an unimaginable height; a subterranean, immense
rumble at a depth too deep for the imagination to fathom. They
meet. And this is the ultimate economy of Ammons's poetry.
This *is* the talk of giants, illustrating the illusion of size: the atom
which can destroy a mountain, the drop of water complex as a
galaxy.

Sometimes this economy has a terrifying quality, and there is
often the sense of the poet moving, carefully, through a world in
which a more acute consciousness has been substituted for the
"normal" illusory proportions. This is one reason why the earlier poems tend to confine overtly defined emotions to isolated
poems, individual incidents. The vast process observed and
reported on is so intricate, so incredibly able in its motions, so
frighteningly economical, that all poetic energy is absorbed into
that observing, that reporting. Conclusions, other than tentative
conclusions on immediate evidence, are postponed, are presently
inappropriate.

A pig, the comfortable familiar of a hundred mornings, will
be slaughtered when the inescapable calendar says so; the indi-

vidual and precious mule will be carted off when the inescapable
financial calendar says so; a marvelous and battered human figure will shine out of the inescapable processes of pain and death.
But what, if anything, this *means* cannot yet assert itself; there is
still too much evidence to be accumulated. The pig will feed
other bodies, the mule will balance a debt; the servant-friend's
gnarled body responds to the demand of toil.

The parallels are too numerous and beautifully varied to
belabor. Among these, the bones of the poet on which the wind
will perform the song the poet did not manage; the glossy flies
winging up from the dead cat's putrefaction; the poet's use of his
tape, which permits and limits.

A THIRD IMPORTANT tension of Ammons's poetry is that of
levels:compensation, and this is perhaps most powerfully represented in the title poem of *Expressions of Sea Level,* one of the
most remarkable poems of its time. It is as though this poetry,
for an instant, laid a finger on a pulsating heart exposed to
touch. "Expressions of Sea Level" is a poem so close to non-
verbal reality that the reader feels he is in the presence of some
miraculously sensitive instrument. That instrument fixes the
position of the poet, the spot from which he works. It establishes
that fractional instant of balance, that living center of a shift so
secret and so momentary as to be almost a metaphor in itself—a
point from which all the infinite interplay, fluctuation, compensation, choices, are redistributed, redefined, again set in motion.

In a body of poetry which must reject, by its very nature, the
appearance of a highly organized overplan, it is no small triumph
that the poems—the very long as well as the very short—show an
almost unbroken parallel in their structure to their conception of
the natural and poetic worlds. The ebb and flow, the periods of
dryness, with catalogued details, provide a duplication of the
poem's intent, a sort of root-tree, shaped like the tree in air.

The form of the lines upon the page turns out to be a physical expression of the poetry's basic element: a dominant sense of form, evidenced in flexibility and a variety of modes and tones. The lines in the long poems—and these are by far the greater number—assert a fundamental character: a breath-oriented, serious but not solemn, *discussion,* varying according to season, mood, the advent and termination of incidents; however indented, stretched, abbreviated, the discussion always maintains the balance between the poetry's intention and the levity of failures, disappointments, the ridiculous and necessary frustrations of actuality. The very real lyric quality in the poems is so conditioned by the other ingredients, humor, information, discoveries, that it can be easily missed.

Humor in Ammons's poems, being the manipulation of proportion, weaves in and out of even much of the serious poetry. It is overt in regard to the poet himself: he sees himself at once as a weed, a fool, and Ezra, the speech of the wind; above all, as a servant to the Muse:

> help me:
> I have this &
> > no other comfort:
> > the song,
> the slight, inner
> unmistakable song you
> give me
> and nothing else! what
> > are you,
> some kind of strumpet?
> will you pull out on me?
> look: I have faith: I
> have faith: come or go:
> I'll always love you:
> I have nothing else:
> I have
> nothing else besides you:

will you tear me
to pieces? I'll go
on without you, until
you come again:

(*Tape* 45)

The poet shoots himself down at the first hint of the portentous.

One major fact has contributed greatly to the strength and toughness of Ammons's writing: the matter of reinforcement. Most of those poets who signally avoid stasis, and the slow process of petrifaction within their own accomplishment, move sequentially, developing forward from past accomplishment by way of experiment, and advance upon new territory. Ammons has moved circularly, in the manner of seasons and tides, reinforcing the nature, the manner, the approaches of his poetry. New growth constantly appears, compelling changes by development, variation, richness, penetration. But what is happening is unmistakably, organically, what was happening in his very first poems. It is not just that one can identify an Ammons poem by its essential tone and flavor; it is that the concerns, the self-admonitions, the scrupulous search, the vast undertaking, are exactly that to which his first poems were addressed. To be able to control so much renewal, to strengthen and deepen new insights and hints, upon so permanent a project, to maintain so much *oneness* and flexibility in such an unrelentingly coherent poetic purpose, is perhaps the most solid of Ammons's achievements.

One of Ammons's preoccupations is the poet's relation to his reader. Ammons works within the tension between the wish and need to communicate, and a vigilant sense of the poet's need for freedom—freedom from the dictation of the reader's taste and approbation. (As for the more sordid dictates of poetic fashion, it would be hard to find any poet now writing more totally free from the taint of other-directed concessions to any sort of bandwagonism.) Dickinson and Hopkins come to mind, but each

was sealed into (or freed by) certain rigid habits of life, while
Ammons's work is freely exposed to an almost unnerving range
of interests. His poetry, owing nothing to any school, group,
clique, critical pressure, has developed its unique tone in a sort
of solitary soliloquy which is simultaneously an open response
to life, and a dialogue with the self. Its originality, so unostenta-
tious as to make only a gradual impression, is amazing—far less
an easily identifiable matter of technique, vocabulary, subject
matter, than of breath, tone and texture. It is this sort of originality which argues best for the permanent value of his poetry.

Ammons's sense of the necessity to communicate accounts in
part for the organic quality of his poetry. Solipsism would be
ludicrous: poetry must be a part of a speak-hear process of
shared discovery. But a refusal of the hearer's influence comes at
the point where any concession would distract the poet from the
quest for his quarry, from the balanced point of a position which
must be constantly realigned. The "Coon Song," having
addressed life, death, survival, defeat, at their deepest level,
starts back abruptly from the reader's "Well, what happened?"
pressure. Within the poem, nothing is inevitable; so the thread is
roughly snapped. The near-solemn vocabulary is abruptly sub-
verted. The coon, having a secret knowledge, will cause the
hounds to disappear, but will end in disorder in the teeth of
hounds:

> now there
> one two three four five
> are two philosophies:
> here we go round the mouth-wet of hounds:

> what I choose
> is youse:
> baby

(*Collected Poems* 89)

There is a very strong pressure on the poet to "reflect his own time." What is his identity—personal, political, social, national—within the parentheses of his dates of birth and death—specifically, the birth and death dates of his life as poet? If any demonstration were needed (which seems unlikely) that poetry of major caliber relates to, and indeed affects, every aspect of its own time, regardless of subject matter or specific reference, Ammons's poetry would afford it. American it is, as earlier noted, by its accent and tone. Its personal and social relevance to its own time comes through the compliment it pays to continuity: it examines doggedly those interactions of environment, characteristics, chance, and law, which shape human history. There is no section in his entire work which is not applicable to our immediate predicament. Unquestionably, a reader's taste for more explicitly considered human problems may be thwarted: Ammons's poetry supplies the key and the energy; it is up to the reader to open any door he wishes.

There is in the work, however, a growing sense of the personal emerging from the poetry, and this must be a consideration in any attempt to understand its present direction. Eighty lives are lost when a plane crashes over Delaware:

> grieved, we
> rejoice
> as a man rejoices saved
>   from death: we beg
> that men be spared
> calamity & the hard turn:
> we make an offering of out
> praise: we reaccept:
>
>   our choice is
>   gladness:

> (*Tape* 17)

Gladness is chosen; but it is a hard and constantly eroded choice. It is mostly in the recent work that human sorrow, of which the early deprivations were foretokens, has become more explicit. It is as though the poet's universe had to be formerly so passionately and protractedly examined that there was no room in the resulting poem for explicit expression of the havoc wrought on human affections and attachments. Eight years ago, a short poem gave full scope at last to sorrow. "Dark Song" (*Collected Poems*) says it all in twelve lines:

> Sorrow how high it is
> that no wall holds it
> back: deep
>
> it is that no dam undermines
> it: wide that it
> comes on as up a strand
>
> multiple and relentless:
> the young that are
> beautiful must die; the
>
> old, departing,
> can confer
> nothing.
>
> (*Collected Poems* 176)

The refusal of the work as a whole to tie itself to the occasional or topical, the stubbornness of its roots in the specific as part of the universal, are what makes the poetry relevant to contemporary problems. The poems are never as discrete as they seem. Just as every choice, every fragment of motion, affects multiple beings in unexpected ways, so the slightest ethical shift affects all human relations. In the poem "Expressions of Sea Level," the secret moment of balance—leagues out, at an undefinable ocean-point—affects the tiny pools of minnows inland. The faintest suggestion of a shift sets in motion life and death forces. It would be nonsense to argue that this sort of poetry has little to do with the terrors and pressures of our daily life.

Although the poems use scientific terms freely, Ammons is sharply conscious of what must be the incorruptibility of the vocabulary in relation to its subject:

> high-falutin
> language does not
> rest on the
> cold water
> all night
> by
> the luminous
> birches:
>
> is too vivid
> for the eyes
> of pigeons,
> heads tucked
> under wings in
> first
> patches of sunlight:
>
> is too noisy to
> endure
> the sleep of buds,
> the holding in
> of the huckleberry
> blossom:
>
> too voracious
> to spin,
> rest
> & change:

is too clever
for the frank
honey-drop
of the lily-pistil:

(Tape 131–132)

Ammons's poetry as a whole can be considered religious in character. It possesses the senses of humility and awe, and a kind of unconquerable expectation. This was foreshadowed in the earliest of books. But it was a preoccupation often submerged for long periods in simply paying attention, that special genius of Ammons. This attention often brought on dismaying results, results never distorted in the service of optimism. Though Ammons now and then reminds his reader of Emerson, there is an unbridgeable gap between the basically firm optimism of the transcendentalist, and the painful, theory-free search of the poet of "Extremes and Moderations" (*Collected Poems*). In "Unsaid," Ammons asked, earlier,

Have you listened for the things I have left out?
I am nowhere near the end yet and already
       hear
       the hum of omissions,
the chant of vacancies, din of

silences:

(Collected Poems 90–91)

Toward whichever side the balance tilts, there is a silence affirming the counterweight:

I know
the standing on loose
              ground:
I know the

violence, grief, guilt,
despair, absurdity:
    the sky's raw:
    the star
refuses our wish,
obliterates us with
      permanence,
      scoop of its
      coming and going:

I know what it is
    to feel around in
    the dark
    for a hold
    & to touch
    nothing:

we must bear
the dark edges of
our awareness:

                      (*Tape* 154–155)

Here, hope is silent.

    and when
    the Florentines painted
    radiant populations in
      the heavens, they were
            not wrong:
          each of
  us,
    says modern science, is
    radiant,
        tho
        below the

> visible spectrum:
> paradise will
> refine our radiance
> or give us better sight:
>   we're fallen
>   now:
>   we may be raised into
>   knowledge & light:
>   lower would be
> longer & longer wavelengths
> to dark's undisturbed constant:
> may we
> not go there
> but ever and ever up
>   singing into shining
> light:
>
> <div align="right">(<i>Tape</i> 52–53)</div>

Here, it is sorrow which is silent.

More and more, in the recent poems, the personal emerges from the universal. But the foundation has been so strongly laid, the range of the search has been so wide, that this increasingly personal element, far from narrowing or weakening the poetry, is itself infused with an extraordinary strength, as though a quintessence of all the natural world had been concentrated in a human emotion.

It is obviously pointless to speculate about the future direction of the poetry, especially in view of Ammons's repeated refusal to impose a pattern, to provide that definition which is the final box:

> when we solve, we're
> saved by deeper problems:
>   definition is death:

                          the final box:
                  hermetic seal:

                                          (*Tape* 171)

But the pressure of a greater freedom to express the personal
(always within the wider context), and the sense that for some
time now he has been ready to draw conclusions, if always the
most tentative, make Ammons's current poetry interesting in a
way that little contemporary poetry attempts to be. It is interesting, also, that the culture which has produced this particular
body of work has been, in general, the most antithetical to its
elements. It is nature poetry from a nation hastily burying itself
in concrete and plastic; a poetry conscious of immense reaches
of time, in a period of changes so frenetic that a cardiogram of
its heart would cause despair; a poetry of humility and patience
in a setting of shrillness; a poetry of immense scope in a rabble
of specialists. Perhaps such a period is best suited to produce just
such poetry.

The one thing which can be predicted is that that scope will
not shrink:

                  is there a point of rest where
                  the tide turns: is there one
                  infinitely tiny higher touch
            on the legs of egrets, the
            skin of back, bay-eddy reeds:
                  is there an instant when fullness is,
                  without loss, complete: is there a
                  statement perfect in its speech:

            how do you know the moon
            is moving: see the dry
            casting of the beach worm
                  dissolve at the
            delicate rising touch:

that is the
   expression of sea level,
the talk of giants,
of oceans, moons, sun, of everything,
spoken in a dampened grain of sand.

                        ("Expressions of Sea Level,"
                              Collected Poems 136)

Ammons's Radiant Toys

David Kalstone

Less than total is a bucketful of radiant toys.
— A. R. AMMONS, *"Cut the Grass"*

P ASTORAL IS HARD reading today, not simply because we
are more removed from "nature" than the city-dwellers
who wrote the first pastoral poems, but because it is a
genre scored with contradictions. Its language, stripped of social
entanglements, can be baffling and abstract, strenuous testings
of the mind against a landscape, as if these were the only really
telling encounters. Its modern exponents—Frost, Stevens and
Ammons among them—seem almost sentenced to write pastoral
poems. "Life is an affair of people not of places. But for me,"
Wallace Stevens wrote, "life is an affair of places and that is the
trouble." Companionable eclogues have long since given way to
solitary discoveries, thoughtful shepherds to epistemologists.

Modern pastoral exposes the problems of modern poetry in
their most extreme forms. Rather than serving as a welcome setting for verse, landscape presents a test of the poet's ability to see
and enter the world, a crisis of observer and object. Poets like
Stevens and Ammons satisfy and frustrate us because, drawn to
the radiance of things of this world, these writers are also the
most ample and abstract witnesses of their own failure to pos-

sess them. In Stevens's words, "It is the human that is the alien, /
The human that has no cousin in the moon" ("Less and Less
Human, O Savage Spirit"). Ammons sees the poet, pastoral or
otherwise, as a "surrendered self among unwelcoming forms"
("Gravelly Run"). His large ambitions and his frequent fallings
away in the face of abundance make Ammons's pastoral poems
sound puzzled and urgent, the frustrations of the most willing,
the most ardent, the most open observer. I cannot agree with
Helen Vendler that Ammons "will have written the first
twentieth-century poetry wholly purged of the romantic." His
not being purged is the problem. He has always had a gift for
recalling romantic promises as if there were fresh ways for them
to be fulfilled: "for it is not so much to know the self / as to
know it as it is known / by galaxy and cedar cone" ("Gravelly
Run"). Yet after these exhilarating prospects come the sobering
performances, the puzzles of the "surrendered self among
unwelcoming forms." What sounded like visionary prompt-
ings—lightning weddings of the self to the outside world—
become bewilderments before his eyes.

To devise in the face of that sense of nature an ample rhetoric
has been Ammons's problem and finally his distinction: to have
invented a pastoral poem at once jagged and discontinuous, but
still open to radiance; to have found a grammar that almost
erases the speaker who uses it. We can see Ammons's claims over
landscape at their most minimal in a recent poem like "Further
On":

> Up this high and far north
> it's shale and woodsless snow:
> small willows and alder brush
>
> mark out melt streams on the
> opposite slope and the wind talks
> as much as it can before freeze

takes the gleeful, glimmering
tongues away: whips and sticks
will scream and screech then

all winter over the deaf heights,
the wind lifting its saying out
to the essential yell of the

lost and gone: it's summer now:
elk graze the high meadows:
marshgrass heads high as a moose's

ears: lichen, a wintery weed,
fills out for the brittle sleep:
waterbirds plunder the shallows.

(*Collected Poems* 288–289)

In this poem summer sensations are almost stunted by reminders everywhere of the approaching inhuman freeze: "the brittle sleep," the cold which "takes the gleeful, glimmering / tongues away." More important, the threat is put in terms of human speech and understanding: "the wind lifting its saying out / to the essential yell of the / lost and gone." Against such odds, against a "yell" that strangles articulation, even the ability to describe, to offer the reader a corner of landscape becomes a form of self-assertion. What serves is an exact sense of the surviving instincts of summer life: "lichen, a wintery weed, / fills out for the brittle sleep: / waterbirds plunder the shallows."

Many of Ammons's short poems—especially those in *Uplands* (1970) and *Briefings* (1971)—end in just such reduced circumstances, whether facing inhuman zero weather, as in "Further On," or doing battle against the "Periphery," the profusion and separateness of the outside world, "thickets hard to get around in / or get around for / an older man." The poem "Periphery," after looking for explanations and for a center that governs the luxuriant border growth, lapses at its close into documentary satisfactions:

>   I came on a spruce
>
>   thicket full of elk, gushy snow-weed,
>   nine species of lichen, four pure-white
>   rocks and
>   several swatches of verbena near bloom.
>   (*Collected Poems* 275)

These precise notations are ultimately shrunken relatives of Whitman's famous catalogues—more modest, but announcing some kinship as in another recent poem, "Breaks":

>   From silence to silence:
>   as a woods stream
>   over a
>   rock holding on
>
>   breaks into clusters of sound
>   multiple and declaring as
>   leaves, each one,
>
>   filling
>   the continuum between leaves,
>
>   I stand up,
>   fracturing the equilibrium,
>   hold on,
>
>   my disturbing, skinny speech
>   declaring
>   the cosmos.
>   (*Collected Poems* 204)

This is not one of Ammons's very best poems. With its awkward bow to Whitman, the "I" seems unsettled, uneasily self-assertive, "standing up" when at other moments in the poem the speaker is pointedly guarded: guarded by the parentheses which enclose the poem ("From silence to silence") and by its otherwise self-deprecating tone, the "disturbing, skinny speech" which contrasts so sharply with Whitman's expansive line.

From the title on ("Breaks": noun or verb? ruptures? bits of fortune? glimpses as through a clouded sky?), Ammons courts a certain confusion. The poem fans out, one simile explained by another, the sound of a woods stream over rocks compared to the "declaration" of new leaves. From that simile within a simile, he pops into the poem "fracturing the equilibrium." The grammar is not entirely clear. He "holds on" like the jutting rock but "declares" like the clusters of sound breaking over it. His "disturbing, skinny speech" is a wry deflation of the stream's "multiple" sound and the "declaring" leaves. No need to labor a simple point, one that helps us understand Ammons's more interesting lyrics. After nature's generous sounds, the assertion of self seems both awkward and a little uncontrolled, an odd placing of the ego. Surprised by fluency, he doesn't appropriate the landscape as Whitman would, though the phrase "declaring the cosmos" might well be Whitman's own.

I am talking about the observer's voice and the assurance it offers us over objects and landscapes. Even Robert Frost's country speakers are sociable by comparison with Ammons's. Frost's wit—his secure rhymes, the way he spreads his net over the sonnet's frame, his puns that catch the eye in a conspiracy of meaning—never allows natural terrors to terrorize form. It is good to have his tone in mind for comparison with Ammons's. Something like "One Step Backward Taken" with its near jingles about geological upheavals in a new ice age ("Whole capes caked off in slices") absorbs catastrophe before it occurs (capes into cake):

> I felt my standpoint shaken
> In the universal crisis.
> But with one step backward taken
> I saved myself from going.

Frost's backward step is also a foreseeing one, a witty preparation.

In a more somber version of disaster, "Desert Places," Frost
looks at a snow scene which threatens to obliterate everything.
From an initial urgency ("Snow falling and night falling fast, oh,
fast / In a field I looked into going past"—insistent participles,
phrases rather than sentences) the poem gathers to a self-
assertion that takes in all the fear:

> They cannot scare me with their empty spaces
> Between stars—on stars where no human race is.
> I have it in me so much nearer home
> To scare myself with my own desert places.

The poem finds a form and assured tone which answer the terror
that remains undiminished. Frost can be homely, witty, and desperate in a single line: "The loneliness includes me unawares,"
asserting by the end a kind of canny control. Balanced sentences
and emphatic rhetoric can replace the poem's introductory
phrases acting out the mind's growing command as it understands its terrors:

> And lonely as it is that loneliness
> Will be more lonely ere it will be less—
> A blanker whiteness of benighted snow
> With no expression, nothing to express.

Always beleaguered by nature, Frost has his witty standpoint,
his one step backward to take. Frost's poems end, have a place
to go, come to rest.

This is precisely what we feel Ammons cannot do: "Stop on any word and language gives way: / the blades of reason, unlightened by motion, sink in" ("Essay on Poetics"). He has his doubts about the finished poem and his own place in it. A few years ago he threaded a book-length poem along an adding machine tape—the poem ended when the tape did—producing a December diary, *Tape for the Turn of the Year.* That was his most flamboyant attempt to turn his verse into something beyond neat gatherings. With *Uplands* and *Briefings,* his most recent short volumes, he was obviously resisting summaries and the idea of books marking stages in a poetic career. They were closer to journals of mental states, each poem an entry finding a form and a scene for a very exact encounter or discovery. The point lay not only in single adventures, but in the continuing, sometimes driven effort: "why does he write poems: it's the only way he can mean / what he says [. . .] / he keeps saying in order to hope he will / say something he means [. . .] / poems deepen his attention till what he is thinking / catches the energy of a deep rhythm" ("Hibernaculum"). The oddest part of that statement is how tentative it is; he keeps writing in order at least to "hope" he'll touch "meaning."

Under such pressures Ammons was bound to value a style that kept moving. "Viable" tells part of the story:

> Motion's the dead give away,
> eye catcher, the revealing risk:
> the caterpillar sulls on the hot macadam
>
> but then, risking, ripples to the bush:
> the cricket, startled, leaps the
> quickest arc: the earthworm, casting,
>
> nudges a grassblade, and the sharp robin
> strikes: sound's the other
> announcement: the redbird lands in

an elm branch and tests the air with
cheeps for an answering, reassuring
cheep, for a motion already cleared:

survival organizes these means down to
tension, to enwrapped, twisting suasions:
every act or non-act enceinte with risk or

prize: why must the revelations be
sound and motion, the poet, too, moving and
saying through the scary opposites to death.

> (*Collected Poems* 343)

Looking askance at "revelation," this poem twins it with danger, scales it down to watching for prey, for the smallest movements. Rather than revelation, there is "the revealing risk"; the "dead give away" is the only moment when the currents of life become visible, palpable for us. The puns and playfulness are part of Ammons's game. Observing, catlike, the rippling caterpillar, the startled cricket, the earthworm prey to the robin, his poem mimics their motion with its own chain of clauses and darting participles. It must, above all, sound offhand, the somber truth buried in the casual opening line. Motion is caught as from the corner of the eye.

Ammons had long since, in a poem called "Motion," talked about the impossibility of ever identifying word with thing. Poems are "fingers, methods, / nets, / not what is or / was." Still he had faith in the music of a poem which

by the motion of
its motion
resembles
what, moving, is—
the wind

underleaf white against
the tree.

(*Collected Poems* 147)

In "Viable" he is more canny, more reticent, and also more alive
to what *compels* him to seek renewals of motion. Poetry—the
movement of poetry—comes closer to reflex and to survival; the
final line of "Viable" only confirms a shadow we have already
felt. Nature's small creatures, the poem admits, are observed not
so much for their own sake as to be a pulse for the poet. He
attempts, through verse, movements as minute as theirs. Motion
reveals; sound, like the robin's call, waits for a reply, tests the air
for "an answering, reassuring / cheep, for a motion already
cleared." The question that closes the poem is rhetorical; there
are no answers to its *why*, only repeated close observation of tiny
actions to relieve an innate and natural "tension." The poet is
alive to risks, taking his prize, hoping to prove for this moment
that he is alive by catching "the energy of a deep rhythm," all the
time acknowledging that he too is ultimately prey. In paraphrase
this sounds like a desperate enterprise, but in the poem such
explicit meanings are subsumed by metaphor until the very end,
absorbed in risk and variety—*sulls, ripples, nudges,* and *strikes.*

A poem like "Viable" is very revealing of Ammons's developed style. Natural facts—an enormous repertoire of them,
closely observed—tick through his verse and make it seem, at
least superficially, a fulfillment of William Carlos Williams's
"No ideas but in things." Ammons's measured, skinny lines
focus our attention on things and parts of things with the insistence of a slow-motion camera.

Yet he is restless adopting that style, even when setting out its
advantages: "I'm doing the best I can, / that is to say, with too
many linking verbs: the grandest / clustering of aggregates permits the finest definition" ("Essay on Poetics," *Collected Poems*
302). The superlatives suggest a fussy version of Williams's
"objectivity." Certainly Williams's notation pulses through

Ammons's short poems, just as the casual, almost random style of the Beats and New York School gives him a way to talk about the provisional and constantly changing voices in his long poems. Those voices contribute to his later verse, but also go against a natural bent, a desire that nature signify or "add up." As a reading of "Viable" suggests, objects may seem like counters in a larger game.

Why then adopt voices close to the minimal and casual, styles which seem least suited to ambitious statement? Certainly the constant struggle of realistic notation and visionary pressure charges these later poems with problematic power and beauty, and explains their curious blurring of the ego. But it is only when we look back to Ammons's early work, poems which reach openly for transcendence, that we see how much he needed the concrete resistance of contemporary objective styles.

Harold Bloom has traced the undisguised Emersonianism of Ammons's early poems. From the very start the poems feared threats to speech: "The pieces of my voice have been thrown / away," he complains in "Rack," and he finds the winds and the sea swallowing his voice in "So I Said I am Ezra" which Ammons sets at the opening of his *Collected Poems*.

> I . . .
> . . . .
> swayed as if the wind were taking me away
> and said
>   I am Ezra
> As a word too much repeated
> falls out of being
> so I Ezra went out into the night
> like a drift of sand

Two threats, loss of speech and loss of self, are fused in a single haunted image ("As a word"). But what kind of speech is it that is constantly endangered or scattered? In "Rack" the poet sees himself ransacking nature: "I must run down all the pieces / and build the whole silence back." What is yearned for—and here the Emersonianism is most strongly felt—is a spectral voice, so complete as to be equivalent to silence. He envisions a speech beyond words, which will offset the threatened loss of identity, a ghostly voice which replaces the merely human "I."

Such satisfactions, rarified and not a matter of earthly fulfill-ment, give an entirely different feel to Ammons's early verse. He faces the shattering abundance of the world, its threat to ego, by making a lunge toward vision, as in the last lines of "Prodigal":

> the spent
> seer, delivered to wastage, risen
> into ribs, consigns knowledge to
> approximation, order to the vehicle
> of change, and fumbles blind in blunt innocence
> toward divine, terrible love.
>
> (*Collected Poems* 77)

Almost ten years later, in "Laser," that same seer trying "to dream of diversity" can admit only one riveting image at a time; and at the close he must suffer an all too human lapse, a fall into a drained and deadened state:

> the image glares filling all space:
> the head falls and
> hangs and cannot wake itself.
>
> (*Collected Poems* 188)

The early poems face no such daily re-enacted deaths. One of their frequent gestures is a welcome abandonment of the world: "I closed up all the natural throats of earth / [. . .] and saying farewell / stepped out into the great open" ("Some Months Ago," *Collected Poems* 5); "I looked down at the ashes / and rose and walked out of the world" ("In Strasbourg in 1349," *Collected Poems* 3); or

Turning a moment to say so long
    to the spoken
    and seen
    I stepped into
the implicit pausing sometimes
on the way to listen to unsaid things
          ("Turning a Moment to Say So Long,"
                    Collected Poems 10)

These poems, awkward and tentative, have not really found the right language for their transcendent adventures. Full of ceremonies and rituals, they try to convince us of vision by using the simplest syntax to recount supernatural events: "I went out to the sun." The effect he is looking for is something like the casual tone of Herbert's heavenly encounters, which convince by their comely, secure, childlike Teachings for another world. One of Ammons's characteristic early structures is the declarative "I" with a verb in the simple past. In another the simple declarative clause is preceded by a present participial phrase: "Merging into place against a slope of trees, I extended my arms." Given the high frequency of present participles in these first poems, there is surprisingly little sense of movement; action is arrested by the completed pasts into tableaux, characters in a frieze as they reach for or just attain transcendence.

These modes do not completely satisfy Ammons, or so one would think from some unsettled and unsettling poems sprinkled among the early rituals. They sound almost masochistic in their desire for change:

With ropes of hemp
I lashed my body to the great oak
saying odes for the fiber of the oakbark
and the oakwood saying supplications
to the root mesh
          ("With Ropes of Hemp," *Collected Poems* 14)

Or:

> A gall-nesting wren took my breath
>
> flicking her wings, and
> far into summer the termites found the heart.
> > ("Song," *Collected Poems* 35)

The second of the two ends in annihilation; the first closes with a metamorphosis, the melting self "returning" to say odes in the night. But both poems suggest more than a yearning for escape. They try to force their way to vision not through ritual exits and tableaux, but by a burial *in* nature, a smothered union with the world.

The dilemma becomes clear to Ammons in poems like "Ritual for Eating the World." A rope hangs mysteriously from rocks. At first it is threatening: a hangman's noose or "god's own private fishing hook." Then, seized as a lifeline, a rope "old mountain / climbers left / dangling," it may be a way to the visionary heights. Finally grasped,

> it broke
> and all through the heaving night
> making day I faced
>
> piecemeal the sordid
> reacceptance of my world
> > (*Collected Poems* 48)

No talk here of reassembling the pieces of his world into a perfect silence. Conflating the hangman's noose—the self-annihilating impulse—and the climber's rope, an active escape, he is able to see the two as related and doomed to failure. The alternative, ever stronger in his poems, is the piecemeal mastery of his *own* world, here awkwardly scorned, but "faced."

Ammons entertains alternatives more fluently in a fine poem
of the same period, "Hymn." Genial, free of the pressures which
make him want to lash himself to nature "with ropes of hemp,"
it truly represents, in Bloom's words, "Ammons's second start as
a poet." Each choice has its separate moment:

> I know if I find you I will have to leave the earth
> and go on out
>   over the sea marshes and the brant in bays

And in the second section:

> And I know if I find you I will have to stay with the earth
> inspecting with thin tools and ground eyes
> . . . .
> and going right on down where the eye sees only traces
> (Collected Poems 39)

"Hymn" does not attempt a resolution. It praises the alternatives and is delicately conditional about ever locating the truth
of nature, equally accepting, as Bloom puts it, that "one part of
the self will be yielded to an apprehension beyond sight, while
the other will stay here with the earth, to be yielded to sight's
reductiveness, separated with each leaf."

Poems like "Hymn" seem a relief for Ammons. Irreconcilable
tensions have surfaced and win equal and clear-eyed attention.
Yearnings once awkward are now absorbed into a style rather
than swamping it. They generate a new kind of poem, as he was
to announce in "Guide": "You cannot come to unity and remain
material: / in that perception is no perceiver / when you arrive /
you have gone too far." The perceiver was realistically to replace
the seer as protagonist in his poems, though the ghost of the
visionary is always there, hinting at unity, rueful and radiant. In
some of his poems the two voices are raised in gentle argument,

or can be recognized prompting together or in counterpoint the
speaker of the poem. In "Gravelly Run" he is open to both:

> I don't know somehow it seems sufficient
> to see and hear whatever coming and going is,
> losing the self to the victory
>   of stones and trees,
> of bending sandpit lakes, crescent
> round groves of dwarf pine:
>
> for it is not so much to know the self
> as to know it as it is known
>   by galaxy and cedar cone,
> as if birth had never found it
> and death could never end it:
>
> the swamp's slow water comes
> down Gravelly Run fanning the long
>   stone-held algal
> hair and narrowing roils between
> the shoulders of the highway bridge:
>
> holly grows on the banks in the woods there,
> and the cedars' gothic-clustered
>   spires could make
> green religion in winter bones:
>
> so I look and reflect, but the air's glass
> jail seals each thing in its entity:
>
> no use to make any philosophies here:
>   I see no
> god in the holly, hear no song from
> the snowbroken weeds: Hegel is not the winter
> yellow in the pines: the sunlight has never

heard of trees: surrendered self among
unwelcoming forms: stranger,
hoist your burdens, get on down the road.
(*Collected Poems* 55–56)

Central to an understanding of Ammons's verse, "Gravelly
Run" is more explicit about its problems (a speaker who reads
Hegel and talks about epistemology) than many of Ammons's
later lyrics were to be. Being explicit at this stage allows him his
casual tone; having aired so much that his earlier poems did not
admit, he can accept himself as the stranger who must "get on
down the road."

What is remarkable about "Gravelly Run" is the modulation
of tone, the range of voices to which it is open. At the beginning
seer and observer seem united. The opening rhythms widen to
visionary assurance ("as if birth had never found it / and death
could never end it"); observation narrows to the utmost particularity (the emphatic consonant-clotted "long / stone-held algal /
hair and narrowing roils"). From that exercise, taking a sharper
license, he imagines the cedars as spires. A rebuke is prompt and
compact. "Reflect," offered as a gesture of understanding, is
drained of its meditative meaning before our eyes. Human gesture becomes nothing but a reflection, a mirror; the poem turns
everything brutally physical, a world of unconnected particles,
his visionary effort merely that of the "surrendered self among
unwelcoming forms."

From this time on the placing of self in Ammons's work is
one of its oddest features. In "Saliences," one of his best poems,
the "I" enters only in its closing third. It has, of course, made
earlier veiled appearances, from the moment, in fact, that this
poem announces its title, which has to do with the interaction of
mind and landscape. Saliences are, as Bloom notes, "outleapings, 'mind feeding out,' not taking in perceptions but turning its
violent energies out into the field of action." The ostensible subject of the poem is a dunes walk like that of "Corsons Inlet." But

an elaborate syntax keeps the "I" from making assertions in any ordinary way:

> Consistencies rise
> and ride
> the mind down
> hard routes
>   walled
> with no outlet and so
> to open a variable geography,
>   proliferate
> possibility, here
> is this dune fest
>   releasing
> mind feeding out,
> gathering clusters,
> fields of order in disorder,
> where choice
> can make beginnings,
>   turns,
>   reversals,
>
> (*Collected Poems* 151–152)

The very notion of a distanced "mind" is provocative. It both acts (feeding, gathering) and is acted upon (ridden down, released). More important, the distinction between the two is almost erased when the "dune fest" begins. We are to be caught in a whirl of motion, self merging with the outer world. The rhythm, the short lines and relentless alternation of noun and participle practically blot out differences between actions of mind and nature. Nouns are suspended in a chain of participial explosions of equal force ("releasing / mind feeding out, / gathering clusters"). The maneuver is vital; you almost feel that the verbal motion is more important than the mixture of abstractions and particulars swept along, and that everything moves, dissolving "before the one event that / creates present time," an event described in the long second section of the poem, the palpable "unarranged disorder" of the wind. Tracing the sequence of tenses here is one way of telling the story: a sweep of present participles through the landscape ("weathering shells with blast, / [. . .] lifting / the spider"); then the wind traced in past participles, a loving dialogue with objects it touches ("wind / shaped and kept in the / bent of trees, / [. . .] the kept and erased sand-crab trails"). All this is done with a Whitmanic force, minimal pauses, the movement constantly aided by repetitions of words and participial endings—but in a shorter line than Whitman's to accelerate the flow.

Only then, after this virtual effacement of the self, does he begin in a third movement to lay claim to the experience: with imperatives ("bend to these / changing weathers") and, finally, with his first use of the simple past tense ("when I went back to the dunes today"). This is the first real admission of a separate observer and leads to what Bloom describes as the "firm beauty" of the last seventy lines, a detailed tracing of "the reassurance [. . .] / that through change / continuities sinuously work." In a recapitulation of the previous day's sights and sounds, all changed but with shades of resemblance (the "saliences" of the title "congruent to memory"), he finds "summations of permanence! / where not a single single thing endures." The confusion of present and past in the memory is full and fruitful:

> much seemed
> constant, to be looked
> forward to, expected:
> from the top of a dune rise,
> look of ocean salience: in
>   the hollow,
> where a runlet
>   makes in

at full tide and fills a bowl,
extravagance of pink periwinkle
along the grassy edge,
and a blue, bunchy weed, deep blue,
deep into the mind the dark blue
   constant:

                     (*Collected Poems* 154)

Is it full tide? Or is the mind thinking ahead to the expected moment of full tide and ocean salience which it fuses with the present feel of pink periwinkle and the blue weed that partakes, for the observer, of land and sea? The evasive *where,* some elided verbs covered by obliging commas—these work to blur present and past in a more relaxed confusion of mind and nature than is felt in the first part of the poem. "Saliences" builds to a close as beautiful as that of Stevens's "Sunday Morning."

desertions of swallows
   that yesterday
ravaged air, bush, reed, attention
in gatherings wide as this neck of dunes:
. . . .
earth brings to grief
much in an hour that sang, leaped, swirled,
yet keeps a round
   quiet turning,
beyond loss or gain,
beyond concern for the separate reach.

               (*Collected Poems* 154–155)

The elegiac close allows for the observer's limitations as well as for nature's "deaths and flights." In fact, the spectator's discretion is one of the poem's great secrets. Manipulating rhythms, but particularly verb tenses—energetic displacements at the outset, subtler swellings at the close—is a way of veiling the observer, without whom, on the other hand, he had come to recognize, no poem exists. Ammons is testing another approach to vision: not claiming it as a seer, but invoking or propitiating it; withdrawing, making us forget he is there; appearing to be close to details, yet minimizing the spectator's presence and powers.

It is here that Williams's devotion to "things" would become useful. The stripped-down lists, the focused notation were indeed to become ingredients of Ammons's *Briefings*, but not, we can see from "Saliences," the only ingredients. Nor, as a poem like "Viable" suggests, was the balance between discrete particular and a suggested visionary pattern always so grandly, so securely achieved as in "Saliences." The pattern elsewhere may be elusive, the details under pressure to yield it up. Ammons's verse is more restless than Williams's lyrics. The most precise details seem only approximate: "there is nothing small enough to conjure clarity with."

"Clarity" is in fact one of Ammons's subjects. But what other poet would illustrate that title with a poem about erosion? Ammons now enjoys giving visionary words like *clarity* a tumble. A rockslide, exposing the stresses beneath what we imagine to be solid, reveals "streaks & / scores of knowledge / now obvious and quiet." The poem deliberately belies its abstract title and the ordinary meanings of *knowledge, obvious* and *quiet,* scaling down the large questions of philosophy and romantic lyric to answers made sensible by discrete and particular encounters:

> After the event the rockslide
> realized,
> in a still diversity of completion,
> grain and fissure,
> declivity
> &
> force of upheaval,

whether rain slippage,
ice crawl, root
explosion or
stream erosive undercut:

well I said it is a pity:
one swath of sight will never
be the same: nonetheless,
this
shambles has
relieved a bind, a taut of twist,
revealing streaks &
scores of knowledge
now obvious and quiet.

(*Collected Poems* 274)

Though we have an illusion of the utmost particularity, the first-person observer is almost incidental, invoked only by a chatty comment, otherwise absorbed or lost in the poem whose principal effort is a "realization" of motion—the motion latent in every knot of geological structure. Specific words don't seem to matter as much as the total assembly of nouns and the illusion that they trace out all geological contingencies. At first it is even hard to tell whether the opening section is governed by "realized" or by "diversity of," all the nouns parallel to "completion"; both effects are forceful. The exertions and knotting of syntax seem again an effort to blur traditional functions of grammar; the poem strains toward the general by being as roughly particular as possible. Series of details are preferred over a sustained rhetorical structure that might suggest a spectator's control over them.

We can see how precarious these claims are by comparison with Whitman's large gestures, appropriating objects for the self. "I think we are here to give back our possessions before / they are taken away," Ammons says in the searching long poem

"Hibernaculum." That attitude makes Whitmanian confidence impossible. No wonder then that the "I" eventually leaves many of Ammons's briefer poems, letting objects take them over, as in "Periphery" and "Further On." The poem exists for him in a continually threatened state, like a sheet of ice:

> for language heightens by dismissing reality,
>
> the sheet of ice a salience controlling, like a symbol,
> level of abstraction, that has a hold on reality and suppresses
> it, though formed from it and supported by it:
>
> motion and artificiality (the impositional remove from reality)
> sustain language: nevertheless, language must
> not violate the bit, event, percept,
>
> fact
>
> ("Essay on Poetics," *Collected Poems* 298)

The violation of fact becomes the death of language: "when that happens abandonment / is the only terrible health and a return to bits, retrials / of lofty configurations."

It is true, then, that in recent poems Ammons characteristically narrows attention to find the smallest details which might confirm a relation between self and nature, that his verse's pressured motion seeks the "energy of a deep rhythm."

> I think I'm almost
>
> down to shadows, yielding to their masses,
> for my self out here, taut against the mere
>
> suasion of a star, is explaining, dissolving
> itself, saying, be with me wind bent at leaf

edges, warp me puddle riffle, show me
the total yielding past shadow and return.
                    ("Schooling," *Collected Poems* 323)

But it is also important and marvellous that in the very best
of his recent work his anxiety is either muted or seen in a new
light: muted, as in "Peracute Lucidity," where the self builds, but
without commenting on it, the very chapel in nature it was prevented from inhabiting in "Gravelly Run."

                    clarity's chapel
    bodied by hung-in boughs: and

    widening out over the pond, the blown
    cathedral luminous with evening glass:
    I go out there and sit

    till difference and event yield to
    perfect composure: then the stars
    come out and question every sound, the brook's.
                    (*Collected Poems* 275)

Only at the end is there a slight rebuke to his confidence, a delicate disturbance that ripples but does not overturn his inhabited
scene.

Elsewhere he sets anxiety in a new key. The setting of "Peracute Lucidity" had "a perspicuity like a sanctuary." "Triphammer Bridge," one of Ammons's most beautiful new poems, takes
the very word "sanctuary" and, turning it over, as if it were a
prism, takes an explicit pleasure in the powers of language that
Ammons seldom allows himself.

    I wonder what to mean by *sanctuary*, if a real or
    apprehended place, as of a bell rung in a gold
    surround, or as of silver roads along the beaches

of clouds seas don't break or black mountains
overspill; jail: ice here's shapelier than anything,
on the eaves massive, jawed along gorge ledges, solid

in the plastic blue boat fall left water in: if I
think the bitterest thing I can think of that seems like
reality, slickened back, hard, shocked by rip-high wind:

sanctuary, sanctuary, I say it over and over and the
word's sound is the one place to dwell: that's it, just
the sound, and the imagination of the sound—a place.

(Collected Poems 319)

Sanctuary: the word itself is the subject, as if Ammons were for
once enjoying the separation of self and nature. Imagination creates its sanctuaries: the bell echoing in gold; the cloud beaches
free of eroding seas and piercing mountain peaks; but also—and
given co-ordinate place—"jail." Still, confinements are shapely
—"massive," "jawed"—transformed despite reminders of an
adverse life: the rains of autumn, the bitter shaping force of
wind, inseparable from the palpable pleasure he takes in shapes
it has made. The poem itself is like the ice of which he speaks: its
past participles, like ice crystals, take the sting out of bitter
action. The difference between real and apprehended, bitter and
sweet, includes all reminders of frailty and a joy, finally, in
repeating the word that has evoked them all, "sanctuary [. . .]
the one place to dwell." The exaltation of the final line, its real
abandonment to the force and pleasure of imagination, recalls
the late, great poems of Wallace Stevens.

Recently, then, Ammons has found ways to step back from
the whirl of the provisional and particular to which, of necessity,
his work has been committed. Perhaps his long poems have satisfied his need for "movement," and he has new notions of what
the short poem can do. "The City Limits," which Bloom praises
so highly, suggests all the hidden threats and difficulties of vision

prominent in *Briefings,* but suspends them in a wonderfully sustained rhetorical structure almost like that of the most controlled and contemplative of Shakespeare's sonnets. Five clauses, repeating, "When you consider the radiance [. . .] when you consider [. . .] When you consider the abundance,"—the *whens* tensing rhetorical springs for an expected *then,* each clause taking in another corner of abundance and vicissitude—finally license the high pleasure and relief of the closing lines: "then [. . .] the dark / work of the deepest cells is of a tune with May bushes / and fear lit by the breadth of such calmly turns to praise." "The Arc Inside and Out," which closes *Collected Poems,* is another example, with its controlled rhetoric, of a firmer meditative order.

But Ammons is unpredictable, full of the subversive bravado of natural and even random facts. There is no way of knowing whether (or when) you will find him desperate to get back to them ("wrestling to say, to cut loose / from the high, unimaginable hook") or on the contrary full of the yearning which Stevens expressed for things beyond "the separate reach":

> Unreal, give back to us what once you gave:
> The imagination that we spurned and crave.
> (*Wallace Stevens,* "To the One of Fictive Music")

The Humor of A. R. Ammons:
The Clown and the Seer

Daniel Mark Fogel

MY FATHER INTRODUCED ME to his new colleague in the Cornell English Department, A. R. Ammons, when I was a senior in high school. For years I had been writing poems, and Mr. Ammons, whose first house in Ithaca was just down Triphammer Road from ours, invited me to come by with some of my poems. After more than twenty years—it was 1964, and Ammons was then, at thirty-seven, my present age—and after three poetry writing workshops with him at Cornell between 1965 and 1974, I can no longer recall what he said about the poetry I brought him, though I do have some distinct memories of the visit: the brilliant blue fall day on the piney bluff where the Ammonses' rented Colonial house stood, the bowls of chocolate chip ice cream Mrs. Ammons served midway through our talk, the sense I had at once, confirmed again and again in later years, of Mr. Ammons's generous, finely tuned receptiveness to student work, and his recommendation that I read Frederick Clarke Prescott's *The Poetic Mind,* a suggestion acted upon promptly and with eager fascination.

Far more detailed is my memory of my first class with Ammons when I was a freshman at Cornell the next fall.

Ammons sat at the end of a u-shaped configuration of wide, long, scarred wooden tables in a room in the third floor attic of Goldwin Smith Hall. He was tall and thin. His already balding crown was fringed with light red hair. He wore a white shirt, no tie, and tan pants. As the first class hour was to begin, he looked nervously around at us twenty or so workshop students seated at the old tables. He seemed almost as if he wanted to run away, but couldn't, a stallion in a narrow stall. Then he broke the expectant quiet of those first moments by abruptly pushing his chair back and standing up. These were his first words as he walked, drifting around the corner of the u of tables and strolling down one side: "I'm trembling. I was born trembling. The only time I stop trembling is when I'm writing poems." As he spoke, going on to define poetry in terms of the high energy released by intense concentration, his voice seemed continuous with the voice in his poems, a voice lofty with metaphysical stress and acute with desire, as in his exquisite early poem "Joshua Tree."

> I must go on
>   consigned to
> form that will not
> let me loose
>   except to death
>   till some
> syllable's rain
> anoints my tongue
> and makes it sing
>   to strangers:
> if it does not rain
> find me wasted by roads:
>   enter angling through
>   my cage
>   and let my ribs
> sing me out.

(*Collected Poems* 59)

There, for most readers, is the quintessential Ammonsian voice. In his pioneering study of *The Poetic Mind* (in 1922—the year also of "The Waste Land" and *Ulysses*—one of the earliest adaptations of the new psychologies of our time to the study of literature), Prescott sees the poet as vatic, visionary: "The poet and the prophet are one" (p. 287). But he also suggests, in applying the term *awe* to the modes of thought intrinsic to poetry, that awe may be tinged by the "playful and genial feeling with which we regard a thing humorous but not quite comprehended" (p. 81), and he later quotes Sir A. W. Ward on "the . . . divine gift of humor" that may touch "the spring of laughter by the side of the spring of tears" (p. 221). There is, aside from the high-strung, quirky, lofty Ammonsian voice, another strain much less widely remarked in Ammons's poetry, though readers who know any quantity of his poetry have surely enjoyed it, chuckled over it, and even laughed out loud in response. What I am referring to, and what I want to highlight in the remarks that follow, is A. R. Ammons's humor. He is, in a word, the only major American poet who is recurrently and unerringly funny.

To begin, we might distinguish humor from wit, in theory at least (since in practice they are often intimately enmeshed with each other). Ammons's wit, which is akin to the wit of the metaphysical poets, is at work throughout his body of work. This wit is integral to the voice of such characteristic pieces as "Joshua Tree." It may be exemplified in the marvelous, explosively involuted conceit of another comparatively early poem, "Reflective":

> I found a
> weed
> that had a
>
> mirror in it
> and that
> mirror

looked in at
a mirror
in

me that
had a
weed in it

(*Collected Poems* 170)

Ammons's humor, by contrast with such cerebral wit, expresses his relish of the ludicrous, the comically incongruous, and the absurd, as well a deeper sympathy with human failings, his own and others'. Ammons's humor may be analyzed in several distinct categories (though in practice the categories often merge or overlap), including simple word-play, jokes involving bodily functions and mortality, jokes at the expense of the poet's own persona, and literary jests such as parodies of poetic conventions and of other poets. Ammonsian humor, despite the lack of critical attention to it, is one of the most formidable and, for me at least, one of the most memorable of Ammons's poetic resources.

All of the forms of Ammons's humor are perhaps subsumed under his notion that the poem is a "play-form" for the release of hidden and unacceptable passions, as he puts the matter in *Tape for the Turn of the Year*: "since there are feelings / (& thoughts) I can't / express / through the forms of / society, / here I make other forms, / play-forms, / to express them through." A couple of pages further on, speaking of such passions and the energies they arouse, Ammons writes lines clearly propaedeutic to a passage in "Summer Session," written more than a decade later. Here are the lines from *Tape for the Turn of the Year*: "like cool it: run it / into approved / channels: / irrigation / in reverse: run it off: / lower the pressure / on the dam" (*Tape*, pp. 105, 107). And here is the passage from "Summer Session," lines that exemplify several of the categories of Ammons's humor that I outlined a moment ago:

friend of mine, brilliant
linguist, told me
a Southern Gentleman screwed
himself in the
penis
with a squirrel's
pizzle:
puzzling:
got it hung in there's how everybody
found out:
doctor had to cut it loose:

let approved channels then be your
contemplation
so you will not wind up in a fix
or fuxy fox, feel the fire asphaltic:
(*Collected Poems* 254–255)

One butt of the preceding passage is of course Ammons's own past poetic persona who had first written of "approved channels" in *Tape for the Turn of the Year*. This is an in-joke for close readers of Ammons. Similarly esoteric, perhaps, is the unobtrusive parody of John Berryman a few pages earlier in "Summer Session." Contemplating his son and other children on the swings at Stewart Park in Ithaca, thinking of how he and his wife will be dead long before the probable span of the children's lives is completed, Ammon writes, "I said think of it by that time / we, you and I, will have been dead / so long / worms yet will scoff at us: / it makes you think / (twice): / what are / a few vaginal weeds in the teeth / compared with the traipsing gluebellies of / candorous maggots: *&* other worms, / all their noise"—a downright funny parody of the closing phrase in these lines from one of the last of Berryman's *Dream Songs*, lines that also take the aging of one's child as a sign of one's own mortality: "my daughter is heavier. Light leaves are flying. / Everywhere in enormous numbers turkeys will be dying, / And other birds, all their wings" (Berryman, p. 317).

Some of Ammons's parodies are funny whether or not one knows the object of the parody. Such is the case, for example, of "Louise":

> I drove down to Aurora
> at 4:15 and picked up
> Louise from work
> and Louise's hair, what a deposit,
> and her eyelashes and teeth,
> her shoulders hung
> with all that seemed to be
> getting away with her sweater,
> and I suggested McDonald's
> for dinner but thought we
> should stop off somewhere
> first and get it over with:
> Louise and I love relaxed
> dinners and that's the
> kind we had: Louise's
> shiny fingers pulled
> french fries out and her
> stomach and hips and thighs
> appreciated the hamburger: by
> then I was feeling real loose
> and easy and thought as we
> left of Louise's ankles and
> toes getting her out of the
> place and of the way her
> mind put it all together
> without even thinking.
>
> (*Diversifications* 67–68)

Funny as is, yes—but this cunning poem is funnier yet when one knows that it is a burlesque of a favorite type of Renaissance love poem, the blason. The persona in a blason praises a woman's beauty part by part in anatomical order from head to foot, concluding with praise of her inner beauty, of the perfection of her soul or heart or mind. (The form was established in the thirteenth century by Geoffrey de Vinsauf. By 1536, numerous French examples were collected in the oft-reprinted volume *Les Blasons anatomiques du corps feminin, ensemble les contreblasons*. Perhaps the best example of the blason in English is Sir Philip Sidney's "What tongue can her perfections tell" in *The Old Arcadia*, a virtual paradigm of the form.) Ammons's catalogue of Louise's features, from her hair, "what a deposit," to her "ankles and / toes getting her out of the place," and concluding with his tribute to her mind, which "put it all together / without even thinking" is a perfect vernacular American sendup of the blason, all the funnier, perhaps, when one grasps its kinship with that other great mock blason in English, Shakespeare's sonnet in which we also descend a ladder of the lady's parts, from "My mistress' eyes are nothing like the sun" to "I grant I never saw a goddess go; / My mistress, when she walks, treads on the ground."

If "Louise" represents, then, a very literary sort of humor, there is another vein of humor in Ammons's poetry that dwells on incongruity and self-deprecation. In one of his poems, Ammons describes his self as a "clown kite" that "rustles / up / to any gust" (*Briefings*, p. 3). There are times, indeed, as this image might suggest, when he seems unable to resist any occasion for verbal pratfalls that serve, at the same time, as comic self-deflations. Here is an exemplary passage closely related to the "clown kite" trope:

> my enormous, airy self splutters like a balloon at its
> inadequate outlet and shoots off spinning enlarging circles

34

into the galaxy—or at least over the fence and treetops or
halfway over the lake: when it gets too dry around here
in the summer sometimes, the little creeks nearly creak

with drought, a dribble of a drop dropping off the
dry ledges: well, I could use a little of that spareness
of form and volume: imagine the luxurious lassitude of

taking five minutes to swell into a drop and then let
go with a lengthy reluctance: the last drop bulbing
from the spent member: but little boys have small

35

emotional bladders and the pressure's terrific: they'd
rather have a string of little wow's every day
than build up to one big blast:

(*Collected Poems* 362)

In "The Wind Picks Up Slick," Ammons shows a flair for the
comic crescendo as he runs through this spiel:

> grain off the old pebble
> pebble off the old stone
> stone off the old rock
> rock off the old boulder
> boulder off the old range
> range off the old divide
> divide off the old tectonic
> jerk off the old jerk
>
> (*Snow Poems* 122–123)

I began by suggesting that the humorous Ammons may be
seen as distinct from the radiantly visionary Ammons that

Harold Bloom has established as the dominant critical image of the poet. But in fact the two voices, of clown and visionary, often lie down together, as it were, in the same poetic bed. For example, there is a delicious comedy in the dialogue between the mountains and Ammons's persona in "Mountain Liar": "What do you think you want to do / They said Oh fly." One of the funnier moments in *Tape for the Turn of the Year* occurs when the poet, writing alone past midnight, imagines himself exhorting a watching crowd to give ground:

> back off there, populace!
> the poet will have a little
> room!
> disburden the area: hey,
> you: git off da stage!
> the poet will take
> a little distance on:
> what?
> can you think these
> "private" things are
> private?
> they were got from
> jokes & dirty books:
> the poet, lawsee, but
> sings to the general
> & claims
> but the murmur in the words:
> have at you, sir!
>
> (*Tape* 68–69)

And yet his poem is, as he asserts a few lines later, a "sacred saying," and its sanctity arises precisely because the poet "sings to the general." Ammons seems to me in such passages very much like the metaphysical poets whose strength derives, as T. S. Eliot observes, from the "alliance of levity and seriousness."

When I summon up before my mind's eye the physiognomy of Mr. Ammons—the strong nose, the twinkling eyes, the fringe of light red hair around the high hairless dome—I see by turns the ascetic poet of radiant visions and the buoyant clown of word-play. They are finally, perhaps, identical figures, for as Prescott puts the matter in *The Poetic Mind,* "the clown and the great creative writer fall psychologically into one class" (p. 1), and A. R. Ammons, when he is not trembling, is more likely than not shaking with inward laughter.

The Solitary Man: The Poetry of A. R. Ammons

Frederick Buell

THE POETRY OF A. R. AMMONS is set in a domain of difficult plainnesses—or rather amidst a wealth of plain things
that have been deepened and made complex by means of
Ammons's ever-continuing, ever-various interrogations of them.
One thinks of his creeks and breezes, his cars that won't start on
winter mornings, all the minute data of nature that he observes
in his backyard or in the course of a short walk. Ammons's
milieu is one that seems so familiar that one might well expect
many Americans to be startled at the fact that a major poet has
chosen it for the setting of his poetry. For, in America, where the
notion of real life is still puritanically plain, that exotic bird,
poetry, almost always seems to be one that will only be found
singing elsewhere. So the expectation often goes; but it is an
expectation that the best of our poets have repeatedly violated,
and A. R. Ammons is certainly one of them.

More specifically, Ammons has located his work in the midst
of the ordinary phenomena of middle-class (white, bourgeois)
American social life and the nature that surrounds and coexists
with its scatterings of separate (the insurance companies say
"detached") single family dwellings. Though identifiable from

its weather and folkways as set primarily in the northeast (New Jersey and Ithaca are responsible for most of the poems), the milieu of Ammons's work is not (save for a few poems of reminiscence set in the South) regionalist in emphasis; one does not feel that Ammons's language, however slangy it becomes, constitutes a regional dialect, or that his settings are done in a tradition of local-color writing. Instead, one would be more accurate in saying that the settings of Ammons's work have the cultural universality of a northeastern suburb, a place that has seemed to embody middle-class life in mid-century America.

Ammons locates the theater for his poems also quite clearly and significantly in time. He does so with great subtlety, for, though he is intensely self-conscious about how he defines himself, a great deal of that awareness is embodied in the concrete details of his poems—in their language and settings—rather than stated. In literary-historical terms, he inhabits a world in which the sublime vistas of nineteenth-century romanticism have contracted in scope to the size of a backyard, but have become, compensatorily, more detailed and even microscopically specific. Correspondingly, the nineteenth-century dream of both nature and the imagination as forms of power has yielded to the cooler and more complicated computer-age image of nature and the imagination as complex forms of information processing, a dialectic of coherence and flow, order and entropy, and the thunder of the romantic millennialist promise of freedom has been pared down (and made thereby truer to the present-day ear) to the note of the conditional affirmation won by the solitary man who survives the adversities, psychic rather than physical, of an isolating winter.

The figure of that man is as deep as it is plain; he is a receptive, thoughtful, and often inwardly extremely talkative seeker, a seeker who, every bit as much as Kierkegaard's knight of faith, is invisible as such in his private domestic setting. Ammons has discovered and mined the enormous solitude of ordinary American life. It is the figure of that man that most interests and compels me in Ammons's work, and it is what most allies him with the tradition of American poetry Whitman inaugurated. As charmingly conversational as Ammons is in his work, he is—he depicts himself finally as—a man who lives and works (in the midst of often giddy ups and downs) against the threatening and profound background of a certain sort of solitude: the solitude each feels in the midst of a domestication that has not succeeded in putting to rest the haunted soul within, a solitude that is indeed heightened by the fact that the world about the haunted soul seems so quiet and so reasonably well-to-do, so rationally disenchanted. Every bit as much as one could with Whitman, one could name a book on Ammons *The Solitary Singer.*

In Ammons's familiar settings we can find, then, a great many social references, for he has created them, at least in part, as a means of heightening his inner solitude. The anxiety that isolates forms a substantial part of these references. In Ammons's work, we encounter the age we live in—the age of the conquest of nature that has yielded comfort at the cost of a growing sense of both our reduced size in the universe and the fear we have done something irreversible to ourselves and our environment. It is an age in which we lead a restricted daily life on top of a thin crust, under which is the potential for overwhelming disaster, disaster that is, however, at an enormous bureaucratic distance from the single individual and thus out of his control. There is an anxious and haunted passivity somewhere within all of the facts of this life, then, and it is something that shimmers on the undersides of even the most breezy and apparently insouciant moments. In the life of the majority of our time, Ammons's work makes us feel, the contortions and potential for tragedy have been driven further inward.

In evoking this sort of social milieu, Ammons is a master of representing a certain sort of detail. It is the kind that shows daily reality to be a cluster of small discomforts, ones that illustrate the estrangement from Reality we collectively experience, in the materially abundant but isolating middle-class retreats we inhabit. These moments in Ammons's work are ones of comic failure, ones which dramatize our private loss and separation at the same time they evoke the experiences that make up our precarious social bond. In a breezy mode, Ammons writes that "the lawnmowers of reality are / whirring on the slopes of absent lawns / and sunday is in the world or part / of it"; the diminutive whirrings of those too-civilizing implements, which do not serve as a broadsword might, to augment the manliness of those walking behind them, here are celebrated, for they represent, whatever their limitations, a return to the common world of fact from the private realm of our own phantasmagoria. But the psychic importance of such a return makes one aware of both the inadequacy of lawnmowers and their like to bear any real burden of communal faith and the ominous presence of what one has returned from—the threat of a Sunday that would otherwise drop out of the world, one that would hold instead the suffocating experience of social and metaphysical isolation. The lawnmower comes from the poem "Summer Session"; it is kin to the car in *Tape for the Turn of the Year* that won't start on a winter morning, and teaches thereby the power of reality, of fact. The car evokes the same comedy, but in a mode of refusal.

One meets a more intensely charged and significant experience of solitude when one steps beyond the social into the natural realm—into the theater that is ultimately, for Ammons, not a theater for mankind. This theater is everywhere still immediately accessible to those who need its dialogues and seek out the sensation of otherness that the dialogues provide; one needs to do no more than step out of one's house into the yard, or to take a small walk. The great wealth of detail and lore about nature that one finds in Ammons's work plays a dramatic role, and yet its most fundamental, as well as most austere, interaction with man is something that represents the futility of such dramatic interaction: nature reveals that it exists outside of dialogue, in non-human otherness and self-sufficiency. To be sure, Ammons finds thousands of marvelous sermons in his stones, but ultimately he finds that the stoneness of the stone exists longest. That note is struck at perhaps its somberest at the end of the poem "Gravelly Run":

> so I look and reflect, but the air's glass
> jail seals each thing in its entity:
>
> no use to make any philosophies here:
>   I see no
> god in the holly, hear no song from
> the snowbroken weeds: Hegel is not the winter
> yellow in the pines: the sunlight has never
> heard of trees: surrendered self among
>   unwelcoming forms: stranger,
> hoist your burdens, get on down the road.
>
> (*Collected Poems* 56)

Old religious practice, nature poetry, philosophy: all are forms of trying to locate something of the human imagination in the world about one; all fail, man is isolated, and must face that quiet and yet awful fact. The only gesture left him is to hoist the burden of his selfhood, and get on down the road. Perhaps the indifference is most powerfully created in the assertion that sunlight has never heard of trees. Even the different parts of the natural world are estranged from each other, ignorant of each other. The vision is both plangent and tough; it is tougher and more plangent than the pathos of man excluded. Without steeliness— without ever sounding like Robinson Jeffers—Ammons allows himself no self-pity. And that is one of the enormously memorable aspects of Ammons's more somber poetry—the work that presents itself as awakened to an alien realm. Self-pity makes a loud noise and is enormously attractive to us in the short run; the sort of concentration on the otherness in things that Ammons displays in "Gravelly Run" disenchants the impulse to self-pity and yields instead an emotionally rich, defeated strength that sustains us in the long run.

Ammons has clearly had some experience with the persistence, concentration, and strength in the face of solitude that the poem evokes. A self-exiled Southerner, an outsider, one who moved in his life from an economically and (as the dominant culture has it) culturally thin background to a milieu that has little understanding or experience of such roots, a literature department in an Ivy League university, Ammons has, with precision and no theatrics, entered and appropriated the culture of New England as thoroughly and skillfully as T. S. Eliot, another emigrant from the South, appropriated that of England. Ammons's journey to New England has not had the effect of gentrifying him; indeed, he has not, as he has said, felt as if he ever could have become a part of New England culture. He has described himself as like the phenomenon of the solitary baboon, the one who, out of a mixture of defeat and desire for dominance, leaves his original group and goes off in the woods on his own. Rather than letting himself be gentrified, Ammons has lived in the New England tradition as a solitary in the woods. And he has done a number of things to those woods by living in them; not the least is the fact that, through him, they have regained some of their original flavor of a-social, or even anti-social wildness. Seen through the eyes of one who is, despite considerable intellectual gifts, always conscious of the fact that he is, by his birth, excluded from the group of those who, both socially and academically, are their official custodians, they are changed, and appear, surprisingly enough, more like they originally were than they have been in years.

To put it more concretely, Ammons has reenlivened the New England tradition in a number of ways. He brings solitude to it again; he rediscovers the primitive force of nature again in an area that we had thought had been settled and socialized. In the course of doing this, he has rediscovered in it—or attached for the first time to it—older and more primitive roots than those explored by the academic students of the tradition. Through Emerson, he has looked back to Lao Tse in the East and, in the West, back to early Greek nature philosophy (most Emersonians stopped at Plato) and Gilgamesh (most stopped at the Bible). He has also, by uniting the New England tradition with contemporary science, enlivened it with something of its old extra-literary strength, the precision and concreteness that originally helped sustain it in its flights into abstraction. In doing so, he has displayed the "terrible precision" that, as he once remarked to an interviewer, is the prop of the solitary, as it is the separate individual's self-created replacement for the support of a group; likewise he has made use of the self-contained cunning that, after Joyce, he has seen as necessary to him in his self-imposed exile. By drawing on these sorts of strength, he has renewed the central emphasis that the New England tradition puts on individualism and self-reliance by incorporating into it a modern sort of urgency, one that has its most powerful root in survival in the face of alienation. Most specifically, he has drawn power by depicting himself repeatedly as surviving the experience of defeat and failure. Ammons comes from what he has called the "rural and defeated" South; he has preferred the legend of Gilgamesh, a legend of failure, to the New Testament of his Protestant roots; and, in his work (despite its frequent high-jinks and high spirits) failure has been a powerful force in both its intellectual dialectic (unity is unapproachable; it means destruction of the self) and its emotional intensities (as in "For Harold Bloom," the dedicatory poem to the book *Sphere*). For a multitude of reasons, then, it should be no surprise that Ammons has had the proclivity, wit, and ability to look into his finally separate and self-existent landscapes, see in the ordinary details of them an enormous weight of fate, and do so with the unselfpitying concentration of a man who is working on his own.

Recently Ammons has, in *A Coast of Trees*, extended his poetic cultivation of solitude significantly. The book's most moving poem, "Easter Morning," achieves an encounter with yet another sort of solitude, an encounter that is perhaps more fearful than that of "Gravelly Run" in that it comes closer to the terrifying experience of solipsism—of suffocation in one's separate self. The world encountered at the heart of the poem is neither the contemporary social milieu, nor the natural realm; it is the province of confessional poetry. We do not learn many of the specific details of Ammons's early personal life; the past is not rendered in narrative, but is evoked as a whole body of memory, one that resists the desire of the poet, who has returned to his homeland to try to resurrect what he can from it.

Part of the greatness of the poem is the way reading it diminishes the confessional work of Lowell, Plath, Sexton, and their many followers. Ammons writes with a virtual renunciation of the effects that have made the confessional poets blaze brightly (and ultimately briefly, I suspect) in reputation as major figures for their age. Ammons writes with a renunciation of psychological and biographical sensationalism. I imagine Ammons could find as much as they in the way of horrors in his private biography; indeed, that is not so mean a feat, as the better work in this vein is usually more dramatic monologue than confessional, strictly speaking. It has an active and inventive element, one that can turn one's father—who committed the offense of dying when one was little—into a Nazi storm trooper. Ammons's confessional, however, is one that understates where the genre usually overstates, and it achieves a far more lasting, profound, and universal self-revelation.

Ammons returns in this poem to a graveyard that holds the bones of his relatives and the other great presences of his childhood; the poem does not say where the graveyard is specifically, but details like the "trinket aunts" who always had something in their pocketbooks like "cinnamon bark" for him locates it essentially. Ammons allows himself—or achieves, one should say, for this small but enormously resonant effect is the result of the practice one finds in *The Snow Poems*—a note of genuine southern gothic (in language that comes from the north) by not letting us know that it is a graveyard he is visiting, until we are there and have met some of the people. The note is an enormously serious one, and the hollow sort of laughter one hears behind it only deepens that seriousness: Ammons writes that these days it's more convenient to visit where he comes from, the reason, we find out later, being that the people he travels to see are all gathered into the same small graveyard.

But the great encounter is to come. Ammons faces the graves and looks their significance for him in the eye:

> the child in me that could not become
> was not ready for others to go,
> to go on into change, blessings and
> horrors, but stands there by the road
> where the mishap occurred, crying out for
> help, come and fix this or we
> can't get by, but the great ones who
> were to return, they could not or did
> not hear and went on in a flurry and
> now, I say in the graveyard, here
> lies the flurry, now it can't come
> back with help or helpful asides, now
> we all buy the bitter
> incompletions, pick up the knots of
> horror, silently raving, and go on
> crashing into empty ends not
> completions, not rondures the fullness
> has come into and spent itself from
> I stand on the stump
> of a child, whether myself
> or my little brother who died, and
> yell as far as I can, I cannot leave this place, for
> for me it is the dearest and the worst,
> it is life nearest to life which is
> life lost: it is my place where

I must stand and fail,
calling attention with tears
to the branches not lofting
boughs into space, to the barren
air that holds the world that was my world
(*A Coast of Trees* 20–21)

I quote the whole of the reminiscence and meditation because
it is too powerful and uncompromising to divide. It states the
difficulties at the heart of reminiscence: one must face the child
in one that will not grow up; one must hear the cry of that child
unanswered then, and more finally unanswered now; and one
must attempt to integrate that child into one's present adulthood
by recognizing that the common fate of man is to experience just
such incompletion and truncation. But pain remains dominant,
pain that lies at the root of the assertion of one's ever limited
selfhood. Ammons yells from the stump of his past without leaving it, and the cry is one of terrible isolation at the same time it
represents a painful, but moving sort of self-acceptance, one that
comes in the recognition that this place is both his dearest and
his worst. Or—the grammar of the poem allows one to hear the
echo of another reading—Ammons stands on the stump silently,
realizing that, no matter how far he might yell, this is the place
he cannot leave. Either way, the agony of self-entrapment by his
past is inextricably interwoven with the consolation of self-
acceptance; the awareness of his private injury, the attempt to
struggle against it, and the painful acceptance of both that injury
and that struggle are simultaneously felt and fused together.

The poem thus takes on the matter of Lowell and Plath—the
terrible facts of childhood trauma, the persistence of that psychic pain, and the isolation of the adult consciousness on
account of and within its early roots. But it finds, within this
material, not an agony of self-aggrandizing self-condemnation
and self-pity—not an agony that perfects one's terrible singularity—but an agony that is experienced, we feel, too completely

for either self-pity or theatrical heroics and that therefore unites Ammons with us, his readers, at the same time that it expresses the completeness of his solitude. Ultimately Ammons discovers in the particular griefs of his personal history the devastating presence of man's common lot, and he becomes a representative figure in his awareness of the fact and consequences of isolating, utterly private loss. The painfulness of Ammons's recognition of the psychic endurance of early trauma is neither sensationalized nor incompletely rendered; and the assertion that this loss represents his place nonetheless is as moving as it is painfully unresolved.

Lowell by contrast, in even a much-anthologized poem like "Skunk Hour," is far less intelligent, mature, and powerful. He strikes a more assertive note; self-aggrandizingly, he condemns himself ("I myself am hell") and yet, interwoven with that self-condemnation is a large dose of self-pity (how horribly I am degrading myself, in creeping about peering in the windows of parked cars, in confessing this in a poem, and in doing so with such a painful display of rhetoric). Ammons has surrounded the child's unstilled cry in himself with an adult consciousness; Lowell's self-conscious self-portrayal in "Skunk Hour" is both too extreme and too insufficiently adult to keep, after its initial impact, its power as long.

Following the power of the center part of the poem—the great refusal that the graveyard presents Ammons with, the refusal Ammons internalizes as both private and representative man—comes the recovery, which is powerful in a different way, one that does not respond, really, to the pain and acceptance of pain that precedes it. Perhaps it is a measure of Ammons's cultivation of strength and persistence in failure that he is an old master at creating what will not move, what represents an impassable barrier of fate, and then going around it; in the words of "Summer Session," "discover for yourselves where / the problems are & amass / alternative strategies: / otherwise its D— & no pussy:." The end of "Easter Morning" simply skirts the agonized arrest of the middle part; and it discovers thereby a different sort of relationship to roots, one that is more hopeful, extroverted, and rationalized.

Ammons, having faced the intensity of his loss, experiences the return from that charged subjectivity to the world of his present circumstances as a kind of sudden burn-out, then recovery. The shapes of the past stand for a moment as flash-burned things hold for a few seconds their own forms, although they have turned to ash; then those forms crumble, and one is back in the "picture-book" sense, for it is just conventional good weather, and it has yielded no resurrections. But present nature follows up on the apocalyptic burn-out of the past with a compensatory experience: Ammons watches the flight of two great birds, which he describes, in its variations and circlings, with an elated exactness—with the elation of one released for a moment from his private cave, one who discovers himself suddenly in the spring sunlight. Ammons is reborn within nature, not from it. This flight he rationalizes, in serene, elevated poetry, as a less agonistic relationship of self with past; in this version, one does not stand and fail. One travels outward and returns enriched: the birds represent "the having / patterns and routes, breaking / from them to explore other patterns or / better ways to routes, and then the / return."

The agony of the solitary man, his awareness of the magnitude of his personal loss and the unalterability of his confinement in himself, is past, as Ammons rationalizes and objectifies his predicament by reading a sermon in the great birds—and by locating himself publicly in American literary tradition with an explicit echo of Stevens. But the other sorts of pain that the poem has evoked do not go away; they remain; and they represent, against the background of confessional poetry, yet another attainment of a marvelous and substantial poet. In "Easter Morning" Ammons has encompassed, with a strength that needs no sensationalism to call attention to itself, the work of his far more self-assertive contemporaries. He has taken his readers, in the context of the modern values and faiths implicit in confessional poetry, as close as one can come, it seems, to a loss of himself in the abyss of solipsism; and he has embodied that terrifying experience as memorably for his age as his great predecessors—poets as different from each other as Walt Whitman and Emily Dickinson—did for theirs.

The Natural Philosopher Returns, Singing

Roald Hoffmann

THE NATURAL PHILOSOPHER never left. But he (and she) lost his way. No wonder—it was getting awfully dark, the smog and stink of the industrial revolution coming down over the Midlands, and there were all these distracting wild noises, romanticism beating its chest. So part of the natural philosopher went this-a-way—into the scientist's seductive and productive play with quality and quantity. And part went that-a-way—in the poet's principled turn of nature into a willing (or conscripted) mirror for the self.

Could one say "too bad," when what was granted us after separation was 175 years of glorious poetry? And the greatest explosion of reliable knowledge of the innards of the beast that humanity has ever seen—this the scientist's boon? Yes, I would say "too bad," for they could have moseyed through the beautiful and terrible landscape of the twentieth century together. As it is, we have had to wait that long for a natural to return, to hold hands with both, for A. R. Ammons.

I read "natural philosopher" in at least three ways: First, *natural* philosopher—in the sense that the poet's use of language, as forethought and Promethean it be (and "forethought" is what the Titan's name means), is natural. What comes easy to Ammons, comes over easy also to us. His poems are not hermetic, and they touch us immediately. Their sagacity is direct. Even his neologisms have the feel of smooth stones, as if they've lain around that creek an eon or two.

Second, Ammons is a natural *philosopher*. His métier is thinking, his mode is contemplative. He talks to us, with us. There is in his stance a standing apart (but hardly one that excludes us), and there is an entering. There is concentration. There is a hunt, a truffle hunt, for essences.

Ammons is a *natural philosopher,* now both words given their equipoise. His search, gentle yet insistent, is for a philosophy of nature—a metaphysics always, an epistemology of openness to the connectedness of things and ideas, its inherent logic, an aesthetics rooted in the wonder of it all, and reinforced by the purposive harmony of his poems, an ethics, even an eschatology of the very real world.

Let me read a poem of Archie Ammons with you, in this light.

The Spiral Rag

Opposites attracting could easing jar to a standstill
or unmoderated blast into mutual annihilation's O; or,
just at the meeting node, veer around each other,

the momentum transforming into spin which would, of
course, generate a whirlpool flow-through, so that the
energies undemolished and still current could find a

place where, slowed, they could give up their terrible
shapes and tendencies and dissipate into the continuum
from which they might eventually return: anyway, the

circle won't do, except as an infinitely extensible outer
boundary: also, the sphere won't do, for some reason
I've forgotten (no transfusing discharge) just surface

extension with only surface flow: but the vortex will
come close to doing because it gives a standing-motion
shape at the central interior so that high formations

finding each other have a way to go: the truest motion's
truest shape's the spiral's inward arc, the inward
turning whirl that promotes a direction for the

meeting that can wear down or fly apart somewhere past
the tightening screw's whirl: whatever, what
a mechanism for averting, for taking in, changing, and

giving out, for holding still while the motion flies!
the mind figures but even though it wants to do well
never comes up with the source of what it comes up with.

(Lake Effect Country 7)

This is about as scientistic a poem as Ammons will give us.
The science is that of vortices—structures ranging from the
mundane whirlpool in your flushing toilet to black holes. I have
seen the partial differential equations that describe vortices—
and they do not tell me as much as this poem does.

What Ammons describes as "momentum transforming into
spin" actually corresponds to one way these equations are con-
ceptually set up. But I am as disinterested in finding those equations in the poem as I am in the Bible anticipating modern science.
No, it is essence we crave, and this the poet gives us—he cap-
tures the fact that a vortex is more than a spirally shape. It is a
mass transport device, for "taking in, changing, and / giving out."

Still more interesting is the dazzling craftsmanship (one of the symptomatic links of good art and good science) of this poem. Like room-temperature butter on bread fresh out of the oven, the workmanship is spread gently, even diffidently. But who else can get away with dangling articles at the end of a line or a stanza? And who can *use* that risky device (the same dangling articles) here to take us past the stop of a line break, there emphasize the break, through the break between article and noun?

We not only read about a vortex, we are made to fly in and out of it, we read faster when Ammons wants us to, we read slower. The simplicity and sophistication of the poet's devices here are astounding. Have commas ever felt heavier than those around ", slowed,"? Ammons is especially masterful at making us walk the tightrope of syntax. So the ambiguity between possessive and contraction (with is), and the curiosity of learning what the heck is possessing what are played out within "the truest motion's truest shape's the spiral's inward arc" to make us accelerate to warp speed right there.

I've said the craftsmanship is dazzling. But Ammons also takes steps to deflect us from his mastery, indeed to downplay it. I take the conversational tone of the poem in this way, his diffident sharing with us that he has forgotten something, or the "whatever." Are these rhetorical strategies, just to hit us with the salient stopping comment of the mind at the end of the poem? I don't think that's all, for I see in Ammons's gambit a parallel to science I like—not the science of the market, of implicit claims to hyper-rationality hyped with a phrase such as "the unprecedented synthesis of a novel conducting polymer by molecular engineering," but the science that lets creation speak for itself, and that speech gives space to the mind to reflect on the ingenuity and labor of the human artificer.

THE FIGURE OF THE whirlwind rises in many of Ammons's poems. I cite but two:

Bottommost

We circle the sinkhole
the coil spins in:
when the speed is close and sufficient,
a tube of nothingness
opens down which
attracted objects mill exodus.

(*Really Short Poems* 65)

and

Planes

The whirlwind lifts
sand to
hide holy
spun
emptiness or erect a
tall announcement
where formed
emptiness is to be found

(*Worldly Hopes* 44)

The first poem includes a "we" that is pretty unusual in an Ammons poem. Part of the philosophical distance, the contemplative stance, is achieved by eschewing the overly personal. The "I" is most certainly there, but think about how different, how less bombastic but no less effective in drawing us in, that "I" is in Ammons compared to, say, Whitman.

These poems move from whirlpools and dark holes to whirlwinds, if not tornadoes. The figure is natural, but the questions are deeply metaphysical: How is nothingness to be defined? How are we to reconcile one of the essential tensions, the quietude sculpted by impelled motion?

The whirlwind or a tempest is the place to ask important questions. It is the locus from which the Lord asks Job: "Who put wisdom in the hidden parts?"

"Planes" also reveals another characteristic of great poetry that Ammons masters naturally. I will call it clumsily "heightening by backtracking" or "turning back to climb higher" or "reverse resonance." Look at the "holy" in line 3 of "Planes." It carries the weight of ambiguity of holiness of the sacred type or just the quality of having holes, plus the third enriching acrophonic relation to wholeness; as we puzzle out whether Ammons is getting religious, the "emptiness" bounces us back. "Holy" becomes the center; the poem caroms back and forth around that word, like a laser beam amplified by mirrors.

That reflection is explicit in another beautiful little poem, "Reflective":

> I found a
> weed
> that had a
>
> mirror in it
> and that
> mirror
>
> looked in at
> a mirror
> in
>
> me that
> had a
> weed in it
>
> (*Collected Poems* 170)

The weeds and mirrors are reflected; the beginning and end, and the incredible focus on a small two-letter word "in." "Reflective," as well as some of Ammons's other poems, do an American turn on Descartes. The natural philosopher is because he thinks, but he thinks because he senses the real world of a dewdrop in a weed, which *is*. Note how deftly this little poem sashays around Bishop Berkeley's ontological dilemma—you don't have the slightest doubt of the existence, forever and ever, of either weed or observer, do you? And each is enriched by being mirrored in the other. What might have been a stumbling into a dismal corridor of endless mirrors becomes a reconciliation of two seemingly disparate pieces of the world. How soft these mirrors are, how they humanize the harsher mirrors we look into each day!

I think this is the best poem in the English language written in words of no more than six letters. And without adjectives.

These poems are so much more than cleverness, they are deeply philosophical. Their span is cosmic, from weed to universe, and their philosophic range commensurably immense. Take "Substantial Planes": An epistemological question is asked, about the meaning of poetry—asked, even if it is distanced from the poet, who will dismiss it. The query is answered by a deft deflection that is metaphysical. Human beings create the foundation, call it worry, from which poetry will surely rise like a mad vine.

The one philosophical element that I feel Archie Ammons's poems lack is that of teleology. I do not bemoan this—the universe, from piddling puddles to reeds, weeds, and galaxies is *accepted*. By him, for us. Indeed, what reason need there be for what is so wondrously with us, replete with its natural intricacies, splintered into a million shards of meaning by human construction, shifting floors, the solid floor? To paraphrase a repeated phrase in the Passover service: "Dayenu"—It suffices.

I see here an interesting difference from that other great natural philosopher poet, Johann Wolfgang von Goethe. Goethe's reached as far as Ammons, from the smallest to the immense. Goethe was different, of course. He gave names to his gods of nature, and as his nature ran its effulgent course, we could only hold our breath in wonder as we read him, as untranslatable as he is.

What is different about Goethe is that teleology matters to him. There is no easy acceptance of a multivalent universe; if Goethe had an idea about the existence of an ur-plant, and an evolutionary mechanism of metamorphoses, then woe for other notions; he writes a poem of the metamorphosis of plants to convince us that the world is the way he wants it to be.

For fun, compare two poems on a similar theme by Ammons and by Goethe:

The Time Rate of Change

You mosey around, idling here and
there for years,
unaware that a waiting is hanging

out for you, and then one day
you feel a light hindrance
like a floating, cut-away spider web

touch your shoulder: and some
years later, perhaps, another,
still light but with a smallish

tug to it, and then one day you
trip and catch in an entanglement like
direction, but the direction is

rope-loose and you don't mind that
much: more years and a fine halter
of dense constraints bites in,

and a kind of speed breaks out,
not just speed but acceleration, and
you begin to look back and also,

and with equal alarm, forward,
and the speed picks up, the direction
narrows, and the speed is light's.

(Brink Road 17)

and Goethe:

Die Jahre

Die Jahre sind allerliebste Leut:
Sie brachten gestern, sie bringen heut,
Und so verbringen wir Jüngern eben
Das allerliebste Schlaraffen-Leben.
Und dann fällts den Jahren auf einmal ein,
Nicht mehr, wie sonst, bequem zu sein;
Wollen nicht mehr schenken, wollen nicht mehr borgen,
Sie nehmen heute, sie nehmen morgen.

(1814)

The Years

The years? A charming lot, I say.
Brought presents yesterday, bring presents today,
And so we younger ones maintain
The charming life that's led in Cockayne.
Then all of a sudden the years change their mind,
Are no longer obliging, no longer kind;
Won't give you presents, won't let you borrow,
Dun you today, and rob you tomorrow.

(translated by Michael Hamburger)

Let me return to Ammons. The philosopher *returns*. He comes back, shuffling along, and he rings the changes on the only words we have, on that evanescent but mind-brick-hard floor. The natural philosopher is *peripatetic,* and Aristotelian like the Aristotle of "Historia Animalium," the one who could describe a murex sea snail in sufficient detail for us to reconstruct the Tyrian purple industry. Ammons's poems are suffused by a sense of entering—as in his great "Corsons Inlet"—and returning. As in the early "Hymn":

Hymn

I know if I find you I will have to leave the earth
and go on out
   over the sea marshes and the brant in bays
and over the hills of tall hickory
and over the crater lakes and canyons
and on up through the spheres of diminishing air
past the blackset noctilucent clouds
     where one wants to stop and look
way past all the light diffusions and bombardments
up farther than the loss of sight
   into the unseasonal undifferentiated empty stark

And I know if I find you I will have to stay with the earth
inspecting with thin tools and ground eyes
trusting the microvilli sporangia and simplest
   coelenterates
and praying for a nerve cell
with all the soul of my chemical reactions
and going right on down where the eye sees only traces

You are everywhere partial and entire
You are on the inside of everything and on the outside

I walk down the path down the hill where the sweetgum
has begun to ooze spring sap at the cut

and I see how the bark cracks and winds like no other bark
chasmal to my ant-soul running up and down
and if I find you I must go out deep into your
    far resolutions
and if I find you I must stay here with the separate leaves

                                (*Collected Poems* 39)

There is a you in this poem. But it is Nature, of course,
hardly the you of most contemporary poems. And yet—it is you.
There are poems of nature, wonderful, evocative poems. But
somehow none today dares to address Nature with the hunger
of incipient knowledge, with the joy for the contents of its cor-
nucopia in the way early Ammons did.

The natural philosopher returns, *singing*. Curiously, A. R.
Ammons's song in my mind absolutely resists musical setting
(unlike Goethe, the singer who can be sung). The ample melody
and counterpoint of Ammons's poetry turns those dangling articles into syncopations, works a prosaic turn such as "Spiral
Rag's" "for some reason / I've forgotten (no transfusing discharge) just surface / extension with only surface flow . . ." into
a riff that has much akin with João Gilberto's "Samba duma
nota" ("One Note Samba"). What rhythm, what verve, what
song in the deceptively gentle register!

And why does the natural philosopher sing? I'll let him tell
us.

Singing & Doubling Together

My nature singing in me is your nature singing:
you have means to veer down, filter through,
and, coming in,
harden into vines that break back with leaves,
so that when the wind stirs
I know you are there and I hear you in leafspeech,

though of course back into your heightenings I
can never follow: you are there beyond
tracings flesh can take,
and farther away surrounding and informing the systems,
you are as if nothing, and
where you are least knowable I celebrate you most

or here most when near dusk the pheasant squawks and
lofts at a sharp angle to the roost cedar,
I catch in the angle of that ascent,
in the justness of that event your pheasant nature,
and when dusk settles, the bushes creak and
snap in their natures with your creaking

and snapping nature: I catch the impact and turn
it back: cut the grass and pick up branches
under the elm, rise to the several tendernesses
and griefs, and you will fail me only as from the still
of your great high otherness you fail all things,
somewhere to lift things up, if not those things again:

even you risked all the way into the taking on of shape
and time fail and fail with me, as me,
and going hence with me know the going hence
and in the cries of that pain it is you crying and
you know of it and it is my pain, my tears, my loss—
what but grace

have I to bear in every motion,
embracing or turning away, staggering or standing still,
while your settled kingdom sways in the distillations of light
and plunders down into the darkness with me
and comes nowhere up again but changed into your
singing nature when I need sing my nature nevermore.

(*Lake Effect Country* 42–43)

What is there left to say about the poetry of A. R. Ammons? Oh, just an infinitude of infinitesimals. That small things matter. And the startling claims of the *the*. Through the way of the *the* Ammons celebrates earthy communion with the insistently particular particulate infinity of—poems, of this world, of no other one. A world worthy of song.

Archie's Heart

Roger Gilbert

ANYONE WHO'S READ even a few poems by Archie Ammons knows that he has a formidable brain. Words like "suasion" and "salience" abound in his work, along with philosophical quandaries like the one-many problem, intricate geometries of center, periphery, sphere and surface, and a host of scientific topics ranging from astronomy to molecular biology. No other contemporary poet has presented himself so unabashedly as a *thinker* as well as an artist. Yet for all its abstraction and erudition, his poetry flows as much from the heart as from the head. Most critics of Ammons's work have attended chiefly to its thematic complexities, its richly intelligent exploration of nature and the human mind; this seems like a good moment to pay some attention to the other major organ that contributes to his poetry. (Archie would insist there's a third organ involved as well, one I won't be dealing with here—read the opening section of *Sphere* for a pithy account of *its* role in creation.)

The impression some readers and critics have of Ammons as a cold, aloof man, unengaged in the lives of his fellow human beings, owes something to his propensity for abstraction, but can also be ascribed to the profound solitude his work so often evokes and even celebrates. Ammons's best-known, most anthologized poems tend to focus on isolated figures wandering through empty landscapes. When an interlocutor appears, it's more likely to be the wind or a mountain than another human being. This aspect of Ammons's work clearly derives from his great nineteenth century forerunner Ralph Waldo Emerson, whom most critics regard as a crucial influence on him (Archie himself cheerfully acknowledged the debt). For Emerson everything always comes down to two basic facts, the Self and Nature or, as he sometimes put it, "Me" and "Not-Me," and all human relationships are dwarfed by this immense bifurcation. Over and over Emerson insists that the self is most powerful when most alone. In a famous passage from his essay "Nature" he describes an epiphany in the forest:

> Standing on the bare ground—my head bathed by the blithe air and uplifted into infinite space,—all mean egotism vanishes. I become a transparent eyeball; I am nothing, I see all; the currents of the Universal Being circulate through me; I am part or parcel of God. The name of the nearest friend then sounds foreign and accidental: to be brothers, to be acquaintances, master or servant, is then a trifle and a disturbance.

Like many American writers, Ammons was haunted by this passage, and echoes it frequently (see *Sphere*, p. 19: "oh it's spring, and I'm more transparent than ever"). But he also understood that the sense of God-like height and perspective Emerson achieves here comes at a terrible price. From this vantage point all human relations, whether intimate ("brothers") or hierarchical ("master or servant"), seem trivial, even annoying. Emerson goes still further in his great essay "Self-Reliance," declaring, "I shun father and mother and wife and brother when my genius calls me." At its most extreme, the logic of the Emersonian self demands a solitude so absolute it leaves no room for involvement in the lives of others, no matter how close.

Ammons both accepts and regrets this logic. Much of his poetry courts the kind of solitary splendor that Emerson espouses, yet often with a certain ambivalence. Consider this poem from his 1981 volume *A Coast of Trees*:

> I'm walking home from, what,
> a thousandth walk this year
> along the same macadam's edge
> (pebbly) the ragweed rank
> but not blooming yet,
> a rose cloud passed to the
> east that against sundown would be
> blue-gray, the moon up nearly
> full, splintering
> through the tips of street pine,
> and the hermit lark downhill
> in a long glade cutting
> spirals of musical ice, and I
> realize that it is not the same for
> me as for others, that
> being here to be here
> with others is for others.
>
> (*A Coast of Trees* 45)

This is a deeply Emersonian poem in which solitude and sublimity commingle. It's surely no coincidence that the speaker's attention comes to rest on a hermit lark, a similarly isolated singer, nor that the bird's song is described as "musical ice." An essential coldness precipitates the poem's conclusion, its apparent rejection of community and relationship. Yet the almost stuttering articulation of that final insight seems to me to betray a profound ambivalence toward its implications, an ambivalence still more powerfully underscored by the poem's title, "Poverty." Here and elsewhere in his work Ammons's declarations of solitude hover uneasily between pride and shame, privilege and privation.

Ultimately Ammons refuses to join Emerson on the path of pure selfhood. While he feels the call of solitude and often answers it, he also recognizes his moral and psychological entanglement in the lives of others, those at a distance as well as those close by. Ammons expresses this double condition beautifully in *Sphere*:

> I don't love anybody much:
> that accounts for my width and most of my height: but
>
> I love as much as I can and that keeps me here but light:
>   (*Sphere* 19)

The first statement is almost shocking in its matter-of-fact attribution of the speaker's magnitude to his lack of emotional bonds. Yet the qualification that follows retroactively calls our attention to the slippery word "much," which leaves a margin for love to abide in, however diminished. (Notice how the word shifts from a negative to a positive in a typically Ammonsian sleight-of-grammar: "I don't love anybody much"; "I love as much as I can.") If detachment from others induces an Emersonian expansion of self, attachment to others supplies the crucial counterweight, preventing the self from soaring into empty space like an untethered balloon (a danger Ammons felt more keenly than most people).

"I love as much as I can": that turns out to be quite a lot. Solitude may be the most prominent element in Ammons's poetry, but his oeuvre contains many poems in which connections to others are central. One such connection, of course, is his relationship to readers. Ammons always insisted in interviews that his explorations of solitude were intended to reach others as solitary as himself: "I imagine other lonely people, such as myself. I don't know who they are or where they are, but they're

the people whom I want to reach" (*Set in Motion* 65). The paradox here is that by giving himself over fully to his own loneliness, the poet may succeed in establishing a deeper bond with
others than could be achieved through more overtly social forms
of address. Ammons explicitly links this vision of poet and
reader to the Emersonian self in a passage from *Glare*:

> that's why the so-called
> Emersonian self is not "imperial"—
>
> the solitary self is alone *in the*
> *world* with a consciousness directed
>
> toward all but by only one, one little
> guy seeing and saying, not speaking
>
> through the megaphones of public
> structures but if to anyone to another
>
> alone, one to one: if those ones
> add up to millions, still they are
>
> single threads unbraided
>
> (*Glare* 98)

Ammons's use of italics to emphasize the phrase "in the world" is
unusual for him, and suggests the intensity of his desire to reconcile the Emersonian ideal of transcendent selfhood with a sense of
community and connectedness. For Ammons, genuine connections can be made only with individuals, not groups. He disliked
the word "audience," with its suggestion of collectivity; like Whitman he saw himself as writing for solitary readers, "single threads
unbraided." (This may be why he gave so few poetry readings—
he seemed to prefer reciting his poems to one person at a time.)
   Yet while all Ammons's poems seek one-to-one connections

with readers, many of them also explore more intimate relationships predicated not on solitude but on communion. In the remainder of this essay I want to consider the place of others in Ammons's poetry, his acknowledgment of and investment in the lives around him despite the call of solitude. This is a neglected aspect of his work, in part because the poems that exemplify it are not usually the ones that appear in anthologies. As I've said, Ammons is best known for poems that feature a lone protagonist in a natural setting contesting with the elements. He established his mastery of this mode in his first volume, *Ommateum* (1955), a book almost completely devoid of sentient beings apart from the speaker. Even here, however, the imprint of other lives can be faintly discerned. Indeed the book's first poem begins by invoking the name of another: "So I said I am Ezra." This famous line, the inaugural gesture of Ammons's poetic career, has been variously interpreted as referring to an Old Testament prophet and a modernist poet, in either case suggesting a bold assumption of authority on the speaker's part. In fact, the Ezra Ammons claimed to have had in mind was a childhood friend, a hunchback who later died in World War II (in which Ammons also served). The adoption of his dead playmate's name thus becomes a complexly elegiac gesture, a way of acknowledging the place of otherness within the self while maintaining a kind of theatrical distance. Of course this significance gets clouded by the poet's withholding of Ezra's true identity in the poem, which allows the name's biblical and literary overtones to resonate. The real Ezra exists in the poem only as a phantom, the trace of a life rather than a fully formed other.

In a series of poems written shortly after *Ommateum* appeared, Ammons gave flesh to the ghosts of his childhood. Turning sharply from the starkness and abstraction of his first book, he began to write with a new vividness of detail about remembered scenes and companions. At first he lavished his attention on animals, like a favorite hog named Sparkle whose slaughter he witnessed:

Oh, Sparkle, when the axe tomorrow morning falls
and the rush is made to open your throat,
I will sing, watching dry-eyed as a man, sing my
    love for you in the tender feedings.

    She's nothing but a hog, boy.

Bleed out, Sparkle, the moon-chilled bleaches
    of your body hanging upside-down
hardening through the mind and night of the first freeze.
            ("Hardweed Path Going," *Collected Poems* 68)

Another poem memorializes the family's snake-bitten mule,
Silver:

Silver came up to the gate and stood head-down enchanted
    in her fate
I found her sorrowful eyes by accident and knew:
            ("Silver," *Collected Poems* 64)

The unabashed sentimentality of these poems will surprise
readers of Ammons who only know his more visionary and
philosophical work. The poet himself may have felt slightly
embarrassed by them, to judge by their absence from his
Selected Poems. Yet the tenderness and empathy toward other
creatures they display informs all his work, if seldom so openly.

    Ammons tempered the pathos of the farm series in another
poem written shortly afterward, "Coon Song." Like "Silver,"
this poem centers on a moment of eye contact between human
and animal; here, however, the encounter is suffused not with
affection but a kind of grim recognition:

        I got one good look
        in the raccoon's eyes
            when he fell from the tree

came to his feet
and perfectly still
seized the baying hounds
in his dull fierce stare,
in that recognition all
decision lost,
choice irrelevant, before the
battle fell
and the unwinding
of his little knot of time began:
(*Collected Poems* 87)

Unlike Silver and Sparkle, this coon is not a domestic animal with a name and a history; its otherness is more absolute, its gaze more opaque. Yet this doesn't keep the speaker from finding a message in it: "reality can go to hell / is what the coon's eyes said to me." Where Sparkle's fate elicits grief, however, the coon's imminent demise arouses a strange anger in the speaker, which he directs with startling vehemence at the reader:

you want to know what happened,
you want to hear me describe it,
to placate the hound's-mouth
slobbering in your own heart:
(*Collected Poems* 88)

Next, as though to distance himself from the voyeuristic blood-lust he ascribes to us, Ammons foregrounds the poem's purely formal properties, specifically its use of indentation:

(all this time I've been
counting spaces
while you were thinking of something else)
(*Collected Poems* 89)

The poem ends with a curiously jaunty tag that further belies the speaker's rage at the coon's fate:

> what I choose
> is youse:
> baby
>
> (*Collected Poems* 89)

Irony, hostility, and artifice all protect the speaker from the horror of the coon's plight, which nevertheless remains palpable in every line. A poem like this suggests that the coolness readers sense in much of Ammons's work reflects not his detachment from the suffering of others but his excessive identification with it.

There are limits, of course, to the empathy humans may achieve with other species. Soon after writing these animal poems, Ammons wrote another poem based on childhood memory, this one focused not on an animal but a weak-minded woman named Nelly Myers whom his grandmother took in as a girl and who worked on the Ammons farmstead. Her abject condition seems to have inspired a fierce devotion in the poet, who movingly records his grief at her death:

> oh where her partial soul, as others thought,
> roams roams my love,
> mother, not my mother, grandmother, not my grandmother,
> slave to our farm's work, no slave I would not stoop to:
> I will not end my grief, earth will not end my grief,
> I move on, we move on, some scraps of us together,
>   my broken soul leaning toward her to be touched,
> listening to be healed.
>
> ("Nelly Myers," *Collected Poems* 127)

This poem is uncharacteristic of Ammons in its naked emotionality and occasionally stilted language; yet its passionate testament to a person others saw as worthless reveals the poet's deep attachment to the lowliest among us, a principle he voices more abstractly in better-known poems like "Still." While Ammons chose not to include "Nelly Myers" or the animal poems in his *Selected Poems,* they all may be found in the wonderful collection edited by Alex Albright called *The North Carolina Poems,* which features a priceless photo of the poet as a tousle-headed, overalled farmboy on its cover.

The expanded edition of *The Selected Poems* does contain what many critics regard as Ammons's masterpiece, "Easter Morning," which also revisits his North Carolina childhood, this time from the perspective of an adult who has outlived most of his kin:

> when I go back to my home country in these
> fresh far-away days, it's convenient to visit
> everybody, aunts and uncles, those who used to say,
> look how he's shooting up, and the
> trinket aunts who always had a little
> something in their pocketbooks, cinnamon bark
> or a penny or nickel, and uncles who
> were the rumored fathers of cousins
> who whispered of them as of great, if
> troubled, presences, and school
> teachers, just about everybody older
> (and some younger) collected in one place
> waiting, particularly, but not for
> me, mother and father there, too, and others
> close, close as burrowing
> under skin, all in the graveyard
> assembled, done for, the world they
> used to wield, have trouble and joy
> in, gone
>
> (*A Coast of Trees* 19–20)

For all its affectionate detail, the aunts and uncles in this passage remain slightly generic (there's the "trinket aunt" genus, for example). This may be because "Easter Morning" explicitly aligns itself with a high Romantic tradition in which loss is universalized and offset by the consolations of nature, and so it can't afford to evoke these relatives in all their particularity. Some twenty years later Ammons returns to the subject of his dead elders but this time individuates them, supplying names and other distinguishing traits:

> the world, so populous, is so decimated: there
> were 40 aunts and uncles: there was Aunt
>
> Blanche, and Uncle Claude, Aunt Mitt, Aunt
> Kate (I loved her), Uncle John (commanding)
>
> and Uncle Frank (soused), and Aunt Lottie,
> Addie, Laura. . . .
>
> *(Glare* 286)

The difference between these two passages provides a measure of the growing warmth of Ammons's later work. Family, friends, even acquaintances become increasingly present in his poems, not just as shadowy others but as intimate participants in the poet's inner life. Growing older, Archie seems to have discovered that he was never as alone as he once thought.

The most intimate of all relationships is, ideally, marriage. Ammons wrote about this subject infrequently, but when he did it was always with piercing insight. He seemed especially moved by very old couples and the afflictions they endured. A poem called "Parting" from *A Coast of Trees* offers a poignant portrait of a woman with Alzheimer's whose slightly more competent husband visits her at a nursing home:

> she watched her
> husband tremble in to call

and shoot up high head-bent
eyes: her mind
flashed clear through, she was
sure of it, she had seen
that one before: her husband

longed to say goodbye or else
hello, but the room stiffened
as if two lovers had just caught
on sight, every move rigid
misfire in that perilous fire.

(*A Coast of Trees* 43)

I know few poems that so artfully balance pain and tenderness, the very condition that parts husband and wife seeming to foster a strange renewal of their love in all its dangerous uncertainty. The physicality of Ammons's language is largely what keeps the poem from bathos: verbs like "tremble," "shoot up," "flashed," "stiffened," and "caught" make the atmosphere of dread and desire almost unbearably palpable. The slightly off-balance repetition of "fire" in the final line completes its vision of love as a heroic ordeal for old as well as young.

Ammons's own marriage seldom receives much attention in his poetry before the nineties, but in that decade he began to acknowledge its centrality to his life—for example by using the pronoun "we" to describe his outings and excursions. His wife Phyllis appears more and more frequently in Ammons's late work as a figure of great strength and serenity, and while these references are often anecdotal, a few poems express his devotion to her more directly. Here is "A Birthday Poem to My Wife":

Have you considered how inconsequential we all
are: I mean, in the long term; but

anything getting closer to now—deaths, births,
marriages, murders—grows the consequence

till if you kissed me that would be a matter
of great consequence: large spaces also include

us into anonymity, but you beside me, as the
proximity heightens, declares myself, and you, to

the stars: not a galaxy refuses its part in
spelling our names: thus you understand if you

go out in the backyard or downtown to the
grocery store—or take a plane to Paris—

time pours in around me and space
devours me and like inconsequence I'm little and lost.
(*The New Yorker,* October 20–27, 1997, p. 192)

I'm strongly tempted to call this the finest love poem of the last twenty years—maybe more. Part of its pathos comes from the way it implicitly sets the solitary splendor Ammons had so long espoused against the exhilarations of intimacy and finds the former sadly lacking. To be alone is no longer a condition of transcendence but of annihilation; conversely, love is now a means rather than an impediment to ascension, as well as a shield against the withering vastness of time and space.

The other person nearest Archie's heart, of course, was his son. John makes cameo appearances in some of the long poems, but again it's not until the nineties that the poet openly voices his paternal love, as in this beautiful lyric from *Brink Road*:

For My Beloved Son

The blackberries that ripened
soon after you left are

ripening again and thunderstorms
after the broken-down winter

are rolling through here again:
I keep looking for the season

that will bring you home:
I don't know how many times

I've put in the seed, watered
the plants, counted the blossoms.

(*Brink Road* 146)

This poem expresses the longing most parents feel for their grown children with a tact and delicacy reminiscent of classical Chinese poetry. The theme might easily yield to self-pity, yet by assimilating his son's movements to those of seasons and plants Ammons renounces any direct claim on him. Only by tending his garden can he hope to nudge the cycles of nature along and so hasten his son's return. The perennial parental wish to be visited has rarely been voiced so mildly, without a hint of reproach.

Where his shorter poems tend to emphasize individual relationships, it's in his long poems that Ammons explores his larger visions of community and connection. I want to juxtapose some passages from his three masterpieces in the long form, *Sphere* (1974), *Garbage* (1993), and *Glare* (1997), that together chart the shifting proportions of head and heart in Ammons's later work. While all of them show the poet's abiding commitment to the human species in both its highest and lowest phases, the increasing particularity of his engagement with others suggests a gradual closing of the gap he had once felt between himself and his fellows.

Sphere is Ammons's most openly Whitmanesque poem, and in it he borrows a key metaphor from Whitman to express his solidarity with others:

it's because I don't want some
thing that I go for everything: all the people asleep with

me in sleep, melted down, mindlessly interchangeable,
resting with a hugeness of whales dozing:

(Sphere 29)

For Ammons as for Whitman sleep is the great uniter, leveling
differences and gathering all humans in its fluid embrace. Yet
while this image suggests utopian possibilities that Ammons
develops more fully later in the poem, it remains fundamentally
abstract in its figuring of people as a single substance, "mindlessly interchangeable." In *Garbage* Ammons offers another
image of utopian community, this one far more local and concrete. Ithacans especially have reason to be grateful that Archie
celebrated their most beloved institution so eloquently:

> an early June morning in early June, we, having
> already gone out to breakfast, pop into the red
>
> Toyota Tercel and breeze down the hill by Lake
> Cayuga to the farmers' market, so bright, so
>
> clear, rows and rows of cars and stalls and,
> beyond, boats docked calm on the glassy inlet:
>
> the people look a little ruffled, like yards
> trying to come out of icebound winters into
>
> springs, the old stalks still there, the space
> of the new stuff not filled out: affliction
>
> here, where the heavy woman, heavier than last
> fall, leans over to swish one knock-knee past
>
> (check that rhyme) the other; affliction there,
> where the wobble-legged man leans over into his

arm crutches, a four-legged progression: aging
women, drooped breasts under loose T-shirts,

hair making a virtue of snow-white or veering
off into an original expression of blue:

toothless, big-bellied, bald, broad-rumped,
deaf: the afflicted, hurts hurting but less

than they hurt at home or, if hurting more,
with some compensation: one absolutely lovely

person, perhaps: the radiance of some babies'
faces, the perfect interest of some boy in mud

puddles: and this is all under the aspect of
eternity, soon to be: but listen to the

good-mornings and how've-you-beens and
were-you-away-any-of-the-winters, along with

the hanging baskets of fuchsia, purple and red
and streaked white, tuberous begonias with the

freshest colors alive, bread, and stall after
stall of vegetables, goat cheese, honey, coffee

plus a live minnequin who is moved to thank you
by coins and bills dropped in a hat: this is

we at our best, not killing, scheming, abusing,
running over, tearing down, burning up: why

did invention ever bother with all this, why
does the huge beech by the water come back every

year: oh, the sweet pleasures, or even the hope
of sweet pleasures, the kiss, the letter from

someone, the word of sympathy or praise, or just
the shared settled look between us, that here

we are together, such as it is, cautious and
courageous, wily with genuine desire, policed

by how we behave, all out of eternity, into
eternity, but here now, where we make the most

of it: I settle down: I who could have used
the world share a crumb: I who wanted the sky

fall to the glint in a passing eye:

(Garbage 69–71)

It's hard to believe the same poet wrote these lines who once
declared "being here to be here / with others is for others." I
don't mean to suggest that Ammons ever repudiated solitude as
his primary condition, but in passages like this one he seems to
have found a powerful antidote to it. The farmers' market is a
kind of earthly paradise, full of bounty and beauty, and while
not devoid of mortal afflictions, these are temporarily offset by
the myriad "sweet pleasures" of human contact. The centrality
of the first person plural here is all but unprecedented in
Ammons's work; note how the pronoun "we" swells from its
initial reference to the poet and his wife to become planetary in
scope: "this is / we at our best." From this expansive height the
poem's focus gracefully contracts again, first to the couple ("the
shared, settled look between us"), and then to the speaker alone
("I settle down"). The settling that occurs in the last lines I've
quoted entails both renunciation and feasting. To give up the
longing for transcendence and totality, world and sky, means to

discover the wealth of the local and the contingent, crumbs and glints that sustain and nourish. Having once ended a poem with the uncompromising assertion "less than total is a bucketful of radiant toys," Ammons is now finally willing to settle for those toys and that radiance.

In *Glare* Ammons revisits the farmers' market but this time moves even closer to its denizens, singling out a particular figure to name and extol:

> the man four-legged with arm braces
> isn't there anymore, and the lady
> too fat to wobble her knees past
>
> each other, where was she, and Mrs.
> Fox, a decisive sharp lady with a
> constant near-smile and a fine-lady
>
> accent, where will her like be found
> again, here by the waters of the
> Inlet, the boats' reflections too
>
> glassy to bob, the gulls crying
> downward swoops, the ducks flicking,
> drawing those huge wedges of
>
> ripples behind them: but here is a
> young man and woman holding hands,
> looking at the vegetables as from
>
> another planet, she with a bottom
> broad & warm for planting, his
> schlong adequate to bed the
>
> deepest seed, and the black dog
> licks the baby's face, the stroller
> bumping to the plank cracks:

even where the air is empty it is
filled with space and sunlight,
the jabber of buyers and sellers:

those who miss the missing will soon
be missing: Mrs. Fox, are you gone,
or do you wait somewhere in a nursing

home and someone else is preparing
your potatoes, mashing them maybe
when they are already cold: are

you healing, may you return, will we
see you again: we hardly knew you,
still now we realize we loved you,

your face set with a smile, your
quick movements, your choice salad
leaves: the market will leave the

shoreline, the giant poplar will
give up more than its leaves, the
ladybugs all frigging this morning

on the green plant or weed will have
to shop this strange place for
the needed damp: the wind almost

totally missing will show up somewhere
else and sing a different song or
maybe the one known here heretofore

(*Glare* 34–35)

Self-consciously a sequel (it even bears the same section number), this passage lacks the expansive lyricism of its predecessor

in *Garbage,* but gains a corresponding warmth and particularity. The relation between the two passages is curiously reminiscent of Ammons's great shore odes "Corsons Inlet" and "Saliences," in the second of which he returns a day later to the beach he'd walked in the first and enumerates all the creatures who have disappeared. The absence of Mrs. Fox and other remembered figures becomes an occasion for both lament and praise, in the manner of the classical *ubi sunt* poem. But new faces have taken their place, like the young couple whose sexual ripeness the poet bawdily celebrates. Transience and renewal mingle in that delicate counterpoint of which Ammons is the contemporary master.

Where the passages I've just quoted lean toward affirmation in their emphasis on community, other sections of Ammons's long poems deliberately seek out less hopeful instances of affliction. Ammons shares Whitman's impulse to incorporate or, in Walt's trope, "swallow" every form of pain and suffering he can imagine. Again *Sphere* is most openly Whitmanesque in its gestures:

I
know my own—the thrown peripheries, the stragglers, the cheated,
maimed, afflicted (I know their eyes, pain's melting amazement),

the weak, disoriented, the sick, hurt, the castaways, the
needful needless: I know them: I love them: I am theirs:

(*Sphere* 18)

This is very close in tone and cadence to Whitman's famous declaration in *Song of Myself* "I am the man, I suffered, I was there"; but where Whitman gives a harrowing catalogue of individual "agonies" (a fugitive slave, a dying fireman, etc.), Ammons contents himself with a quick series of abstract epithets. Once again, he moves toward a more concrete rendering of this theme in *Garbage:*

what of so much

possibility, all impossibility: how about the
one who finds alcohol at eleven, drugs at seventeen

death at thirty-two: how about the little
boy on the street who with puffy-smooth face and

slit eyes reaches up to you for a handshake:
supposing politics swings back like a breeze and

sails tanks through a young crowd: what about the
hopes withered up in screams like crops in

sandy winds: how about the letting out of streams
of blood where rain might have sprinkled into

roadpools: are we to identify with the fortunate
who see the energy of possibility as its necessary

brush with impossibility: who define meaning
only in the blasted landfalls of no meaning:

who can in safety call evil essential to the
differentiations of good: or should we wail

that the lost are lost, that nothing can be right
until they no longer lose themselves, until we've found

charms to call them back: are we to take no
comfort when so much discomfort turns here and

there helplessly for help: is there, in other
words, after the balances are toted up, is there

a streak of light defining the cutting edge as
celebration:

(*Garbage* 90–91)

Two days after Ammons's death, Robert Pinsky chose these lines
to read in his memory on the PBS News Hour, perhaps because
they manifest a social conscience the poet himself often denied
having. Like Whitman, Ammons was driven to acknowledge the
ubiquity of human misery while maintaining his essentially affirmative posture. Here the strain of that effort becomes palpable.
Unlike the market passages, these lines offer no pastoral images to
soften the pain and brutality they document. The tentative questions that frame Ammons's instances of horror ("how about . . .")
betray genuine perplexity, as though the poet were forcing himself
to confront a set of facts he'd managed to evade till now. While
the passage eventually moves toward a renewal of the celebratory
strain, its troubled questions remain unanswered, its impulse to
grieve for the lost unrefuted. The balance may come out on the
side of celebration, but the very process of toting it up, integer by
bloody integer, serves to darken and disturb that result.

As he did with the farmers' market, Ammons follows up on
this theme in *Glare* while narrowing his focus to a single embodiment of it:

> she said, it's hard to have hope
> when there is no hope: she'd run
>
> back and forth looking after people
> till her legs wouldn't work: she
>
> would send her legs a message and they
> either wouldn't get it or wouldn't
>
> do it: she just lay there, poor
> thing: I told her to have hope: she

said there wasn't any, or not enough
to pay much attention to: she died:

the adopted son she staked her life
on was shot dead by somebody at the

7-11: just a month or so later:
she didn't know about that: I reckon

she got off just in time: you'd be
surprised, though, how folks can get

over something like that and keep
on trucking, if they have legs: she

didn't: nope: but she didn't know
anything about the son: pretty

lucky: old lady

(*Glare* 99)

The two basic sources of human suffering, disease and violence, intertwine here in a grim fable that parodies the Whitmanesque impulse to find some element of good in the worst afflictions. If Mrs. Fox stood for all the losses that deprive us of accustomed pleasures, this nameless woman exemplifies loss as a relief from pain, both present and to come. No large rhetorical gestures sublimate the wrenching specificity of her story; the poet simply presents her case with a kind of sardonic shrug. Even his minimal effort to draw some comfort from her fate lacks conviction, as line break and colon interrupt and elongate the closing phrases so that they almost seem choked out: "pretty / lucky: old lady." In this passage, written at the end of his career, Ammons has moved so close to another's pain that any attempt at celebration feels hollow.

Archie never really stopped celebrating, of course, even in the face of death. (The opening section of *Glare* ends "come, let's / celebrate: it will all be over.") Even as his own health declined, he remained warmly engaged in the lives of others. I'd like to end this essay by reflecting briefly on the place of friendship in his life and poetry, but to do so I must shift to a more personal register. I was privileged to know Archie for about thirteen years, during which I benefited incalculably from his wisdom, humor, and encouragement. For a poet who presented himself to the world as a misanthropic loner, he was amazingly gregarious, often sitting in the Temple of Zeus or in his office with the door open just waiting for visitors to drop by for a chat. He loved to talk, about anything and everything, from sports to politics to sex and other bodily functions. (He could be incredibly bawdy, and incredibly funny, often at the same time.) I've never known anyone as addicted to conversation; much of his later poetry was really a refinement and intensification of the unbuttoned everyday talk he loved so much. Some lines from *Garbage* capture this love with his usual mix of lyricism and goofiness:

> I
>
> don't know anything I want anybody to believe or
> in: but if you will sit with me in the light
>
> of speech, I will sit with you: I would rather
> do this than eat your ice cream, go to a movie,
>
> hump a horse, measure a suit, suit a measure:
>
> (*Garbage* 73)

Many mornings as I passed through Zeus to get my coffee I'd decline Archie's invitations to sit and schmooze for a few minutes, explaining that I had to go prepare my class (which I did); I'd give anything to go back and have those missed conversations now.

While Archie was fully capable of being gruff when he felt put upon, he was unfailingly generous and kind to his many friends, who included colleagues, former students, neighbors, and fans. And yet he seems never to have realized just how much of himself he gave away, to judge from a heartbreaking passage in *Glare*:

> sometimes I get the feeling I've never
> lived here at all, and 31 years seem
>
> no more than nothing: I have to stop
> and think, oh, yeah, there was the
>
> kid, so much anguish over his allergy,
> and there was the year we moved to
>
> another house, and oh, yes, I remember
> the lilies we planted near that
>
> siberian elm, and there was the year
> they made me a professor, and the
>
> year, right in the middle of a long
> poem, when I got blood poisoning from
>
> an ingrown toenail not operated on
> right: but a wave slices through,
>
> canceling everything, and the space
> with nothing to fill it shrinks and
>
> time collapses, so that nothing happened,
> and I didn't exist, and existence
>
> itself seems like a wayward temporizing,
> an illusion nonexistence sometimes

stumbles into: keep your mind open,
something might crawl in: which

reminds me of my greatest saying:
old poets never die, they just scrawl

away: and then I think of my friends
who may have longed for me, and I say

oh, I'll be here the next time
around: alas, the next time will

not come next: so what am I to say
to friends who know I'm not here and

won't be back: I'm sorry I missed
you guys: but even with the little

I know I loved you a lot, a lot more
than I said: our mountains here are

so old they're hills: they've been
around around 300 million years but

indifference in all that time broke
itself only to wear them out: my

indifference is just like theirs: it
wipes itself clear: surely, I will have

another chance: surely, nothing is
let go till trouble free: when

I come back I'm going to be there
every time: and then the wave that

comes to blank me out will be set
edgy and jiggling with my recalcitrance

and my consciousness will take on weight
(*Glare* 121–123)

I suspect we all have moods like the one expressed in this passage, in which life feels illusory, the years we've traversed insubstantial. But not all of us respond as Archie does here, with regret for the friends he feels he's abandoned. Poetry was his ultimate vehicle for making himself present, for giving his consciousness weight and substance, and from now on it's only in his poetry that he will be there every time. But speaking for myself and for the many others who sat with him in the light of speech, I want to say: Archie, you were here.

The Titles:
A. R. Ammons, 1926–2001

Helen Vendler

> *I hope my philosophy will turn*
> *out all right and turn out to be a philosophy so as*
> *to free people (any who are trapped, as I have been)*
>
> *from seeking any image in the absolute or seeking*
> *any absolute whatsoever except nothingness:*
> ("Hibernaculum," Collected Poems 379)

POETS INVITE US into their volumes by the titles they choose; and at the end of a poet's life, the work often becomes symbolically represented by the successive volume-titles: we can think of Robert Frost's *North of Boston* and *New Hampshire*; or Eliot's *The Waste Land* and *Four Quartets*; or Lowell's *Life Studies* and *History*; or Bishop's *North and South* and *Geography III*. Now that, to our grief, the canon of A. R. Ammons's work has closed, what will we find of him symbolically present in his volume-titles? There are nineteen of them— not counting such titles as *Selected Longer Poems*—and they are:

> *Ommateum, with Doxology* (1955)
> *Expressions of Sea Level* (1964)
> *Corsons Inlet* (1965)

Tape for the Turn of the Year (1965)
Northfield Poems (1966)
Uplands (1970)
Briefings: Poems Small and Easy (1971)
Sphere: The Form of a Motion (1974)
Diversifications (1975)
The Snow Poems (1977)
Highgate Road (1977)
A Coast of Trees (1981)
Worldly Hopes (1982)
Lake Effect Country (1983)
Sumerian Vistas (1987)
Garbage (1993)
The North Carolina Poems (1994)
Brink Road (1996)
Glare (1997)

We begin with the 1955 *Ommateum, with Doxology*, the title
of that slim vanity-press volume that brought in, as royalties for
its first year (as Ammons once told me) four four-cent stamps,
and that is now, as a rare book, valued almost beyond price. (All
Ammons's trade books were published by Norton.) Alexander
Pope, in *The Essay on Man*, had asked, ironically, "Why has not
man a microscopic eye? / For this plain reason, man is not a fly."
Ammons's title, refuting Pope, tells us that he aspires to the fly's
compound eye that sees its surroundings from every angle, not
merely from one. This god's eye—or fly's eye—view commands
an instantaneous and spatial omniscience. In his Foreword to
that first volume, Ammons announced his lifelong themes: "fear
of the loss of identity, the appreciation of transient natural
beauty, the conflict between the individual and the group, the
chaotic particle in the classical field, the creation of false gods to
serve real needs." And he defined his poetic form: "While maintaining a perspective from the hub, the poet ventures out in each
poem to explore one of the numberless radii of experience. The

poems suggest a many-sided view of reality; an adoption of tentative, provisional attitudes, replacing the partial, unified, prejudicial, and rigid."* The word *Ommateum* reminds us of Ammons's training as a scientist; he is the first American poet to use scientific language with manifest ease and accuracy, as part of his natural vocabulary—and this is one of his great contributions to the language of modern poetry. But an even greater contribution is his exposition of a philosophical view of humanity built on the constructs of modern science: we are matter that came from energy and that will dissolve back into a slush of energy. Ammons did not find this view of life incompatible with the deepest human affections and gratitude for them, as the second half of his title tells us; nor was it incompatible with his conviction of the importance of the invisible realm, from the perfect spheres of geometrical abstraction to the physical laws governing the immense motions of the universe to the creative human spirit itself. *Ommateum, with Doxology,* a title combining science and thanksgiving, bravely began Ammons's heterodox form of poetry.

The titles of the two following volumes, *Expressions of Sea Level* (1963), and *Corsons Inlet* (1965), reflect Ammons's experience of the Atlantic shore. Though he was born inland, Ammons grew to know the sea well in his wartime Navy watches in the Pacific. In New Jersey, walking by the sea, he came into intimate relation with the coastal landscape. The poem that made him famous is the title poem of his third volume, *Corsons Inlet,* which is less an ars poetica—though it is that—than a poem declaring itself for freedom and variability and a consciously expanding mental universe. Though psychic terror is still present in the poet, it arises now from nature and not from the pulpit threatening divine wrath. Order, as Ammons

---

* Set in Motion: Essays, Interviews, & Dialogues, by A. R. Ammons. Ed. by Zofia Burr. University of Michigan Press. The Foreword was originally published in *Ommateum, with Doxology* (Philadelphia, Dorrance 1955).

sees it, is not an imposed and static system, but rather something that springs from an accumulation of small physical events, "orders as summaries," and with this view, the poet finds, "there is serenity":

> no arranged terror: no forcing of image, plan,
> or thought:
> no propaganda, no humbling of reality to precept:
>
> terror pervades but is not arranged, all possibilities
> of escape open:
> (*Collected Poems* 151)

"Corsons Inlet" symbolizes experience as a walk—a different walk each day, with no permanent stopping-place—a conviction insisted on by Ammons's lifelong use of the colon in preference to the period. Like the compound eye of *Ommateum*, "Corsons Inlet" aspires to a form of omniscience, but Ammons now locates omniscience in a temporal unfolding, as he embraces it in a walk, rather than in the instantaneous glance of a compound eye. The poems of the two New Jersey volumes testify not only to Ammons's lifelong capacity for attachment to a specific place—first, his North Carolina farm country, and, after New Jersey, Ithaca—but also to his love of persons—especially Nelly Myers, the household helper in his childhood—and of animals—Sparkle, his hog, and Silver, his mule.

Ammons's intense response to the unscrolling of time, which he first acted out fully in the walk around Corsons Inlet, was repeated in the quixotic enterprise of composing a long poem in short lines on a roll of adding-machine tape, resulting in the 1965 volume *Tape for the Turn of the Year*. In that poem, Ammons charts not only the absolute length of a fragment of time, but also the changes, even the most minuscule ones, taking place within it. The wintry "turn of the year" often found the poet depressed; in both *Tape for the Turn of the Year* and the

1977 *Snow Poems* there is a time of complete cessation of poetry, weeks of cold and darkness in which no poem stirs in the mind. Ammons's strong responses to the deaths and resurrections of the natural world mirrored his own oscillation between extreme emotional poles—from panic to joy, or from miserable anxiety to hope. His great poem, "Easter Morning," to which I'll return, finds a redemption from such torturing extremes of feeling in the simultaneous eddyings and order of the natural universe, symbolized—when the desolate beginning of the poem comes to a conclusion—in the varying but stable routes of great migratory birds, one of the many signs of the turn of the year always observed by the poet.

Ammons continued his habit of drawing titles from place names and landscape in the 1966 *Northfield Poems* (from Northfield, New Jersey, where his wife Phyllis came from and where they lived after their marriage), the 1977 privately printed *Highgate Road* (named after a road in Ithaca) and the 1970 *Uplands,* as well as in the 1994 *North Carolina Poems.* Despite their titles grounded in the earth, the first three of these often rose sharply to philosophical abstraction. In them Ammons formulated his shapely poetical helices, poems inhabiting the upper regions of his worldview. But in the 1971 title *Briefings,* Ammons departed from his place-titles to call attention to form itself rather than to content: the very short poems of *Briefings* offered, like the items in Thoreau's notebooks, briefings on and briefings to the world expressed in epigrammatic concision.

Although Ammons brought the short abstract lyric to a quintessential perfection in *Northfield Poems, Uplands,* and *Briefings,* he also wanted to write the sort of poetry that, in Beckett's words, "includes the mess" of life. Writing long poems is a way to include the mess, and the oscillation between very short poems and very long poems is one that has attracted many of our poets: we can see it in Blake and Wordsworth, Merrill and Ashbery, as well as in Ammons. Long poems are not congenial, perhaps, to the "purest" lyric poets, those without any sustained wish to expound a "philosophy" or to burden their poems with novelistic detail: George Herbert, Robert Herrick, Emily Dickinson, and Elizabeth Bishop come to mind as such poets. But Ammons, like Wordsworth, had a life-project: it was to formulate the consciousness of the poet as it must operate in a secular, scientific, and, above all, information-laden environment. "The Growth of a Poet's Mind"—the subtitle given on publication to *The Prelude*—would equally well describe Ammons's long poems. They delineate the intellectual and imaginative scope of the poetic mind in the twentieth century, as Wordsworth did in the nineteenth century.

Sphere, Ammons's 1974 volume, adopts a title belonging to solid geometry and chooses a subtitle—"The Form of a Motion"—apparently more proper to calculus and the physics of dynamic systems than to poetry. About the volume and its title, Ammons once said:

> *Sphere* had the image of the whole earth, then for the first time seen on television, at its center. I guess it was about 1972. There was the orb. And it seemed to me the perfect image to put at the center of a reconciliation of One-Many forces. . . . The earth seemed to be the actual body around which these forces could best be represented.
>
> (*Set in Motion* 103)

Such a title draws our attention to the Platonic side of Ammons's mind—the side that wanted to draw in a lyric a perfect two-dimensional arc, and then from it create, via a long poem, a perfect three-dimensional sphere and set it in motion. The extreme idealism of Ammons's yearning for achieved perfection struggled with his refusal to accept a perfection that could not include lowly things, ever engaged in an evolutionary dynamic.

Sphere, we are not surprised to find, was followed by a counter-truth of dispersal in the 1975 volume of short poems called *Diversifications*. Diversification of species is a formal drive of Darwinian selection, as natural to poets as to flora and fauna; and with this title Ammons is again, as he was in the earlier title *Briefings*, creating an aesthetic pun: versification, when multiplied, yields diversifications—in this case a multitude of short, pungent lyrics, closing with the longer lyric "Pray without Ceasing," in which the poet, usually apolitical in verse, mentions, and judges, the war in Vietnam.

Ammons's 1977 title, *The Snow Poems*, offers us a return to the natural world after the abstract titles *Briefings, Sphere,* and *Diversifications. The Snow Poems* suggests that the weather, as the most complex of visible dynamic systems, is the best symbol for human moods. For Ammons, the weather plays the role that color plays in painting (and we might recall that Ammons was an abstract painter in his spare time). Just as each collocation of colors has for both painter and spectator its own emotional weight, and each collocation of words, for both writer and reader, has its own atmosphere, so the weather—down to its minutest aspects—determines the "feel" on our skin and our senses of any given day. Ammons (resembling in this Hopkins and Frost) was an expert weather-watcher; he could sense the humidity, the temperature, the wind-direction, the cloud-movements, the weight of snow on a branch, the strength of ice-retaining twigs, the force of water as it splits rock. His assemblages of weather-facts are in truth assemblages of soul—facts; but his role as reporter on the soul did not prevent the *Snow Poems* from being also a theater of the absurd: its Sternian pages allow typewriter doodles, concrete poetry, verbal games, collapses into bathos, jokes (including dirty jokes) and almost anything personally embarrassing to the writer. Ammons fought a long battle with lyric decorum, determined as he was to represent fully even the unpleasant aspects of daily life, even if such a resolution meant—as in a late poem published in *The New Yorker*—reporting on lugging jugs of urine to the doctor's office for tests. Characteristically, the early errand, depressing in itself, reveals to the poet the beauty of dawn snow, untouched but for his footprints.

A Coast of Trees, the volume published in 1981, has a title that does not give us much information; we see in it a landscape of earth, water, and trees. This is Ammons's way of giving us the generality from which the poet must deduce his minute particulars, as the title poem, "Coast of Trees," affirms: "with nothing, we turn to the cleared particular, not more / nor less than itself." A coast of trees is a landscape distinctly different from Ammons's perennial mountains, biblical desert, or back yard or farm or creek. A coast is a humanly friendly, but larger-than-human, vista; because it has trees it must have water and shade and birds and grass, and is therefore a place conceived of as beautiful; but it is also uninhabited. The title gives us nature as habitable but as yet uncivilized, the rural but not the agricultural or the domesticated. It is not sublime, and therefore not Wordsworthian or Shelleyan; it is not yet acculturated to man, therefore not Frostian; it has no fauna, therefore not Mooresque; it is not urban, therefore not Williamsesque. *A Coast of Trees* is a painter's title, and reminds us of Ammons as a painter in words. *Lake Effect Country* (1983), which follows *Worldly Hopes,* is another reminder of Ammons's domestication in Ithaca, where the most salient geographical fact is the presence of Lake Cayuga, which modulates the weather it undergoes, just as the idiosyncratic spirit of the poet modifies the successive weathers of the soul inflicted on him.

Worldly Hopes (1982), on the other hand, is a title drawn from Ammons's Protestant upbringing. We all know what worldly hopes come to, in religious systems; but if we are not religious, what can we have but worldly hopes? Ammons's secularism operates always in a dialectic with religious language, to which he often resorts as the best formulation we yet have of certain longings and certain dilemmas. But he always uses religious terms in a secular, and sometimes ironic, context, as he does in this title. The volume allows itself bursts of anger, as in the poem called "The Role of Society in the Artist": after initially repudiating the artist, society grovels to him once he becomes famous, and the artist, although he pretends gratitude, "every night went out / into the forest to spew fire / that blazoned tree trunks and set / stumps afire." Such occasional bitterness puts into relief the self-conquest that generates Ammons's characteristic mildness and humor throughout his work.

The 1987 title *Sumerian Vistas* came to Ammons's younger readers as something of a surprise. How did we get from Ithaca to Sumer? Older readers would remember the Sumerian grave and its inhabitant described in "Requiem," a poem from *Expressions of Sea Level*:

> Returning silence unto silence,
> the Sumerian between the river lies.
> . . . .
> The incantations, sheep trades, and night-gatherings
>   with central leaping fires,
> roar and glare still in the crow's-foot
> walking of his stylus on clay.
>
> (*Collected Poems* 47)

Sumer is the culture where writing began, in the cuneiform inscriptions made on clay tablets; and the poet's reversion, in the title *Sumerian Vistas*, to the ancient world reminds us of another of Ammons's invocations of ancientness. His first symbolic name for himself, voiced in 1955 when he was in his late twenties, was the biblical and prophetic name Ezra, adopted in order to give himself—an acutely shy and unrecognized person—authority to speak. He eventually placed this self-naming as the first item in his 1971 *Collected Poems*:

> So I said I am Ezra
> and the wind whipped my throat
> gaming for the sounds of my voice

. . . .
Turning to the sea I said
    I am Ezra
But there were no echoes from the waves
                        (*Collected Poems* 1)

Every poet must somehow insert himself into the ancient as well as the modern: Ezra and the Sumerian scribe embodied Ammons's claim to be part of a prophetic and inscriptive genealogy stretching back, in its vistas, as far as the historical eye can see.

Ammons's 1993 title, *Garbage,* was surprising in a different way. It seemed parodic. Can a book of poems be called *Garbage*? Can one go lower in a title-search? *Garbage* turned out to be, of course, a great book-length poem about death. If you look at bodies from a materialist position, you know that all organic materials become garbage: they are destined to be buried and to rot, or to be incinerated and turned to smoke— "unity's angelic spire / rot lit in rising fire" ("Lofty," from *Highgate Road*). With equanimity, humor, curiosity and vivid particular interest, Ammons sees a mound of garbage heaped up beside the Florida interstate—his first inspiration for the poem. Later, he visits the Ithaca garbage dump, where the debris of human culture, pushed by the front-loader into an almost bottomless pit, is incinerated to the screams of hungry gulls haunting the perimeter for food. Mortality is seen steadily and whole as the poem rises and falls; and, as matter is piled up uselessly to moulder, or fed to the fire to burn, *Garbage* gathers itself into interior smaller lyrics, disperses itself into bits and pieces, and becomes a sustained tragic and comic meditation on the Heraclitean conversion of matter into energy.

The 1996 title *Brink Road,* on the other hand, speaks (literally) of human inroads on the virgin landscape. There is a road called Brink Road (carefully defined by Ammons in the Acknowledgments as lying "off NY 96 between Candor and Catatonk"); it has been built because human beings have come

to live in upper New York State; it has been named by its origi-
nators; it has a location and direction and destination; it makes
a human demarcation of the natural world; and, symbolically, as
the poem "Gung Ho" tells us, recalls to us by its name the brink
of death on which Ammons now stands:

> Arriving takes
> destination
>
> out
> of destination:
>
> the grave's
> brink,
>
> to late
> years,
>
> dismantles remnant
> forwardness.
>
> (*Brink Road* 153)

The title *Brink Road* reminds us that Ammons is not only a poet
of nature: he is also a poet of the constructed. In his work we
see—besides roads—houses, garages, hospitals, automobiles,
nursing homes, and garbage dumps, those places and things that
human beings have had to build or dig or invent in order to
make life livable. Ammons regards these cultural artifacts with
the same dispassionate interest he bestows on nature and its
phenomena. This dispassionateness, combined with his equal
and balancing sense of human pathos, gives Ammons's poetry
its special tone of objectivity. One can't imagine associating
Ammons with any sort of special pleading—not even for the
geographic and temperamental categories into which he himself
might be said to fall: the Southerner, the misfit, the genius, the

neurotic. He contemplates himself with ironic inquiry, just as he observes his neighbors and everything else. I can't forbear to quote the poem "Boon," from *Brink Road,* in which Ammons resuscitates an old genre, the dialogue between the soul and some divine principle. "Boon" speaks of three qualities of Ammons's verse: its universality, its constant drive toward inception and fresh being, and its tragic awareness:

> I put my head
> down low
> finally and said
>
> where then do I
> belong: your
> belonging
>
> is to belong nowhere:
> what am I
> to be:
>
> your being is to be
> about to be:
> what am I to
>
> do: show
> what doing comes to:
> thank
>
> you
> for this office,
> this use.
>
> (*Brink Road* 106)

The virtue of brevity is combined, in Ammons, with the virtue of loquacity, which we see at work in the book-length poems such as *The Snow Poems, Sphere* or *Garbage*. The title *Sphere* speaks of wholeness, summation; *The Snow Poems* speaks of that number of months in which Ithaca sees some sort of snow, from sleet to ice-storms to blizzards; *Garbage* speaks of the endless recycling, in the universe, of matter from its macro-version in human life through mortal decay or incineration to its resurrection in atomic and molecular form. These large subjects require, for Ammons, entire volumes, in each of which poetic process dominates over lyric product. Or rather, as in each of these volumes the expanding discourse coalesces over and over into incorporated lyrics, we see poetic products in their own self-creation and self-extinguishing, rather than in a realized stasis. Although these books owe something, in their large-limbed motion, to Wallace Stevens's long meditative poems, Stevens's poems are divided into cantos that are orderly, measured, isometric, while Ammons's long meditative poems give themselves over, recklessly, to a stream of consciousness that can pass from a pang of grief to the reckoning of the repair bill at the garage, from a surging love of wife and son to the chilly movement of galaxies. The sheer arbitrariness of consciousness is one of Ammons's great formal challenges, one he rises to by an appearance of randomness. I say "appearance," because in Ammons's poems the musical unfolding of a stream of consciousness has its own selectivity of pace, tone, and syntax. The volatility of the speaker's language keeps the reader turning the pages for fresh samples of the enchanting and lonely mind performing its concerto of American English.

Ammons's last book-length poem, *Glare* (1998), derives its title from a few lines obscurely buried halfway through the volume. But those lines are among the most searching, and the most devastating, of Ammons's autobiographical revelations. We had been told, by the 1981 poem "Easter Morning," that Ammons's baby brother had died, and that the death had left the adults in the family undone, so much so that they could not afford to be aware of the blow the death had inflicted on their quiet but exceptionally intuitive four-year-old son, who never recovered from that irreversible loss. But we had not known, until *Glare* was published, the event that preceded the death. The poem shows us the parents, accompanied by a neighbor and their small son, taking the sick child, at night, to the woods. There they halve a sapling at its middle, and pass the child through the split in the tree-trunk which is then bound together to heal. The parents resort in desperation to this uncanny act of folk-medicine in the hope of saving the sick baby by sympathetic magic. But the observance of the superstition did not prevent death; and a truth—the rock-bottom glare of extinction—was revealed to the poet-to-be that he has never since been able to suppress in memory:

> I see the eye-level silver shine of
> the axe blade the big neighbor carried
>
> at our house at dawn, and I see the
> child carried off in arms to the woods,
>
> see the sapling split and the child
> passed through and the tree bound
>
> back: as the tree knits, the young
> rupture heals: so, great mother of
>
> the muses, let me forget the sharp
> edge of the lit blade and childish
>
> unknowing, the trees seeming from
> our motion loose in motion, the deep
>
> mysteries playing through the ritual:
> let me forget that and so much: let

me who knows so little know less:
alas, though: feeling that is so

fleeting is carved in stone across
the gut: I can't float or heave it

out: it has become a foundation:
whatever is now passes like early

snow on a warm boulder: but the
boulder over and over is revealed,

its grainy size and weight a glare:

(*Glare* 94–95)

The dynamism propelling such a passage is visible in everything Ammons wrote, short or long. To him, a poem is an action,
bodily and mental; as it passes from its beginning to its end, it
describes a curve comparable to a geometrical curve—a parabola,
an ellipse, a circle. Every poem starts, for Ammons, with a gesture that goes on to complete itself, ending in a spot other than
the place where it had begun. That is why so many of his best-
known poems (such as "The Eternal City," "Transaction" and
"Easter Morning") have to do with reconstruction following
destruction, life following death, motion resumed after a catastrophe. Because Ammons believes in inclusivity as an aesthetic
principle, the body of the poem has to be open to anything the
real body can contain or sustain, from wounds to excreta.
Because Ammons is a symbolist, his poems can be read as moral,
quasi-biblical, parables of the emotional life; he himself says as
much in the Foreword to *Ommateum*: "The imagery is generally
functional beyond pictorial evocation of mood, as *plateau*, for
example, may suggest a flat, human existence, devoid of the
drama of rising and falling." There was, Ammons has said, no
book in the house when he was growing up except a rarely

opened Bible;* and the psalms and the parables heard at Sunday School and in sermons meant more to him, I think, than the historical parts of the Old and New Testaments (which are rarely mentioned in his poetry). The psalms, as lyrics chiefly of suffering and praise, spoke to the deepest motives of his own later poems; and the parables, as abstractions of life, may have been for Ammons models for his own tendency towards symbolic incident. He has often spoken in interviews, too, of the effect on him of the hymns sung in church, where it is always true that "the imagery is functional beyond the pictorial evocation of mood."

As we evoke his titles, Ammons's spirit becomes present to us, as it walks over uplands and by Corsons Inlet, through lake-effect country and Brink Road; as it looks back to Sumer while taping the turn of the current year; as it scrutinizes—with and without irony—worldly hopes; as it makes small briefings and large gestural spherings; as it notes with its ommateum the infinite forms of snow through an Ithaca winter; and as, in the last two of its book-length diversifications, it describes the glare of the harshest reality, the endless recycling of human bodies into elemental fire and ash.

We never know, with respect to a contemporary poet, which poems will seem most valuable to posterity. But it seems to me certain that "Easter Morning"—which I first saw with amazement and gratitude in the pages of *Poetry*—will last. It is Ammons's elegy in a country churchyard, and is conscious, I am sure, of its lineage from Gray's elegy. "Easter Morning" belongs to Ammons's beginnings in Whiteville, North Carolina, where "there were 40 aunts and uncles" (*Glare*) but it knows the migratory distance he has traveled since his beginnings. It is the saddest of poems as it opens: "I have a life that did not become," and yet it becomes even sadder as it tells why that stunted life could not progress beyond the tragedy of his little

---

*On another occasion, Ammons said that the only book that he had besides textbooks was a torn portion of *Robinson Crusoe*.

brother's death. It becomes even sadder as it sees this event as typical of all human life rather than singular to his own; and it bursts out in its most violent statement:

>   now
> we all buy the bitter
> incompletions, pick up the knots of
> horror, silently raving, and go on
> crashing into empty ends not
> completions,
>
>   (*A Coast of Trees* 20)

Not stopping at the tragedy of death alone, the poet's Easter morning in the family churchyard progresses even to extinction of meaning and intelligibility in the "flash high-burn / momentary structure of ash." Yet the poem ends with what Ammons calls "a sight of bountiful / majesty and integrity"—an ending of the sort Thomas Gray, with his wistful quiet classicism, could not have written, but which marks this poem as distinctively American in its turn to wildness and the width of sky. I want to close this glance at Ammons's evocative titles by reproducing "Easter Morning," the poem that rewrites the most sacred of Christian myths in ordinary American locutions, the poem I always come back to as I remember Ammons, our astonishing, touching, and much-missed great poet.

> I have a life that did not become,
> that turned aside and stopped,
> astonished:
> I hold it in me like a pregnancy or
> as on my lap a child
> not to grow or grow old but dwell on
>
> it is to his grave I most
> frequently return and return

to ask what is wrong, what was
wrong, to see it all by
the light of a different necessity
but the grave will not heal
and the child,
stirring, must share my grave
with me, an old man having
gotten by on what was left

when I go back to my home country in these
fresh far-away days, it's convenient to visit
everybody, aunts and uncles, those who used to say,
look how he's shooting up, and the
trinket aunts who always had a little
something in their pocketbooks, cinnamon bark
or a penny or nickel, and uncles who
were the rumored fathers of cousins
who whispered of them as of great, if
troubled, presences, and school
teachers, just about everybody older
(and some younger) collected in one place
waiting, particularly, but not for
me, mother and father there, too, and others
close, close as burrowing
under skin, all in the graveyard
assembled, done for, the world they
used to wield, have trouble and joy
in, gone

the child in me that could not become
was not ready for others to go,
to go on into change, blessings and
horrors, but stands there by the road
where the mishaps occurred, crying out for
help, come and fix this or we

can't get by, but the great ones who
were to return, they could not or did
not hear and went on in a flurry and
now, I say in the graveyard, here
lies the flurry, now it can't come
back with help or helpful asides, now
we all buy the bitter
incompletions, pick up the knots of
horror, silently raving, and go on
crashing into empty ends not
completions, not rondures the fullness
has come into and spent itself from
I stand on the stump
of a child, whether myself
or my little brother who died, and
yell as far as I can, I cannot leave this place, for
for me it is the dearest and the worst,
it is life nearest to life which is
life lost: it my place where
I must stand and fail,
calling attention with tears
to the branches not lofting
boughs into space, to the barren
air that holds the world that was my world

though the incompletions
(& completions) burn out
standing in the flash high-burn
momentary structure of ash, still it
is a picture-book, letter-perfect
Easter morning: I have been for a
walk: the wind is tranquil: the brook
works without flashing in an abundant
tranquility: the birds are lively with
voice: I saw something I had

never seen before: two great birds,
maybe eagles, blackwinged, whitenecked
and -headed, came from the south oaring
the great wings steadily; they went
directly over me, high up, and kept on
due north: but then one bird,
the one behind, veered a little to the
left and the other bird kept on seeming
not to notice for a minute: the first
began to circle as if looking for
something, coasting, resting its wings
on the down side of some of the circles:
the other bird came back and they both
circled, looking perhaps for a draft;
they turned a few more times, possibly
rising—at least, clearly resting—
then flew on falling into distance till
they broke across the local bush and
trees: it was a sight of bountiful
majesty and integrity: the having
patterns and routes, breaking
from them to explore other patterns or
better ways to routes, and then the
return: a dance sacred as the sap in
the trees, permanent in its descriptions
as the ripples round the brook's
ripplestone: fresh as this particular
flood of burn breaking across us now
from the sun.

Archie's Sphere

David Lehman

W E LOVE BEST THE DISCOVERIES we make on our own. In October 1970 I went to Cambridge University in England for two years of graduate study. In that month's issue of *Poetry,* then edited by Daryl Hine and wielding an influence unmatched today when many more poetry magazines exist, there appeared poems by John Hollander, Richard Howard, and Josephine Jacobsen and, in the back of the magazine, lively prose criticism. Hollander had written on Harold Bloom's version of Yeats, Howard on John Ashbery's *The Double Dream of Spring,* and John Koethe on James Schuyler's first collection. All these made an impression, but it was the poetry of A. R. Ammons—lyric poems, brief and spare, a baker's dozen of them—that took the top of my head off.

The literary love affair thus begun preceded my acquaintance with the poet (whom I met on a visit to Ithaca, New York, in 1976) and survives his death at age 75 on February 25, 2001. Our friendship, gathering momentum after I moved to Ithaca in 1980, blossomed on occasion into a collaborative literary enterprise. We worked together on *The Best American Poetry 1994,* on Archie's *Paris Review* interview (1996), and on a gathering of his prose pieces, *Set in Motion* (University of Michigan Press, 1996), among other projects. I shall miss the man terribly. I already do. But I have his poems to console me. Great numbers of them: Archie was a prolific poet, who wrote sometimes on a daily basis (as in *Tape for the Turn of the Year* and *The Snow Poems*), though he liked to complain, when you met him for lunch or coffee, that he hadn't written anything in years. A few weeks after this mournful pronouncement you would learn that he had a new book coming out. He was always writing, at least until the stroke he suffered in 1998 and the subsequent illnesses that consumed his last three years. The protestations to the contrary were just Archie's way of warding off what he would welcome—it was what Richard Howard might call an "apotropaic" gesture. It was also one way he had of dealing with his anxiety.

Archie maintained that anxiety was the source of his writing. "Anxiety's Prosody," which Donald Hall chose for *The Best American Poetry 1989* and Harold Bloom for *The Best of the Best American Poetry, 1988–1997*, states the case. The poem begins in a homely enough manner, likening the process of composition to the making of a stew:

> Anxiety clears meat chunks out of the stew, carrots, takes
> the skimmer to floats of greasy globules and with cheesecloth
>
> filters the broth, looking for the transparent, the colorless
> essential, the unbeginning and unending of consommé:
>
> > *(Brink Road* 29)

The poet is in effect a master chef (who knows, as he liked to tell me, that "you don't have to know everything to be a master of knowing") and an agent of anxiety. At the end of the poem, "anxiety burns instrumentation // matterless, assimilates music into motion, sketches the high / suasive turnings, skirts mild natures tangled still in knotted clumps." Writing brought Ammons a temporary relief, his version of a "momentary stay of

confusion," in Frost's famous phrase. Writing enabled him to
attain the state when, as he puts it in "Anxiety's Prosody,"
"patience and calm define borders and boundaries, / hedgerows,
and sharp whirls." If the transmutation of anxiety produces
poetry, Ammons welcomes the influence of anxiety, which
almost seems like a realist's way of defining inspiration. In a
note on "Anxiety's Prosody," Archie observed that anxiety
"tries to get rid of everything thick and material—to arrive at a
spiritual emptiness, the emptiness that is spiritual."

A number of Ammons's poems do seem to achieve a transcendent emptiness and calm. Consider the resolution of "The
City Limits" ("and fear lit by the breadth of such calmly turns to
praise"), of "Triphammer Bridge" ("that's it, just / the sound,
and the imagination of the sound—a place"), and of "Cascadilla
Falls" ("Oh / I do / not know where I am going / that I can live
my life / by this single creek"), each a little miracle of closure. In
each case the resolution achieved works in direct proportion to
the amount of energy released in the poem, as if, in Ammons's
adaptation of Einstein, energy equals anxiety transformed into
matterless motion multiplied by the speed of light squared. The
effectiveness of the resolutions owe something as well to
Ammons's mastery at line-breaks, which rivals Robert Creeley's.

Back in October 1970, before I knew that the A. in A. R.
stood for Archie, I read his poems in *Poetry* with some astonish-
ment. To my knowledge no one else besides Ashbery was writing
with the same appearance of ease (*sprezzatura*) in a diction so
unusually blended of the humble and the magnificent, about
subjects as tricky as the fear of death. "Play," for example,
opens:

> Nothing's going to become of anyone
> except death:
>   therefore: it's okay
> to yearn
> too high:

the grave accommodates
swell rambunctiousness &

ruin's not
compromised by magnificence:
(*Collected Poems* 272)

Notice how the staccato lining creates one surprise after another—"death" in line two, "okay" in line three, the sudden outburst of polysyllabic abstractions ("swell rambunctiousness"), the remarkable conclusion. In "Play," the brute fact of "the common disaster" awaiting us all at the end of our lives turns into a liberation, the permission to "drill imagination right through necessity." And how does one do that? One starts in the natural world. "So," the poem instructs, "pick a perch— / apple bough for example in bloom."

Ammons's lining may resemble that of William Carlos Williams in some ways, and there are other elective affinities linking Ammons to the author of *Paterson*. Ammons acknowledges the debt in a poem written in the early 1960s, when he lived on the Jersey shore. These are the opening lines of "WCW":

I turned in
by the bayshore
and parked,
the crosswind
hitting me hard
side the head,
the bay scrappy
and working:
what a
way to read
Williams!

(*Collected Poems* 147)

Unlike Williams, however, Ammons would never limit his ideas to things. In his "Essay on Poetics," he runs Williams's well-known proclamation through his own transformational grammar, with the result that "the symbol apple and the / real apple are different apples, though resembled: 'no ideas but in // things' can then be read into alternatives—'no things but in ideas,' / 'no ideas but in ideas,' and 'no things but in things': one thing / always to keep in mind is that there are a number of possibilities." Another thing to keep in mind is that the speaker means what he says though he seems to be putting an ironic spin on his words, which may make him grin and you chuckle.

Experimenting with short lines, sometimes typing poems on adding machine tape to limit the length of his lines, Ammons aimed to shift the movement of a poem from across the page to down the page. He wanted, he wrote, a "downward pull," a "certain downward rush to the movement, something like a waterfall glancing in turn off opposite sides of the canyon." Landscape as metaphoric for verse is entirely characteristic of Ammons, and so is the effort to act on the resemblances he apprehends behind motions and movements natural (a waterfall, a comet) and man-made (the rhythm and pattern of poetry). At the end of *Sphere: The Form of a Motion*—a subtitle that Ammons liberated from its parliamentary origin in a Cornell University faculty meeting—the reader feels he or she has traveled on a ride that "beats any amusement park by the shore: our Ferris wheel, what a / wheel: our roller coaster, what mathematics of stoop and climb." That ride is the rotation and revolution of the planet captured in the bend and swerve of three-line stanzas. The image or conceit that engendered the poem was the orb itself as photographed from outer space. It is an image that made Ammons feel he could write about anything and everything on earth and beyond, and in the spinning of the orb on its axis as it revolves around the sun he had found a motion to meditate on and turn into the intricate turnings of verse.

On the colon Archie has something of a patent, the way

Dickinson does on the dash. The use of colons where periods would be expected—in book-length poems such as *Sphere* and *Garbage*—is a crucial element of Ammons's versification. Unlike the comma, semicolon, ellipsis, or period, the colon looks two ways; it works somewhat like an equal sign, suggesting that what precedes the mark and what follows it are part of a continuum. In "Composition as Explanation" Gertrude Stein had declared that modernity required a "continuous present" and perhaps no one heeded the injunction as brilliantly as Ammons, whose colons continually postpone closure and create the illusion of perpetual motion until an arbitrary end (the end of a tape, for example) is reached.

In retrospect, the thirteen poems in the October 1970 *Poetry*—which included "Mountain Talk," "Here and Now," "Project," "Reversal," "Working Still," "Play," "Cougar," "Dominion," and "Admission"—still seem to me as good a door-opener to this brilliantly original poet as a novice could want. On display in these works, all reprinted in Ammons's *Collected,* are his sly wit, his characteristic movement from the scientific to the spiritual, his fresh and immediate relation to his natural surroundings, even his distinctive punctuation (call it his "colonization") and his rhetorical affection for words like "nevertheless" and "so" and "therefore" as the hinge word in a poem. Above all in these poems you find Ammons's distinctive habit of allegorizing the landscape, presenting the encounters of the lonely American self with the grand indifferent universe. In characteristically peripatetic poems, Ammons occasionally presents an animated, colloquial dialogue between a mountain and a man, with the wind as one favorite subject and height as another. This happens in both "Mountain Talk" and "Reversal," as in the earlier "Close-Up" and subsequent "Classic."

Ammons was always more comfortable writing about, or addressing, a part of nature than another human being. As he writes in a later poem ("Poverty"), "being here to be here / with others is for others." The one personage striding forth in the thirteen poems in the October 1970 *Poetry* is the neighbor in "Dominion." Being perfectly indifferent to the cosmos, the poem's Mr. Schafer is perfectly uninteresting. Asked if he will "get up to see the comet," Mr. Schafer says no:

> he has leaves to rake
> and the
> plunger on the washing machine isn't working right:
>
> he's not amused
> by ten-million-mile tails
> or any million-mile-an-hour
> universal swoosh
>
> or
> frozen gases
> lit by disturbances
>
> across our
> solar arcs
>
> (*Collected Poems* 201)

Amused at the unamused Mr. Schafer the poet reserves his wonderment for a natural event that he is almost uniquely equipped to translate from the scientific to the poetic.

For a more stimulating conversation partner than the errand-preoccupied Mr. Schafer, Ammons turns to the mountain "across the way." Like Wordsworth, Ammons is not a social poet, but a solitary walker who pauses now and then to confer with a willow or a contemplate a rock ("a poem like a rock is silent but inexhaustible"), then returns home to type up his musings. The dialogue with a mountain becomes a parable in "Close-Up," in which the mountain, "reluctant to / admit my praise could move it much / shook a little / and rained a windrow ring of stones / to show / that it was so." Dusting himself off, the poet realizes that getting close to greatness may endanger his health with no appreciable benefit. The poem ends on a sublime note of pathos when the "friendless" mountain, isolated in its greatness, "said / it couldn't help / itself." The double meaning of that last phrase—it couldn't give itself assistance, and it couldn't prevent itself from raining stones on those who would climb it—adds to the poem's impact.

The philosophical problem of the one and the many, which Ammons also phrases as the problem of "focus" versus "comprehensiveness," has long vexed him into poetry. It is an epistemological problem with literary consequences, and it's an example of the way Ammons brings philosophy as well as physics to bear on his poetry. The problem of the one and the many is simply stated: Does reality inhere in disparate phenomena or is there some unifying principle rolling through all things? And on a practical level, how do you capture the essence of a particular thing without losing the larger picture of which it is part? The more narrow your focus, the greater the danger of obscuring the whole; but the more comprehensive the sweep of your gaze, the more will the minute particulars blur into vagueness. So what is the writer to do? How will the artist reach a condition of unity without sacrificing the multifariousness of things? One reason Ammons is attracted to the image of a mountain (whether encountered in nature or along the side of an interstate highway in the form of a gigantic garbage heap) is that its triangular shape suggests a way of depicting the one-many problem, unity versus diversity, the summit versus the base. For Ammons, the mountain—and what else is the mound of trash that gave rise to his long poem *Garbage* (1993)—is a compelling image: pyramidal, hierarchical. Ammons is drawn to hierarchy as a concept and as a word; his work is full of puns on both the "higher" and "Archie" parts of the term. The mountain stands for hierarchy and for "massive symmetry and rest," but it also signifies "a changeless prospect," "an unalterable view," as Ammons writes in "Mountain Talk." At the apex of the mountain there is the unity of a single point in space, elevated, unchanging, but it comes at the expense of the multiplicity of phenomena at the base. "So," the poet says, using a favorite connecting word: "so I went on / counting my numberless fingers," preferring to continue "along a dusty highroad" instead of stopping at the mountaintop.

By temperament Ammons is a poet who would dismantle the hierarchies that he seeks and find the sacred not in the high places alone but among the weeds and the lichen and the beggars with stumps instead of legs. In "Cougar," the poet tells us he "gained insouciance" by being "Deprived like the cougar / into heights." The key word here is "deprived." In "Still" he writes of looking high and low and of finding in the end that "there is nothing nothing lowly in the universe":

> at one sudden point came still,
> stood in wonder:
> moss, beggar, weed, tick, pine, self, magnificent
> with being!
>
> (*Collected Poems* 142)

At such moments Ammons seems to fulfill his own earliest prophecies in his "I am Ezra" poems: he sounds like a prophet possessed of spiritual truth.

When, in "Reversal," Ammons declares that "the mt in my head surpasses you," the actual "mt" accuses him of "arrogance." On whom or what does the mountain pin the blame? "The wind in your days / accounts for this arrogance." The wind, we learn in "Project," is nothing else than the initiating wind of creation, animating all things, itself invisible, like the breath that drives the waves and leaves in Shelley and that makes the harps of nature burst into song in Coleridge:

> My subject's
> still the wind still

difficult to
present
being invisible:
nevertheless should I
presume it not
I'd be compelled
to say
how the honeysuckle bushlimbs
wave themselves:
difficult
beyond presumption

(*Collected Poems* 214)

Ammons comes as close to the American sublime as we get in modern poetry. In his work you find a sort of secular religiosity—M. H. Abrams calls it "natural supernaturalism" in his study of the great English romantic poets. Romantic that he is, Ammons seems to apprehend the divinity at the heart of natural things, or in the teleology of natural processes. The wonder is that he insists continually on rubbing the nose, his own and his reader's, in the unsavory wastes of civilization, like the "flies swarming the dumped / guts of a natural slaughter or the coil of shit" in "The City Limits," perhaps his most celebrated shorter poem. Of the monumental garbage dump that triggered the writing of *Garbage,* he commented, "My hope was to see the resemblances between high and low of the secular and the sacred. The garbage-heap of used-up language is thrown at the feet of poets, and it is their job to make or revamp a language that will fly again. We are brought low through sin and death, and hope that religion can make us new. I used garbage as the material submitted to such transformations, and I wanted to play out the interrelationships of the high and the low." In the moment of vision that preceded the composition of *Garbage,* Ammons saw the dump as a sort of American church, with the garbage man as priest and the stench functioning as incense.

Not religion but poetry provides the transformative agency in Ammons's poetry. Not orthodoxies of the church (though the rhythms of Sunday school hymns affected him profoundly) but a scientific understanding of natural phenomena girded his faith: "The whole world changed as the result of an interior illumination" that occurred to Ammons when he served in the South Pacific on a naval destroyer escort during the waning days of World War II. "The water level was not what it was because of a single command by a higher power but because of an average result of a host of actions—runoff, wind currents, melting glaciers. I began to apprehend things in the dynamics of themselves—motions and bodies—the full account of how we came to be a mystery with still plenty of room for religion, though, in my case, a religion of what we don't yet know rather than what we are certain of."

Ammons's short poems are lyric outbursts, aptly characterized as "briefings" or "diversifications" (to cite two Ammons titles). Most of his great short poems, from "The City Limits" to "Corsons Inlet," were written in one sitting. He can be wonderfully informal ("Here and Now" begins "Yes, but") or cheeky (his poem "Shit List" brilliantly exemplifies the catalogue or inventory form). There are moments when the poet feels discouraged: "I can't think of a thing to uphold," he confesses in "Working Still." But there are visionary moments when the eye of the observer merges with the object of its contemplation, and the thought and the image are one, as in the title and text of "Reflection":

> I found a
> weed
> that had a
>
> mirror in it
> and that
> mirror

looked in at
a mirror
in

me that
had a
weed in it

(Collected Poems 170)

This poem's shapeliness is manifest. As an object lesson in lining and line-breaks it's up there with Williams's canonical "Red Wheel Barrow." Roald Hoffmann, Ammons's Cornell University colleague, who won a Nobel Prize in chemistry in 1981, has written eloquently about the mirror image. "Note how deftly this little poem sashays around Bishop Berkeley's ontological dilemma—you don't have the slightest doubt of the existence, forever and ever, of either weed or observer, do you?" Hoffmann concludes: "This is the best poem in the English language written in words of no more than six letters."

An American romantic in the line of Emerson and Whitman, Ammons asserts the prerogatives of the self in opposition to the demands of community. Tired of symposia in which the faculty debate "the role of the artist in society," he inverts the terms in his mordant poem "The Role of Society in the Artist." He crafts a parable in which "society" sends the young poet an "invitation to go to / hell." By the time the poet achieves some recognition ("society . . . said it liked my unconventional / verses best") it's his turn to do the rejecting, so he "invited society to go to hell." "Correction" defends and explains Ammons's Emersonian refusal of any political imperative:

The burdens of the world
on my back
lighten the world
not a whit while

> removing them greatly
> decreases my specific
> gravity
>
> *(Collected Poems* 237)

As is often the case with Ammons, what is distinctive is the rhetorical hinge in the middle of the poem ("while"), the surprising change in vocabulary as the poem abruptly ends ("specific / gravity"), and the lining, the distribution of twenty-two words over the course of the poem's seven lines. The effects—including the alliterative linking of "greatly" and "gravity" and the double meaning of "lighten"—are subtle. The wit is at the service of wisdom.

In Ammons's long poems you get a sense of freedom in composition that recalls the emphasis on improvisation in Abstract Expressionism. Long poems are the way he would "manage the multifariousness of things and the unity of things" by finding a single organizing image or gesture that would lend coherence to a discourse capable of encompassing everything, associatively, from abstract philosophical questions to the quotidian details usually left out of the short poems. My current favorite of Archie's long poems is his first, *Tape for the Turn of the Year,* which chronicles the period of December 6, 1963, to January 10, 1964, in daily entries that I found particularly inspiring as I embarked on my own project of writing a poem a day in 1996. *Tape* begins with an address to the muse, to whom the poet explains the nature of the enterprise and pleads for help:

> because I've decided, the
> Muse willing,
> to do this foolish
>> long
>> thin
>> poem, I
> specially beg

assistance:
help me!
a fool who
plays with fool things:

so fools and play
can rise in the regard of
the people,
provide serious rest
and sweet engagement
to willing minds:

and the Muse be manifest:

(Tape 2)

The poem originated, Archie explains, when he saw a roll of adding-machine tape in a housewares store and decided to "penetrate / into some / fool use for it." This is "serious novelty" indeed: the choice of the tape is decisive in determining the shape of the poem. The challenge for the poet is whether his mind can be "as long as / a tape / and unwind with it." It is characteristic of the author that he quickly undercuts his own eloquence. The second day's entry begins: "today / I feel a bit different: / my prolog sounds phony & / posed."

The freedom to reverse himself, the faith in a vernacular American that could climb to the peaks of lyric intensity or sink to the sewer, the mastery of his own prosody and system of punctuation—these are aspects of a poem that seems to have grown organically, and observed itself in the act. It is full of weather reports, opinions, memories, diary notes. For the writer it was marvelously liberating to conduct this "conversation with a / piece of paper" that will outlive the circumstances of its occurrence. I have read the end of this poem aloud on several occasions and each time I find my eyes filling with tears when I reach the moment when the poet says, "Muse, I've done the best

/ I could: / sometimes you ran out / on me / & sometimes I ran
out on you." And on to the last lines:

> the roll has lifted
> from the floor &
> our journey is done:
> thank you
> for coming: thank
> you for coming along:
>
> the sun's bright:
> the wind rocks the
>   naked trees:
>   so long:

(Tape 205)

A. R. Ammons: *Pilgrim, Sage, Ordinary Man*

Bonnie Costello

"SCOPE ELUDES MY GRASP . . . there is no finality of vision," rhapsodizes A. R. Ammons at the end of "Corson's Inlet." His death has left us, however, with the pattern of his thought over fifty years of writing. How, he often asked, shall I stand (or walk) to behold the flow? What clothes shall I wear? What wine shall I drink? The poet of mobility improvised a variety of stances. On this protean figure we must now impose the inevitable tripartite structure of a life and catch him as he transfigures himself: from pilgrim, to sage, to ordinary man.

Ammons's explicit, Emersonian theme is motion as it mediates the one and the many. But in each of these overlapping but sequential phases, Ammons understands the theme differently and constructs a fresh relation between self and nature. In the first phase, Ammons writes fables and parables in which he wanders into a highly ritualized, elemental wilderness, nonhuman but spiritually animated. The animism protests against a grasping rationality. These are poems of an anxious cogito, looking for validation of the self and, ultimately, for a home in the world. This desire remains in tension with a sense of motion as dispersal. In this phase, then, Ammons retains the fiction of a disembodied, noncontingent consciousness that can locate itself within the infinite, but this fiction is continually on trial and in tension with the life of the self at the center of these lyrics.

In the second phase, Ammons's stance is more detached and prophetic, his language more gnomic and didactic. Ammons gives up animism for scientific discourse, even as he continues to entertain a religious rhetoric alongside it and to evoke the sublime. Thus he creates an impersonal authority at once rational and visionary. The speaker apprehends processes, organizations, and ecological networks rather than focusing on particular units or entities. Hence he can contemplate entropy without real exposure; entropy is simply the means of motion. Though "scope eludes [his] grasp," he has identified with the motions he describes; he has made a "home in motion." Particulars exist here as representatives of "the many" and the geography is ultimately a geography of mind, uncharted and dynamic, endlessly traversable, but implicitly (through the spatial metaphor) whole and abiding. The pilgrim poems are future-oriented, looking for an apotheosis of wider being. These poems dwell in a continuous present. They appear more pragmatic, the metaphor of the walk conceding to perspective and provisional vision, but their acknowledgment of limit is framed in a rhetoric of endless renewal and possibility. Ammons may declare that "Overall is beyond me," but it is still very much alive in synecdoche, which evokes a grand dynamic unity overriding local transitions. The aesthetic is Whitmanian: more centripetal and centrifugal than truly decentered.

In his third phase, Ammons is not pilgrim or seer but ordinary man, and the poems are much more concerned with the contingent and partial. Here Ammons confronts the past, especially as it exists as debris in the landscape of the present. The "overall" falls away as a referent, and the poems focus on transition and adjustment rather than the overriding or even microcosmic shape of flux. Ammons's emphasis on the ordinary is not a form of domestication, however. Indeed, the ordinary is strange, uncanny. It is here, paradoxically, that Ammons is least "at home" in the world, at least in an ideal sense, for the ordinary, as Stanley Cavell has pointed out, is associated with human limit and mortality. Nature in this phase involves the body directly, its entropy part of a cycle that excludes the accompaniment of a transcendental self. Mind itself is embodied, and cognition is behavior and navigation, not a mirror of the world. Entropy is still understood in relation to ecological cycles, but the language of evolution, with its dynamic of retention and waste, and its material account of human behavior, brings a new emphasis. The voice of the ordinary man is the most personal in Ammons's work. The world is truly decentered, but the poem is centered in a finite, unfixed self. Home is not in a sublimated "motion" but in "the writing of this poem." "Home is where the doodle is."

The figure of the pilgrim (or "ephebe" as Harold Bloom has called him) initiates Ammons's work and occupies him well into midcareer. Nature is the scene of the pilgrim's search, but it is not the object of that search. Ammons's directive to readers in *Ommateum* (1955) to avoid literalism and impressionism should continue to inform our reading: "the imagery is generally functional beyond pictorial evocation of mood, as plateau, for example, may suggest a flat, human existence, devoid of the drama of rising and falling." Nature, for Ammons, is parabolic. Natural ecologies model behavior in other affiliated spheres—psychological, economic, aesthetic—and instantiate a pattern of being that overrides distinctions between the natural and the human. "These poems, then, mean to enrich the experience of being; of being anterior to action, that shapes action; of being anterior to wider, richer being." It is precisely these affiliations that draw Ammons to nature, and it is in the examination of such affiliations, rather than in the primacy of the natural world, that he can be read as a "nature poet."

In these poems the lyric subject approaches landscape in the desire to locate voice and thus identity within the world of the not-me. Voice is the manifestation of self ("I say, therefore I am") but voice must be given away for the self to participate in integral being. Voice is experienced as a unity that must be dispersed into plurality in order, paradoxically, to attain a wider unity. Motion is the traversal between the one and the many. The poems vary in how they structure these rituals of relinquishment, but each encounter repeats it. Indeed, existence seems to require such repetition. The famous opening poem of *Ommateum* introduces us to this anxious cogito:

> So I said I am Ezra
> and the wind whipped my throat
> gaming for the sounds of my voice
>   (*Collected Poems* 1)

The poem's elemental landscape, consisting of the sea, dunes, and night, is not so much a place as a condition of dispersal in which the wind is the agent and the antagonist of the poet's fragmented, separate selfhood. The opening line hints at that fragmentation, where the "so" suggests ongoing narrative, a prior origin to which the self might return. "I said I am Ezra," the poem implies, because I doubted that I was, because the condition of individual existence is contingent and partial. Indeed, nature besieges the voice almost immediately, its authority ultimately cast to "the dunes of unremembered seas." The middle of the poem presents images of fragmentation and dispersal (broken fields, ripped sheets) associated with the location of self in the body, where the voiced identity has no power and "falls out of being." In "turning to the sea" the poet surrenders but also tropes, establishing the authority of the self in a new connection to the world. The struggle to merge the partial with the infinite can be heard in the verbs, which suggest reciprocal motions: "the words were swallowed up" or they were "leaping over." Indeed, the prepositions (up, over, into, in, from, among)

of the poem propel the voice beyond its singularity into a potential, infinite destination. In the end the "I Ezra," which had been
separated from the infinite and threatened by dispersion, goes
out to it, regaining poetic authority while embracing fluent
being:

> so I Ezra went out into the night
> like a drift of sand
> and splashed among the windy oats
> that clutch the dunes
> of unremembered seas
>
> (*Collected Poems* 1)

Each of these early poems presents a version of this narrative,
the effort at an articulation of the self. In place of objective validation the poet finds temporary release from singularity into
infinite, dynamic being. The variations in the poems derive from
the obstacles encountered in the transition from one to many,
and the rotating structure of unity and brokenness. Individuated
voice opposes nature's motions, so the pilgrim must "throw
away" his voice in the enumeration of particulars. This becomes
itself a meaningful vocation for the pilgrim-self, his way of inter-
secting with the infinite, so it must repeatedly "gather up" the
"pieces of [the] voice" in order to throw them away again.
Nature "answers" the poet's call not because it has spiritual
force but because the poet's voice has dispersed itself among the
elements, split itself off from an initial self-identity. But again the
structure of the poem promises a larger, redeemed identity. Like
the "night" and the "unremembered seas" of the first poem, the
"unwasting silence" in "The Pieces of My Voice" portends
something beyond fragmentation and dispersal: an integration,
through the death of a singular self, into a transcendental whole.

Again and again in these poems the pilgrim exposes himself
to the transience, erosion, and fragmentation of nature (figured
as wind, sand, sea) in order to be gathered up into a voiceless

infinite. Each poem plots this movement differently, but it is often mapped according to a vertical/horizontal logic, the self as a force for "building up" or "running down," while nature "goes by," "sidewinds," and levels. In advancing this ritual Ammons draws on an alliance but also a distinction between the voiced-I and the seeing-eye. The former defines an original unity, which must become dispersed. The latter defines an expansive consciousness, which can collect what is scattered. But there is no sacrifice of visionary power in these rituals of self-sacrifice. "In the Wind My Rescue Is" articulates a pleasure in release from the ordering, hierarchical mind, but the images of multiplicity and extension that form the first and third stanzas depend on the central image of gathering. The pleasure of caprice informs the "loose dreams" and "unknown tongues." In yielding human power to the erosive force of nature, Ammons projects a new identification of the self with freedom from the partial and restrictive structures of individuation. It is a movement out of singularity and location into the wider parabolas of bliss. Death is not a "Terminus" but a transit to the infinite:

> I sat in my bones' fragile shade
> and worked the
> knuckles of my mind till
> the altering earth broke to
> mend the fault:
>
> I rose and went through.
>
>   (Collected Poems 69)

Similarly we find in "Mansion" that a "ceding" of the self to the dispersing wind is also a "seeding" of the self into a transcendent position, a higher "mansion" of consciousness. A fictional bargain, even a kind of courtship, takes place in this poem between the self and the wind, which enacts the movement from one to many to one. Again sight expands identity as consciousness projects beyond the body and stands outside it "watching" from an extended location. The languages of brokenness and redemptive unity merge in the puns. The body has already been identified with the landscape ("tree of my bones") when the poet says to the wind:

> stroll my dust
>   around the plain
> . . . .
> and when you fall
>   with evening
>
> fall with me here
>   where we can watch
> the closing up of day
> and think how morning breaks
>
> (*Collected Poems* 76)

A binary logic (close/open, fall/rise, think/watch, cede/seed) organizes the movement from brokenness to redemption, suggesting the struggle to overcome part/whole tensions. In each of the poems I have discussed so far, indeed in all of the pilgrim poems, Ammons builds a narrative or meditative structure out of this problem of the one and the many. Literally, each poem involves a crisis or impasse—the individual voice threatened by the outer world, access to the infinite blocked by embodiment, etc.—which the lyric subject tries to overcome by an adjustment of his understanding or positioning of his self.

"Cascadilla Falls" offers another study of the one/many examined in terms of the cogito, the central matter of the pilgrim's encounters. But it sets the stage for a reconstruction of the lyric subject from pilgrim to sage. The poem is still a kind of parable, but Ammons introduces a realist effect by naming the site and evoking a scientific discourse of vastness. The poet comes to dwell with the infinite in terms that affirm the engendering power of the self. The landscape refutes his narrow authority as the lineation runs grammar over the falls, projecting a decentered, plural reality of "motions" beyond volition and consciousness. While the poem narrates a failure on the part of the lyric subject, its form restores a one/many harmony.

> I went down by Cascadilla
> Falls this
> evening, the
> stream below the falls,
> and picked up a
> handsized stone
> kidney-shaped, testicular,
>
>   (*Collected Poems* 206)

These opening lines of the poem show the cogito turning in on itself. Knowledge leads to unknowing and unknowing threatens identity. Anthropomorphic thinking presents a potent ("testicular") self; the stream flows from the body (projected onto the "kidney-shaped" stone). But as knowledge becomes inconceivable except in mathematical terms ("800 mph earth spin . . . 30,000 mph of where the sun's going") it threatens to overwhelm this initial perceiving identity. The stance of the lyric beholder and natural historian conflicts with the superperspectives of science, and knowledge is severed from experience and mastery. Ironically, the metaphors, which initially empowered the speaker, now threaten him. The stone, having been associated with the body of the speaker, comes to "dead rest." At the same time, the dropping of the stone delimits the orphic power of the speaker; he relinquishes metaphor, returning the stone to its stoniness.

The scientific language should not distract us from the classic elements of the poem—the falls and stream as figure of many/one, stasis/motion; the sky as a figure for the infinite or higher unity; the poet, at the closing, gazing at the sky and crying out when his knowledge fails him. The "turn" toward the sky is itself a trope (like his turning from the wind in "So I Said Ezra"), if a trope of supplication. He pauses here ("stood still") in the collision of the one and the many, an incongruity figured in the contradiction at the end: "I do / not know where I am going / that I can live my life / by this single creek." But the disavowal of knowledge is in another sense a move toward integration. He "doesn't know" but he "can live." In dropping the stone the poet symbolically relinquishes his hold on a narrow unity, abandoning it to "other motions," to the torments of multiplicity.

I have suggested some of the narrative and imagistic elements that contribute to this movement. The representation of motion reinforces the crisis, as the imagery of falls and stream define a directional flux quite different from the rotational order of the universe. The prepositional energy of the poem suggests the pilgrim figure seeking transcendent integrations—we start with "by" (location), move to "up" (appropriation, as in "take up"), then "into" (integration, assimilation), "around" (circulation, displacement), move to "of" and "into"; "to" and "from" imply a crossing marked by "over," then "to" moves out again, pulled back to "by." These prepositions of location and dislocation, of placement and anticipatory transcendence, mark out Ammons's poem as modern in its intense tension and bidirectional pull between one and many, finite and infinite. Yet the poem in its whole structure does satisfy the paradigm/myth, as it moves from individual to cosmic to their juxtaposition at the end stanza. Indeed, the movements toward this culmination are sequential since this is a narrative, its syntax transitive, not substantive. Each stanza represents a state, dramatized by end words—the "and" of the first stanza breaking out of the narrow unity, entering multiplicity; the "haul" indicating a turn toward wider unity; the "dropped" indicating the failure to reciprocally take that universal into the self; "broke" given a line of its own to accent the failure of the initial unity, but the "turn" suggesting not only a trope but a supplicant's openness to the infinite. "Oh" is a variation on the "O" of apostrophe, uttered to the sky by all poets. The end of the poem shifts to present tense and moves out of the narrative into the reflective. The "single creek" at the end of the poem has plurality inside of it, becoming the form of motion. The word "live" is carefully displacing "know" here. Thoreau went to Walden to "know life." Ammons must be satisfied to live it. But to live life by a single creek is to live in relation to all the multiple motions of the universe.

As Ammons promised in his introduction to *Ommateum* these poems give up "partial, unified, prejudicial, and rigid" orientations for a "many-sided view of reality" and "an adoption of tentative, provisional attitudes," but their aim is for a new, expansive oneness "of wider, richer being." The emphasis in the pilgrim poems is on this widening rather than on any provisional attitude or pluralistic understanding. The desire to assimilate world to mind remains a valued impulse, though one that is inevitably frustrated, for "the unassimilable fact leads us on." In "Staking Claim" and "Plunder" we recognize in the world's recalcitrance a route to the sublime in that the "total" is not calculable or effable but infinite. Discrete human forms are measured against the "roundness and withdrawal of the deep dark," and the imagination pursues this darkness even as the possessive mind relinquishes it. In the meantime, a "bucketful of radiant toys," or poems, allows the infinite, through metaphor, to penetrate the finite.

AMMONS WILL RETURN to the stance of the pilgrim throughout his career, but beginning with his second book, *Expressions of Sea Level*, a different stance begins to emerge, one relatively impersonal, comprehensive, and didactic. Where the medium of the pilgrim poet is ritual gesture, the medium of the sage is abstract proposition and example. The revelation of pattern dominates here over the articulation of self. Problems of identity fall away and the self becomes a node of consciousness through which the shape of the world reveals itself. Where nature in the pilgrim phase is variously the ally or antagonist to the poet's will, here it is the embodiment of dynamic design, often articulated in abstract titles. Critics have emphasized Ammons's interest in "ecological naturalism," and certainly the greater particularity, the assimilation of "facts" from the biological and earth sciences, and especially the emphasis on cycles, habitats, and cooperative behaviors in the natural world, resonate with developments in the environmental movement. Still, the natural environment is not the subject of these poems so much as a resource for exemplifying and troping their subject, which is "the form of a motion."

Ammons draws on natural imagery to give authority to his vision of pattern, and to remove it from the social and psychological attachments it inevitably has when embodied in human institutions. There remains an experiential element to these meditations in which knowledge is a process, incomplete and subject to the shifting conditions of observer and observed world. But an expansive, visionary posture and generalizing impulse prevail. The prophet-subject identifies with motion rather than being subject to it. Ammons's particular challenge is to reconcile this Thoreauvian idea of dwelling with his Emersonian emphasis on motion. "Can we make a home in motion?" he asks throughout his career, and explicitly and affirmatively in *Sphere: The Form of a Motion* (1974). In what I am calling the sage poems he begins to identify the text and the landscape as parts of a dynamic patterning where mind and world, thought and its object, become intertwined. Neither is firmly grounded in the other. Thus the power terms that motor the narrative of subject/object relations in the pilgrim poems fall away. While Ammons remains attached to a figure of "mirroring mind" it is clear that the model of cognition is not really the mirror but something more mobile and improvisatory (rather than ritualized, as before). Mapping may be the operative term for what the mind does, rather than mirroring, if we accept the map as an instrument of navigation rather than an objective diagram of reality.

Designed though it is to convey a Whitmanian plurality, the prophetic stance remains selective in the nature to which it attends. This phase is initiated with "expressions of sea level," not sermons on mountaintops. Ammons grew up in the mountains of North Carolina, but from early on he eschewed the iconology of the mountain, which in our culture has signified stability, endurance, remote imperial power, sublimity, and transcendence. The early poems of dispersal involve a repeated dismantling of hierarchical organizations. A poem still in the pilgrim mode, "Mountain Talk," makes this preference explicit, glancing at the "massive symmetry and rest" of the mountain and its "changeless prospect," but rejecting its "unalterable view," and he repeats it in "A Little Thing Like That" from *Brink Road* (1996): "I have always felt, / as one should, I think, shy / of mountains." In this middle phase Ammons need not dismantle hierarchical orders because he has set his gaze where nothing builds too high. In giving the seashore a central role, Ammons follows an American tradition of leveled, horizontal relations, of many as one, and of a permeable boundary between stability and flux. The seashore is precisely not a home, though it may be a habitat. It provides a simple, generally uniform, horizontal image with a maximum of local change and adjustment. It thus becomes an ideal figure for a decentered world. It is in this gnomic phase that the colon arises as a major signature of Ammons's work, a sign with multiple, ambiguous significations, marking permeable boundaries, tentative sponsorships, as well as analogical possibilities. Similarly, the preposition "of" emerges in this phase to create metaphors yoking concrete and abstract terms and to override the subject/object dichotomy.

Ammons's walk poems, central to this phase, are in a sense what the pilgrim poems grow into. The sage's poems are not emblematic (they do not convey idea by reducing and abstracting image), but analogical. The sage moves freely in and out of a representational scene, geography of mind and geography of landscape, text and referent, allowing for the play of contingent vision without restriction to a narrow perspective. In the pilgrim poems the one/many relation is experienced as a crisis or problem, whereas the walk poems present this relation as a primary dynamic of form. The pilgrim figure seeks a home, whether by mastery or by submission; he seeks to colonize or become accepted into the infinite. The prophet figure in the walk poems already identifies with the movement he conveys. Since the one/many is not a problem to be resolved but a reality to be apprehended and experienced, these poems are less sequential or narrative than they are serial and reiterative. Since the speaker identifies with the movement of reality, he does not need to discover it in a teleological process, but rather enacts it in an improvisatory process backed by a confident metonymic system. The tendency to evoke an infinite unity at the end, without claiming a "final vision" for the poet, is even clearer in "Saliences" than in the more famous "Corsons Inlet":

> where not a single thing endures,
> the overall reassures,
> . . . .
> earth brings to grief
> much in an hour that sang, leaped, swirled,
> yet keeps a round
>   quiet turning,
> beyond loss or gain,
> beyond concern for the separate reach.
> (Collected Poems 155)

One feels that the poem's own rounding off is confirmed here, despite the clamor against the "separate reach."

    The precursor to Ammons's prophetic voice is clearly Whitman, and, like Whitman, Ammons tends to identify the one/many paradigm with America. This is particularly true in "One:Many" which, like most of the prophetic poems, announces its procedure:

> To maintain balance
> between one and many by
>   keeping in operation both one and many:
> > (*Collected Poems* 138)

The poem again locates vision initially in the experiential, and in a descriptive, narrative form. "I tried to summarize / a moment's events," he tells us, and goes on to instantiate the one/many in terms of a description of natural objects and events at "creek shore." This section of the poem then embodies the one/many balance even as it stands, in terms of the poem as a whole, for the one, yielding in the next section to the transpersonal many of the American continent and its *e pluribus unum*. Careful not to make his path across the continent a "straight line," the prophetic mind zigzags from California to Maine and from Michigan to Kansas, integrating cultural and natural images and overriding all dualities. The device of the list becomes, again as in Whitman's poetry, a major formal embodiment of the one/many balance, and Ammons's use of it is careful. In this poem the list has a centrifugal force out from the I, so that the I is released even as it continually penetrates back into the plurality through anaphora ("I tried to think . . ."; "I considered . . ."). The list functions oppositely in the second section, where the I does not provide the hub from which details spin out, but rather intrudes with personal commentary upon the manifest plurality:

> Art Museum, Prudential Building, Knickerbocker Hotel
> (where Cummings stayed);
> of North Carolina's
> Pamlico and Albemarle Sounds, outer banks, shoals,
>   telephone wire loads of swallows,

of Columbus County,
     where fresh-dug peanuts
     are boiled
     in iron pots, salt filtering
in through boiled-clean shells (a delicacy
true
as artichokes or Jersey
asparagus): and on and on through the villages,
                             (*Collected Poems* 140)

The parenthesis, like the colon, becomes a device for interpenetration of the one and the many.

Because Ammons is constantly announcing his own practices, criticism has seemed very redundant. But in the behavior of the poem, rather than in its subject matter or discursive content, we find aesthetic and emotional satisfaction. "Poetry is action," and "poetry recommends," by its behavior, "certain kinds of behavior." Ammons's reflexivity is itself a particular kind of poetic behavior. "Terrain," for instance, after launching a description by way of metaphor ("the soul is a region without definite boundaries"), enters into the second term, forgetting its sponsorship. But, within that second term, the one/many dynamic, which is the real subject of the poem, is reiterated in landscape terms. The soul/body or self/landscape dichotomy is transposed into a network of landscape relations, and duality vanishes. The gnomic proposition that opens the poem yields to a perceptual/experiential model as the poet uses present tense to bring forward the landscape, reversing tenor and vehicle. The "like" in the line "It floats (self-adjusting) like the continental mass" recalls us to the initial metaphor, but the sponsorship of simile is weak and yields altogether to description, which enfolds simile rather than extending it: "river systems thrown like winter tree-shadows." Nature's internal resemblances displace a Cartesian model of mirroring mind. The correspondences of soul/region convert to correspondences within the geography itself—"where it towers most / extending its deepest mantling base." The second stanza of this poem adjusts the intersections that have become too symmetrical, so that "floods unbalancing / gut it, silt altering the / distribution of weight." "Weight" brings us back from illusion to the presence of the poem; we feel the weight not in the referential silt but in the "nature of content"—the weight of the "soul," which is the subject of the poem. This extraordinary interpenetration of consciousness and its object returns us, cyclically, to the poem's opening, but only momentarily.

The poem seeks other means of mapping the one/many/one paradigm. The images of imbalance are followed by images of dissolution:

> a growth into
> destruction of growth,
> change of character,
> invasion of peat by poplar and oak: semi-precious
> stones and precious metals drop from muddy water into mud:
>   (*Collected Poems* 90)

The region is coming apart into multiplicity and separateness (after the earlier symmetry and correspondence). The landscape endures a kind of crisis of multiplicity and separateness—"whirlwinds move through it / or stand spinning like separate orders: the moon comes: / there are barren spots: bogs, rising / by self-accretion from themselves." But if the orders that initiate the poem are entropic, the stanza recuperates with a structure of collision moving toward the "poise" of "countercurrents." The stanza divisions mark an overall pattern presiding in the shifts in focus and organization. The stanza I have quoted moves away from the large geographic model of continental plates and river systems to a more local model of "habitat." The "region" is now far more liquid—it does not just contain lakes and rivers and marshes but is itself "a crust afloat." In this model the sponsoring unity ("the soul" or "continental mass") gives way to a "precise ecology of forms / mutually to some extent / tolerable"—a strange phrase in which precision and approximation must somehow become compatible. But at the same time this "precision" moves to an increasingly imprecise language, a mysticism of "the soul" quite different from earlier geological references. Description turns back into heightened metaphor and visionary stance: "foam to the deep and other-natured: / but deeper than depth, too: a vacancy and swirl: // it may be spherical, light and knowledge merely / the iris and opening / to the dark methods of its sight." The phrase "whirls and stands still" cues the poem to rest in the interpenetration of imagination and earth: "the moon comes: terrain." This gesture marks the poem's unity, providing a double refrain—one internal to the poem, one echoing the title to complete a cycle.

As "Terrain" indicates, particularity in the prophetic phase derives from enumerative rather than descriptive rhetoric. The most eloquent example is "The City Limits," which realizes vision in form. The relation of one and many inheres in the play of the unifying syntax and pluralizing diction: "when you consider // that air or vacuum, snow or shale, squid or wolf, rose or lichen, / each is accepted into as much light as it will take." The heavy enjambment works with the lexical diversity to maximize freedom in form and to create the sense of expansion the poem wishes to convey emotionally. What Randall Jarrell said of Whitman applies here: Ammons's lists are "little systems as beautifully and astonishingly organized as the rings and satellites of Saturn." Here the polarities indicate not only range, but also tension resolved, dualities overcome—good and evil, life and death, nature and culture, high and low. Collisions in the diction ("natural slaughter," "storms of generosity," "gold-skeined wings of flies") have a liberating effect within the constancy of "the radiance." Collisions become chords in the one/many harmony. The coordinating conjunction "or" creates an array of oppositions held in tension: "snow or shale" in textural or "rose or lichen" in visual parallel. Not too much is made of these arrangements. They remain local and metamorphic, yielding to other terms of connection. Similarly the anaphora that binds the list shifts its position in the line so that litany does not become harangue.

The pleasures of the prophetic phase are many and it is still the phase readers most associate with Ammons. It delights in the revival of form in inexhaustible substance, the rediscovery of pattern in particulars. "Scope is beyond me" not because the beholder's vision fails but because motion is the essential nature of this pattern. What this mode gives up, largely, is the self's direct, experiential engagement with the life it beholds. Motion remains theoretical, a matter of spectacle rather than impact. For all their apparent spontaneity and contingency, these are poems of thoughts more than thinking, life viewed more than felt. By making a home in motion, in its form, the sage evades its force.

IT IS PERHAPS inevitable that the pilgrim should become the sage, and there are clear continuities between the two stances. But Ammons wrote *Snow Poems* (1977) against the sagacious stance of *Sphere*. Out of this new, rough, improvisatory, impious, and antitranscendent language of *Snow Poems* came Ammons's poetry of the ordinary man. Of course in a sense Ammons had adopted this pose throughout his career. *Tape for the Turn of the Year* (1965), for instance, with its daily account of whims and weather, hardly suggests philosophic authority. But within the offhand rhetoric and playful reference to the page is a strongly didactic and generalizing impulse characteristic of the prophetic phase:

> don't establish the
> boundaries
> first,
> the squares, triangles,

boxes
of preconceived
possibility,
and then
pour
life into them, trimming
off left-over edges,
ending potential:
    let centers
    proliferate
    from
self-justifying motions!

                  (*Tape* 116)

In *Snow Poems* he qualifies: "I don't insist / on the meaning, only the facts." He names predilections and possibilities rather than revealed truths (however provisional). Slippery phonemes and chiasms sabotage propositions ("whorey bottom / or bottomless horrid"); lists amass words more than things, subverting propositions; double columns divert linear reading. This is poetry of the mind in and on the body, the human body (sexual, mortal) and the body of language. Broad laws of physics and geology, so important to the middle phase, play little part in this raid on matter and manner.

In this last phase of his work Ammons increases the element of transition and adjustment, in contrast to the encompassing continuities of the earlier work. He enters perspective, orients the mind to a particular alignment of reality, and then abruptly alters it. Where the prophetic voice continues, it is now the voice of Proteus, as he indicates in an essay collected in *Set in Motion*.

You remember that Proteus was a minor sea god, a god of knowledge, an attendant on Poseidon. Poseidon is the ocean, the total view, every structure in the ocean as well as the unstructured ocean itself. Proteus, the god of knowledge, though, is a minor god. . . . It was presumed that Proteus knew the answers—and more important The Answer—but he resisted questions by transforming himself from one creature or substance into another. . . . But the vague question is answered by the ocean which provides distinction and nondistinction.

(*Set in Motion* 14–15)

In midcareer Ammons stays close to the ocean (hence the shore poems), and to Poseidon, even as he traces out the "provisional stabilities" and "saliences" that form the waves and dunes. But in the later work he is more interested in Protean metamorphoses. Shifting thoughts and orientations take turns in the foreground. Poetry, Ammons writes, is "a linguistic correction of disorder," not the disorder of the world corrected by art, but the disorder of a former idea which has lost its power through the introduction of new fact. These poems are indeed "linguistic corrections" in this sense, often marked in the middle by transitional conjunctions like "but," "still," "yet." The model of the poem as epistemological quest is least relevant to this last phase of Ammons's writing. Increasingly, he thinks of poetry as exemplary action and behavior rather than epistemology.

As the poet withdraws from the extremes of sea and wilderness, and from the frontiers charted by science, he turns his attention to the everyday but always astonishing world of his backyard, his greenhouse, and his local environment. There are fewer lists in this phase because the imagination is less voracious. (*Garbage* [1993] is the exception that proves the point, since the lists there imply waste and disorder rather than unified plurality.) In place of the prophet's expansive rhetoric Ammons offers more focused descriptions. Nature in this phase is local, ordinary, and thoroughly mixed up with the human. We are part of nature (the mind inextricably embodied), and "nature" is our construction (we shape it visually and invest it with value and meaning).

The prophetic phase is broadly ecological in its thinking:

"ecology is my word: tag / me with that." From this natural philosophy Ammons derives a "moral order." But later Ammons is
less willing to be tagged. In *Glare* (1997) he will not let "the
man from *Audubon* . . . profile, defile, or maybe / just file" him.
"First we artificialize nature / then we naturalize artifice." He
tends to place environmental pieties in a historical perspective:

> our destructive rage
>
> against the unmercifulness of nature has
> put us in need of saving environmentalists, who
>
> have perhaps never happened
> upon a nest of rattlers: we had to
>
> tear down half the woods to have a door to keep
> the wolves away from: don't tell me that
>
> fetches of wind and slugs of rain erode the
> fields; where is the cabbage to come from:
>
> (*Glare* 181–182)

If he imagines nature often as a cooperative system, it can also
be a "nest of rattlers." It includes cooperative interactions of
stable, cyclical ecosystems, but also the dynamic, competitive,
and one-directional changes of evolution. Both patterns map
existence for Ammons.

The visionary phase concerned matter and energy as material
for the abstract form of motion. Later Ammons focuses more on
"motion's holdings," retentive structures, than on motion itself.
As he turns his attention and adapts his stance to the ordinary,
this amassing, schematizing tendency gives way to a greater
sense of materiality. The material may seem ethereal as it
descends into microscopic organization, or as substance con-
verts to energy, but while the world is endlessly metamorphic, it

is less easily transfigured to a metaphysical state. In *Snow Poems* Ammons begins to talk about trash. The mortal body, in particular, resists transcendence. Ammons comes to terms with death rather than overcoming it.

In the pilgrim poems, death of the self is a vehicle by which the soul or consciousness enters a more expansive state. In the sage poems, death is part of a larger motion to which the mind aligns itself. But for the poet of the ordinary and for the poet as ordinary man, death is real and not merely transitional. Rot, compost, garbage, bodily decomposition, the "low" forms of scavengers and parasites, come into the foreground. It is the body, not the mind, which dwells in motion. Where oneness had been held to a transcendent, abstract realm before, the realm of the soul or radiance, here it is the realm of matter. The embodied mind has the authority of experience, but not of transcendental vision. "The spirit dies, but the body / lives forever, run out of its limits // though and caught up into others." Unlike Whitman, Ammons often represents the soul or spirit as fragmentary and intermittent.

This shift in Ammons toward materialism aligns him more with late Thoreau—especially in the *Journal*—than with Emerson. Though he is "not a palpabilitist" he is nevertheless increasingly a poet of matter who unifies the world not at the level of ideas but at the level of substance and energy. Thoreau had "great faith in the seed" and so does Ammons, who sees independent but interactive agents establishing the unity of life. If death is surpassed it is not through transcendence but through transformation, the Darwinian principle of the world's unending flux.

Throughout the pilgrim and prophetic stages, one feels, despite the constant "balancing" of one and many, that oneness is the goal of cognition even as it is restive within any "partial reach." Plurality is in a sense what the pattern must endure on its way to a greater roundness. Synecdoche infuses microscopic detail and refers to the grand metaphor of all reality. In his sense of the All, with its laws of motion superseding particulars, Ammons follows Emerson. But in the late phase he reverses the paradigm; oneness is nodal and intermittent, not comprehensive. Parts do not as readily confer a whole. Reality is, in a sense, always local. This, too, draws him closer to Thoreau. But in his late acknowledgment of loss, and of the accumulative force of the past, Ammons removes himself even from Thoreau.

Ammons's sage lives in a continuous present. "Tomorrow a new walk is a new walk," without a trace of the yesterdays to pollute it. While some interest in habitats, renewable cycles, and cooperative systems carries over from the middle phase, the concept of change in the late work is couched much more in evolutionary terms of extinctions and adaptations. The past is not redeemed as living memory, or easily metamorphosed into today's fresh orders. It lingers as debris, as bits of unfulfilled order, as loss. ("I have a life that did not become," Ammons begins in "Easter Morning.") This is another anti-Emersonian aspect of the new work. The past has no authority, but neither is it easily brushed aside. It accumulates as "garbage," "and there is no way, finally, to throw anything away." These poems explore a variety of responses to death, including mourning, but what they almost never do is evade death. Transfiguration and redemptive possibility remain strong impulses in the late poetry, but their work is more exposed, more strenuous, more provisional, and more uncertain.

These aspects of late Ammons come to full, eloquent expression in his remarkable "Ridge Farm." That this will be poetry of adjustment and discontinuity rather than continuous motion he tells us in canto 5:

> recalcitrance, fluency: these:
> too far with one and the density
> darkens, the mix slows, and bound
> up with hindrance, unyielding, stops:
> too far with the other and the bright

> spiel of light spins substanceless
> descriptions of motion—
>
> ways to be held free this way,
> staggering, jouncing, testing the
> middle mix,
> the rigid line of the free and easy
>
> (*Sumerian Vistas* 5)

This is poetry of "staggering, jouncing, testing"; life achieves its freedoms in breaking apart held orders. Little shocks and surprises assault the imagination, such as the unforeseen, peripheral detail that widens scope (as in "Corsons Inlet"), and reversals, sometimes grotesque reversals, as when a dead mole appears in the watering can with which the poet attends to an abandoned but resilient plant. Indeed, it is in the ordinary that Ammons finds the truly strange.

Ammons puts greater faith in observation in this period. Some of the most eloquent passages of "Ridge Farm" are purely descriptive, removing discursive content to embody pattern in image. Tension is rife:

> The lean, far-reaching, hung-over sway
> of the cedars this morning!
> vexed by the wind and working tight
>
> but the snow's packed in, wet-set,
> and puffed solid: the cedars nod to
> an average under gusts and blusters:
>
> yesterday afternoon cleared the
> sunset side of trees, the hemlocks
> especially, limbering loose, but
> the morning side, the lee, sunless
> again today, overbalances:

the grackles form long strings
of trying to sit still; they weight
down the wagging branchwork snow stuck
branch to branch, tree to shrub,
imposing weeds

(*Sumerian Vistas* 3)

The poem starts with a weight, a double weight in fact, of ice
and grackles. But the second, bird-weight carries with it the possibility of lift. The cedars are "lean" and "far-reaching," yet
"hung-over." The enjambment makes that hangover a form of
freedom, overriding a boundary. Wind seems an agent of this
stress but a narrow unity sustains itself since "the snow's packed
in." The movement of the cedars, "limbering loose," arises in
the recollection of yesterday's afternoon sun, but the dullness
"overbalances" with its unifying force, connecting branches,
tree to shrub, shrub to weeds. But again "imposing weeds" suggests the possibility of a disruption of this grim order. Since
"imposing" begins a new line it takes on the value of a verb.

Thus, while weight and confinement, the burden of ice and
snow, dominate the opening canto, we anticipate transition.
Ammons sets imagination at the brink, like a composer introducing half a cadence. We await the completion of the pattern in
the movement. A partial, retentive oneness must break out into
a more expansive vision. The last canto of "Ridge Farm," culmi-
nating a longer, closing movement, evokes "light" as a discontinuous but perennial presence. It "breaks out" in fresh
configurations, closing the cadence with a descriptive passage
that stands against the first for its redemptive possibility.

yesterday I
looked upbrook from the highway and
there flew down midbend a catbird to
the skinny dip, found a secure
underwater brookstone and began, in a

> dawnlike conclave of tranquility, to
> ruffle and flutter, dipping into and
> breaking the reflective surfaces with
> mishmashes of tinkling circlets.
>
> (*Sumerian Vistas* 41)

The poem that began in ice ends in a brook. A line of restless grackles has become a single catbird finding a toehold. But the sequence does not suggest a continuity of today and tomorrow. The poem begins with "this morning" and ends with "yesterday." This is not the Emersonian prophet of unimpeded radiance. Circles suggest unity, but arise in a myriad of "mishmashes," not horizons expanding out from the eye. Faith is located in plural, intermittent outbreaks of light. The images above maximize the interpenetration between order and disorder, tranquility and flux, one and many, rather than schematizing plurality into abstract patterns and motions. We arrive at the brink of revelation. These moments follow regularly upon images of ordinary mortality, such as the death of a mole. What the poem does not promise, however, is a transition into a vision of the overall. This is a "real brook" of "deep en-leafing" and "certain bends," yet the "tinkling circlets" suggest the imagination glimpsing visionary possibility.

For late Ammons, as for late Stevens, another poet of the ordinary, reality includes the imagination. "If you don't eat the imaginary potato . . . your real capacity to imagine illusion lessens." Ammons's poetry is especially antipastoral in this late phase, testing the pastoral's comfortable balances with frank images of intrusion and threat, disease and despoliation. Nature and man are co-contaminants. But the debunking rhetoric gives way throughout "Ridge Farm," and in later poems, to luminous moments in which the imagination finds some reciprocity with the material world: "still ponds, swallows / plinking them with fine lines . . . nipper fish catching / a chink in the mirror as a / web." In earlier work "nature" was a stable referent, for all its motions, a thing separable from the human configuration of it, something to which the mind went out. But here "nature says nothing— / it has nothing to say" so he "fills nature with my unintentionality," tropes its nothingness. Of course there is ordinary nature: the sexual and mortal body, material being. But Nature, as the transfiguration of the ordinary, is a necessary illusion: "Bernie said he wasn't much interested / in nature but if we didn't have it we'd have to / think of something to take its place."

On one hand Ammons acknowledges the sublimations that go into our pastoral construction of nature: "I love nature especially if there's / a hospital nearby and macadam or / glass in between." We separate ourselves from integral being by denying death, by dividing ourselves from death: "I like nature poetry / where the brooks are never dammed up or / damned to hauling dishwater or / scorched out of their bottoms by acids." But such declarations are set against an insistent confrontation with "the real" as it is known by the nose: "spilldiddlings from the / assholes of filthy sheep." And it is just such denials that lead to abuses: "We can horse deeply in with / irresponsibility's ease; that's what / they say: / I'm afraid nature's going to send the bill: it usually does: / ferocious tallywhacker."

Glare, Ammons's most unflinching confrontation with the ordinary, nearly relinquishes those redeeming moments of luminosity and coalescence that characterize "Ridge Farm." This long poem refuses sentiment, illusion, consolation; it looks at death as the final funnel. *Glare* is not radiance and contains no tincture of the sublime. It's even a little menacing. "Ridge Farm" kept the visionary element alive in local glints and glimmers. But where are they when the light of day is so intense? An often endearingly humorous, but hardly ingratiating, voice tells the truth about oneness, that it's down and out, not up and through: "In time all the stories become the same story; / the energies play out and the hole at the end / contains everything." Yet the poet swerves (with a "meanwhile") from this digestive void, acknowledging "joy" that can "break out anywhere." The "Strip" which names the first half of the poem is Ammons's sign of the infinite, not transcendent, cycle of generation and decay. This once sublime pattern, this "invisibility," may be an "opacity." The transcendental "Overall" reduces to "the sum of too many things to talk about" except in the jerky, improvisatory, discontinuous, scatological, and anxious mental registers of "Scat Scan," as the second part is called. *Glare* is not an epistemological poem at all. It is ordinary in the sense that it claims no position of mirroring mastery. It is, rather, a record of the embodied mind.

Ammons has shuttled regularly in his long career between long and short poems, an alternation expressive of his fascination with the one/many relation. Thus, while the long poem *Glare* ruminates on the large movements of being into nothingness and back, *Brink Road* registers local moments of transition. *Brink Road* is Ammons's fullest exploration of the poetics of adjustment. The poet as ordinary man abides through shifts of orientation, more local and episodic than paradigmatic. The poems repeatedly move from a burdened or dispirited state to one that observes and enables progression. Vision is less about truth than about belief. The poet reconfigures nature in order to make spiritual adjustments. Indeed, the eye is less reliable than before as a vehicle of knowledge and renewal; the imagination corrects the eye's narrow disclosures. Where the prophetic poems celebrated a continuous present, the late poems acknowledge holding patterns and impulses, the human desire to keep what belongs to time. Mobility involves wreckage and debris; the present scene is overlaid with the shards of past structures. The image of the stream runs throughout these poems as a figure by which the mind might train itself to mobility, but the overall experience is of transition rather than fluency, of perspective rather than transcendence. In their emphasis on adjusted vision these poems take us back to the pilgrim poems, but their focus is no longer on cognitive authority. Identity seems to be something inevitable but unfixed, like temperament, rather than an essence in need of transcendental proofs.

Ammons employs a similar poetic structure to convey each of these transitional moments. Each short lyric is divided by a conjunction (but, still, meanwhile, whereas, even) that reverses or redirects the logic of an initial image. Rather than conveying a continuous present, the poems register abrupt transitions in being, set against a background "unity of void." The opening poem of the volume, "A Sense of Now," serves as a template of others.

> Rock frozen and fractured
> spills, a shambles,
>
> and tiers of time pile into,
> shatter through
>
> other tiers or angle up
> oddly, brightly lined with
>
> granite or talus, a jumble,
> "metaphysical debris":
>
> but the stream finding its
> way down a new hill spills
>
> along the right ledges, shifts
> the schist chips about and
>
> down with becoming coherence,
> and moss beds down ruffling
>
> shale edges dark gray
> to green, and the otter

drinks from sidepools
almost perfectly clear.

(*Brink Road* 3)

Surprisingly, the sense of now is not one idea but three, without obvious summary or confluence. The paratactic poem is edgy, jumpy, and restless in its movement through these orientations. Indeed, in the first frame disorder is the principle ("fracture," "shambles," "jumble," "debris"). The sense of now includes the past; a former order has collapsed. What appears is "oddly" configured, not obviously patterned. The term "spills" suggests waste, which "piles up" in an accumulation without coherent design. The abstract summary—"'metaphysical debris'"—is itself discontinuous, the quotation marks highlighting the disjunction. But the phrase brings into focus the abstraction latent in the rocks as "tiers of time." The second frame features motion over its effects. "But" marks a shift in which the "spills" of the previous clause become libation more than waste. The movement from solid to liquid allows the "becoming coherence" (lovely and emergent) to gather agency. The mind does not make a home in such motion, however, only beside it. The poem has moved from wreckage to fluency and will close in figures of tentative dwelling. It shifts again, now to the "moss" that "beds down" on the shale. An organic image, the moss softens the figure of retention, converting "gray" to "green." The otter, like a surrogate for the poet, partakes of the liquid element through the sidepools (now rock and water, retention and flow, converge). The sense of now is a still moment "almost perfectly clear." Qualifiers of this sort characterize the last phase of Ammons's work. He does not celebrate incompleteness as evidence of the infinite, so much as proof of human limit. Human concern, as he puts it in "Ridge Farm," is "a frail butterfly, a slightly guided piece of trash."

Fragmentation rather than continuity characterizes human concern, as these three-part poems suggest in their structure. The next few poems in *Brink Road* repeat, with variation, the structure of adjustment established in "A Sense of Now." And in each of these poems Ammons, the ordinary man, seeks an acceptable balance rather than an absolute truth, some sort of phenomenological "regularum." Thus in "Establishment" the eye produces "invitations, deceptions" and indicates translucence while the mind asserts "hard rock." A third, closing image integrates mind and eye in a phenomenal truth in which "rock-grain" is "cracked and felt into" by "tense roots," a figure of idea taking hold as phenomenal truth and vital ongoing. Each poem begins with some image of necessity blocking creative progression—a rock slide, a storm toss, an impenetrable ridge—but makes an adjustment to refuse terminus and desolation while allowing for tentative order. The pragmatist principle that "belief at any cost serves life" is enacted in the poetry by the imagination turning always toward some angle of vision that will affirm—affirmation is something life requires more than knowledge. So in "Standing Light Up" Ammons begins with avalanches of stone, mud, snow, cast off in a "but so what" that turns abruptly to an affirmation of spirit. Such adjustments are not as facile as the conjunctions suggest, however. Ammons strains the syntax to register the work of restoring flow and contriving new order. Even the syntactically awkward title marks this strain. Contractions and possessives in the poem add to the confusion, indicating how objects separate and reattach in a network of associations and events: "what outleaps / the insides of summits thunder's rumble has / never jarred." The refusal of "jarring" forces is itself achieved by the phonic order more than the grammatical or semantic orders, making us "halt and listen."

These linguistic strains remind us that our orientations are under construction—they are not passive discoveries but behaviors that preserve life. So for instance in "First Cold," a first patterning of "white on white" of snow to petal is aesthetically satisfying but sterile. The "milling" of life in seasonal change produces a new patterning in the imagination of the beholder, of gold on gold, bees and the sun. The descriptions provide a "shifting dynamics between artifice and emergence"("Next to Nothing")—between one construction of reality and another emerging as "motion / undermines meaning with meaning" ("Flurries"). Motion is not just theoretical; Ammons conveys it by moving from one form to another. To hold is human, Ammons seems to recognize in this volume, and to change is natural. Human adjustment is then the appropriate response to nature.

The poem "Fascicle," while it does not launch or conclude the volume as it might, tells us something about lyric poetry as Ammons understands it in this last phase of his career.

> There's a rift of days sunny (not too windy, not
> too cold) between leaf- and snowfall when
> raking works: away on a weekend, you could
>
> miss it and rain could sog everything slick-flat
> or gusts could leave no leaf not lifting
> off the ground: stick
>
> around the house, a big sheet ready, a strong-caned
> rake strung tight, and catch the sun
> just when it stills the air dry: that's likely
>
> to be before some cold front frost-furring
> the saw-edged leaves glistened brittle, clouds
> tightening the horizon: then the white leaves fly.
>
> (*Brink Road* 10)

The model of poetic activity is not the pilgrim's quest or the prophet's visionary excursion, but the simple, domestic work of raking leaves. Whitman stands silently in the background of the poem, but Dickinson prevails. This one-sentence "fascicle" is something less audacious, more contingent, and less transcendental than Whitman's *Leaves of Grass*. The lyric gathering is not comprehensive; it arises in a "rift" (marked by the parenthesis). Again the sense of loss and failure haunts the poem ("sog everything slick-flat"; "no leaf not lifting") and must be dispelled. The gathering at the center of the poem is entirely transitional. It belongs not with cosmology but with the domestic images of the house and the bedsheet/winding sheet (the "strong-caned" left at the end of the line anticipates an old man's chair and stick, not rake). A "catch" of the sun, or holding of energy, makes the dispersal at the end not a failure (as it is logically, and in terms of the poem's narrative), but a release. Liberation comes when "the white leaves fly" after the "tightening [of] the horizon." The thrust of all these poems, what makes them ordinary, is their attempt to overcome the fear of death through images of gathering and release. The leaves are "white" presumably because of the frost, but, as the domestic "sheet" suggests a paper, so the "white leaves" suggest as well a literary dispersal, something countering the death this image also projects. The poem could not end with the success of the catch. But that success allows the final dispersal to become double, overcoming the desolate, anxious language of the poem's opening.

In Ammons's last phase we see a nature poetry finally loosed from sagacious abstraction. Ammons answers the Over-Soul's call to theory with the compelling, tangible struggles of the ordinary man to put himself on the side of motion and flow. Death must be transfigured and it is transfigured, not through confident reference to a transcendental vision, but through local exercise in "the giving up of oneself away," through "simplicity and the breaking surf."

Rereading Ammons's Long Poems

James McConkey

NEARLY ALL THE BOOK-LENGTH poems of A. R. Ammons were written on adding machine tape that unrolled during their composition on his old typewriter. To compose a poem on a continuous strip of paper is to write it either without revision or with the revision a part of its ongoing movement. Ammons's long poems are journals of a particular sort, the record of a consciousness focused on the transcription into words of the associations it is currently making —a consciousness capable of contradictions, moments of brilliant illumination, as well as moments of comic absurdity, self-deflation, and depression.

Ammons—Archie to his acquaintances—was a prolific poet. He wrote book after book of poems of various lengths, one collection (*The Really Short Poems of A. R. Ammons*) consisting of poems so brief that some are epigrams or puns. "Coward," for example, contains five words: "Bravery runs in my family." Another, called "Their Sex Life," requires an additional word: "One failure on / Top of another." These two poems reflect the pure fun Archie could find in words and phrases, while others, like "Small Song," carry that playfulness a step further into an impression with the haunting quality of a fine haiku: "The reeds give / way to the / wind and give / the wind away."

That quality, along with much else, exists in the collections of poems of a more conventional length. Though not in a collection, one such poem—the dedicatory poem to Harold Bloom that precedes the book-length *Sphere*—strikes me as one of the grandest poems written in English in the twentieth century, moving as it does through narrative to an end made inevitable by its action. Though they vary in intensity, I admire Archie's achievements in the shorter forms so much that they influenced my response to those that fill up a book. In reading the long poems as they became available over the years, I found myself always looking for the more concentrated poems they contained, individual poems often so lyrical that I thought of them as arias in an opera that went on too long. The remainder of the material struck me as a series of recitatives—that is to say, mere prose pieces, however carried along these segments might be in the rhythm that marks the whole work. To me, the book-length poems resembled the notebooks poets sometimes keep which give us an insight into what goes on in their minds as they are searching for the ideas and images that, once discovered, will burst into creative song. I wanted to hear those songs, without being privy to the process that created them.

Probably the prejudice I brought to my reading of these long poems is shared by others who think of the ideal poem as a concentrated expression that manages—through the author's selection and ordering of its images, through those sounds that become soundings—to imply so much more than its apparent subject permits that it expands in the reader's mind, becoming, paradoxically or not, an expression of what is beyond the ability of language to convey.

My response to the long poems was complicated by my attitude to my own writing. I am a writer of prose rather than poetry, a prose writer who is particularly dependent upon the spiritual resources of personal memory to justify and connect the various autobiographical experiences I am recalling. At the very least, I want my words and phrases to pay tribute to a unity or wholeness that lies beyond my ordinary life, and to do that to the best of my ability I revise as I go along. Archie was my friend and colleague over the decades, and I felt, in my private conversations with him as well as in his poetry, the kind of mutual, if unstated, understanding that one has for another whose intuitions or feelings are similar, however different the circumstances of their lives or their political leanings. He was a poet and I wrote prose, so I never felt myself in competition with him, never experienced envy at his growing fame—though I admit I was puzzled that it had much to do with the book-length poems that he turned to with greater frequency in his later years. And I also confess that my initial intent in writing this essay was to rescue the arias from the recitatives that surrounded them.

To achieve such a goal, though, meant that I had to reread those book-length poems, to give them a more attentive reading than I had managed during Archie's lifetime. They contain some typos that he missed, and some repetitions that he might not have intended—though, given this mode of writing, it is hard to determine that. (He once told me, with apparent surprise at the fact, that the book editors he worked with never suggested changes of any kind.) The width of the tape determines the length of a line in such books as *Tape for the Turn of the Year* (1965), *Garbage* (1993), and *Glare* (1997). In *Sphere* (1974), the lines are somewhat longer, for here Archie seems to have used conventional typewriter paper, his line endings determined by the bell that rang in accordance with the right margin he had set. In these long poems, Archie sometimes complains of the restraint he has imposed upon himself by this method, but in interviews published in local papers he remarks that they provide the discipline poets once found in more conventional forms, such as the sonnet. In rereading the later book-length poems, I could see that he had developed an intuitive control of his self-imposed form that had been lacking in *Tape*, his fledging attempt—the one responsible for my prejudgment of the others. In the later poems, the line lengths vary from one book to the next, for the tapes are of differing widths. Combined with stanza lengths that also vary from book to book, the lines capture a mental rhythm in keeping with the thoughts and feelings being expressed.

Technical matters of this sort constitute what I first noticed in rereading the long poems. Necessary though they may be to the greater appreciation I now have for those poems, such matters, discussed with pertinent examples from the poems, wouldn't make for lively reading in a personal essay like this one. Instead, I will engage in the kind of associative digression that Archie himself continually employs. The question of what constitutes a proper line seems to be of extraordinary importance to poets, particularly those who have dispensed with traditional forms. I once invited Denise Levertov to Cornell as a participant in a yearlong festival devoted to Chekhov. A quarrel over this issue of the line had brought a disruption of the friendship between Archie and Denise, something they both regretted. Archie readily agreed to have dinner with Denise and me at the Statler Hotel on the Cornell campus, and accompanied me to the nearby house where she was staying. They were happy to see each other. My attempt at peacemaking would have been successful had not Archie stopped to admire a bed of yellow flowers as we were walking to the hotel. "My, aren't those lovely flowers, Denise?" he said. "What do you suppose they are?" She replied, "I thought you were a nature poet, Archie. Those are *daffodils*." The frigidity following that exchange withered the bloom of their rediscovered pleasure in each other's company. At dinner, they wouldn't speak to each other, addressing all their comments to me.

Unlike the book-length poems that follow, *Tape* concludes with a summary of the journey the reader has taken with him, the final entry containing these lines:

                                   I
                         showed that I'm sometimes
                         blank & abstract,
                         sometimes blessed with
                         song: sometimes
                         silly, vapid, serious,
                         angry, despairing:
                              ideally, I'd
                              be like a short poem:
                              that's a fine way
                              to be: a poem at a
                         time: but all day
                         life itself is bending,
                         weaving, changing,
                         adapting, failing,
                              succeeding:

                                                  (*Tape* 204)

   In rereading those lines, I saw them as Archie's reply from the
grave to my objection that he was providing the process along
with the songs that emerged from it. So it is life itself, life in all
of its changes—that is, life as a *process*—that is his subject, and
it is a falsification of whatever constitutes "truth" or "reality" to
freeze into ideal form any segment of it. He expresses such a
view elsewhere, as in these lines from *Sphere*:

                         I don't know about you,
        but I'm sick of good poems, all those little rondures
        splendidly brought off, painted gourds on a shelf: give me

        the dumb, debilitated, nasty, and massive, if that's the
        alternative: touch the universe anywhere you touch it
        everywhere:

                                                  (*Sphere* 72)

—though here, of course, he is moving beyond his or anybody's life to an expression that may sound metaphysical but has a basis in scientific knowledge of the elements from which we, and everything that surrounds us, are composed. But to "touch the universe anywhere" is not to immobilize it, for everything in nature (upward from the electrons of the atom and downward to the strange behavior of the smallest particles) is in motion.

Archie studied biology at Wake Forest University, and for the rest of his life was alert to ongoing scientific investigation, to its continuing discoveries and puzzlements—responding especially to those, I would guess, that are connected to his poetic sensibility and knowledge of himself as a person of changeable moods who meanwhile is moving through life to the death that is foreshadowed by the various ailments of his later years. I'm revealing no secrets in saying that Archie's ego was strong and yet tender to slights (like the one he perceived as he was trying to renew his friendship with Denise), or that he felt anger and some long-held resentments as well as generosity, love, and compassion: his own poetry testifies to that, and recognizes (especially toward the end of his career) his failings.

It would be reductive, though, to say that Archie's altering emotional states explain his mode of composition in the long poems or in any of the others. All of us demonstrate mutability as we move toward death, though we assume (I know I do) that a constancy of belief or character holds, despite all changes. In opening a needed and especially rewarding essay about Archie's "heart," about the depth of his feelings for others, Roger Gilbert says that readers of Archie's poetry realize "that he has a formidable brain. . . . No other contemporary poet has presented himself so unabashedly as a *thinker* as well as an artist." It is true—something Archie was as aware of as any reader—that he was drawn to abstractions to a far greater degree than most of us. In rereading the book-length poems, the ones that permit the development or orchestration of those abstractions, it struck me more forcefully than in the past that motion—not linear motion, but motion in the shape of arcs and curves—is essential to everything else the abstractions (as well as the poems themselves) contain. The curves have a basis in knowledge that the universe is expanding, that space itself curves—possibly back on itself. Even "salience," a favorite word in the poems, has its physical equivalent, for example in the jutting forth of energy from the radiant but self-consuming globular mass that permits us life; in its human equivalent, such projections represent the extent to which we can rise on occasion above the ceaseless motion of our lives and of everything of which we are part to gain a clarity of perception or at least to perceive the curve of the horizon that still may limit our seeing.

Many of us who knew Archie have commented on the similarity between his poetry and the nature of his conversation, particularly in his daily coffee-house discussions with friends. His conversation digressed from any current topic, leading to remarks as unexpected as they were either serious or comic (and frequently bawdy: sex for Archie could be as ridiculous as it was crucial to human continuation and human song). The abstractions found in his long poems, though, are not part of the conversational play that he enjoyed and, I think, needed, for the sake of human contact and the insight of others. (In the poem "Summer Place," he says, "I don't want to be by myself: I don't / want anybody else to be by himself much: I don't mind being / alone: it's loneliness that gets me.") Those intellectual abstractions, part of the solitary poet's thoughts as he sat at his typewriter (and removed as they are from more purely human considerations), are crucial, I would guess, to one of the reasons he gives for writing the long poems—that (as he says in *Glare*) the act of concentration, even more than the thinking itself, "means / the attention is directed outside / and focused away from the self, away / from obsessive self-monitorings" and all the "misery" waiting to be recalled. That Archie's memory could bring him torment is apparent in his perverse invocation, earlier in this same poem, to the "great mother of the muses"

(Mnemosyne) to help him forget a memory from childhood he won't clarify, though it probably refers to the burial of a younger brother; to help him forget the memory of a feeling that however

> fleeting is carved in stone across
> the gut: I can't float or heave it
>
> out: it has become a foundation:
> whatever is now passes like early
>
> snow on a warm boulder: but the
> boulder over and over is revealed,
>
> its gritty size and weight a glare:
> rememberers of loveliness, ruddy
>
> glees, how you cling to memory, while
> haunted others sweat and wring out
>
> the nights and haste about stricken
> through the days:
>
> (*Glare* 94–95)

My quotation here is as lengthy as it is to communicate its power, as part of one of the many poems I had initially chosen as examples of the arias that are self-sufficient (or nearly so). In writing this particular song, did Archie have in mind such extollers of memory as I, who find in memory—however painful certain of the events that are recalled—the desire for unity and oneness that defines the soul?

This essay, like Archie's long poems, is a contemplative process, and what I didn't realize until this moment—not at a typewriter, but at the computer that aids my revisions—is that the major abstractions in Archie's work, whatever their scientific basis, serve him in the same spiritual capacity that memory serves me. That is to say, they serve a purely human need—the need of the psyche for union, for a oneness beyond our mortal grasp. If everything in nature is in motion, the forms of that motion to be represented in arcs, curves, and saliences; if the universe has been expanding since its creation from an apparent nothingness, where is the center to be found? At any given moment, right here, or anywhere. (After all, to "touch the universe anywhere," is to "touch it everywhere.")

And what is true of space is equally true of time. *Garbage* contains a meditation on a number of interrelated matters, the question of meaning and meaninglessness being the central strand. It includes these lines:

> it is
> fashionable now to mean nothing, not to exist,
>
> because meaning doesn't hold, and we do not exist
> forever; this *is* forever, we are now in it:
>
> (*Garbage* 88)

That's a brave statement from one who, as he grew older, frequently thought of the finality of death. And it is especially brave, given the context in which it is found, for he has just been referring to space as well as time—to the immensity of the cosmos, to "the terror of the / unimaginably empty and endless," to "the core-fire of the galaxy" which permits us—"cellular brushfires" that we are—to "burn cool in a way-off arm." Whatever burns consumes its fuel: in the universe, as in any closed system, entropy increases as available energy decreases. Stars shrink and die, humans die and their bodies shrink: for both, silence ensues from the loss of motion and light. Of course, even though the universe itself eventually may return to its beginnings in the silent emptiness, new stars and new humans are constantly being born from dust, cosmic or otherwise.

Though this phraseology is mine, knowledge of a similar sort is included in Archie's abstractions about motion, and has its psychical equivalent in his views about poetry and his own poetics. "The purpose of the motion of the poem," he says in *Sphere,* is to bring the "focused, awakened mind" to "no-motion" where that mind can "touch the knowledge that / motions are instances of order and direction occurring / briefly in the silence that surrounds." The lines that follow stress the importance of silence to renewed creativity, and the passage concludes with an apostrophe addressed "to the spirit-being, great one in the world / beyond sense."

Many writers that I admire—from Augustine to Annie Dillard—have been attracted to silence, as if in silence one can hear the voice of God. Archie's abstractions might be his way of recasting the religious beliefs so prevalent in the rural and impoverished North Carolina of his childhood. To my knowledge, no other poet has constantly struggled against the insignificance that science has brought to us by using science itself to provide us with a sense of a possible unity pervading the cosmos.

Archie's abstractions might seem a cold comfort, at best; but I find them linked to the warmth of the "heart" that Roger Gilbert so properly emphasizes. *Glare,* his final long poem, opens with a return to his long-standing preoccupation with the vastness of the cosmos, one of whose errant motions—in the shape of a boulder, say—might bring an end to all our activities long before Earth is consumed by the sun whose expanding size will foreshadow its own diminution in death. Given such an ultimate cessation, though, "it is not careless to become too local." In the broadest sense, this means that if "the greatest god / is the stillness all the motions add / up to, then we must ineluctably be / included," and "it is / nice to be included, especially from / so minor a pew." In a more specific sense, such insight gives significance to all our endeavors to learn and know everything about the landscape now lying before us; and, at least for me, it gives significance to the humble details from Archie's life that follow this abstraction, details with intimate connections to the lives of others: "peanut butter and soda crackers / and the right shoe soles" for icy sidewalks. It is so obvious that I shouldn't need to add that meditations of this sort, no matter how abstract, are connected to Archie's compassion and love, as well as to his need for informal conversations with friends.

Archie's beliefs are to be found in his abstractions; whatever the modifications that may come to them, their details are consistent from the first long poem to the last. His voice remains an affirmative one, though the struggle for affirmation becomes more pronounced after *Sphere,* the most affirmative of them all. *Glare* contains two sections, the first of which—"Strip"—shows Archie at the height of his powers, as my references to it indicate; the following and much briefer section demonstrates, above all else, his need—his stubborn will—to go on, despite his declining health and the drugs that seem to be inhibiting his ability to remember, to make quick associations. Nevertheless, its title—"Scat Scan"—is a triple pun, the most obvious being its connection to a CAT scan, one of which probably helped in the diagnosis of his own ailments; but "scat" is also a jazz term for singing in which meaningless syllables are improvised, the voice joining the other instruments. Improvisation, though, has always been part of Archie's explorative process. (Its importance to him, in writing as in life, is emphasized here in his comment to himself, "if you can't get going you / might as well get gone, goodbuddy.") The third pun, of course, is in the reference, however ironical, to the excrement of wild animals.

But this section, whatever the faults or hesitancies caused by poor health, concludes with a song as lyrical as any of his devising, one which considers the structures we need for our upholding, and asserts they are made

                                        of no
   earthly thing but of will, blank will, which

acquires nor wields weight but simply insists
that it is as it is, right through the ruins of

truth which melts to reservation and contradiction
right through the rigors of all loss, no more

nothing than the nothing at the end it joins:

(Glare 293)

This song is part of all of Archie's singing:

                            it is a sad song but
it sings and wants to sing on and on and when

it can no more it wants someone else to sing:
to sing is everything but it is also specifically

to dive the stave into marshy passageways and
bring relief and the future singers in. . . .

(Glare 294)

A celebration of Archie's achievements—an "Ammons-fest"—was held for him at Cornell in April 1998. It was the kind of large public event that, despite his appreciation of sensitive and informed praise, he always dreaded. (His health was continuing to decline, and Adam Law, his physician as well as mine, was in attendance, for he admired Archie's poetry and the mind that it revealed while worrying ever more about his condition.) Archie had donated his papers to the Cornell archives, and, to express its gratitude, the library held a reception for him. That reception required a brief response from him, and he probably gave a gracious one; but all that I can remember from it is that he said that I was responsible for bringing him to Cornell. When I objected that this wasn't wholly true, he said that yes, it was: the matter was settled, at least in his mind.

After the celebration was over, I wondered at the reason that Archie had said what he did. Could he have realized, from my words with him at the time he gave his initial reading at Cornell—a reading that so impressed many of us that we wanted this then shy and obscure poet to join the faculty—that I felt a particular kinship with him?

I hope so; it certainly accounts for the nature of this essay, and of all that I learned while writing it.

A Gentle Luxury:
Remembering A. R. Ammons

Alice Fulton

THE FIRST TIME I SAW A. R. Ammons he was sitting at a crowded table in a sunken cafeteria, surrounded by full-sized plaster casts of the Elgin Marbles. It was April 24, 1980, the day of the Carter administration's failed attempt to rescue the Iranian hostages. Having accepted a graduate fellowship at Cornell, I was visiting the campus to get a sense of what lay in store for me. I had the usual worries about meeting a poet whose work had touched me, along with some less usual worries implanted by the comments of several of his former students. Wear a skirt, they said. He doesn't like assertive women, so be quiet and smile a lot. This bleak advice made me wonder what aspects of my self might be held hostage for the next two years. I felt a little like a zoologist learning gestures of appeasement before meeting the chief gorilla. I was determined to forget all I'd heard and decide for myself. But trying to forget was like trying not to think of white elephants: I could think of nothing else.

On the morning of the meeting, assertively attired in pants, blazer, and mournful face, I went to Goldwin Smith Hall to meet Professor Ammons. We were to meet in the Temple of Zeus, and I wondered at first if that was what they called his office.

Although this was to be my first glimpse of the Elgin Marbles (albeit in plaster), I think I hardly noticed how surreal they looked amid the steamy light and frayed furniture of the cafeteria. My powers of observation were concentrated on the long-limbed, pink-pated individual whose face I recognized from book jackets. With his handshake, Archie managed to convey courtesy, democracy, irony, and welcome all at once. He produced a chair, wedged it into position around the jammed table, and began introducing me to everyone. Apparently, the talk had centered on the botched hostage rescue until I appeared, when attention politely shifted to me. Archie began by saying how much he'd liked the poems in the chapbook I'd sent him when I applied to Cornell. He then introduced a theme that was to crop up frequently over the next two years.

"Well, we're happy you want to join us here. We'll be grateful for your presence. But I have to warn you that we have nothing to teach you. Your poems are there already."

Was this humility? Or was I being dismissed with praise? When I suggested that I had plenty to learn from him, the gist of his comments was, "Maybe you can pick something up by hanging around, but formal instruction isn't my method." In retrospect, I see this as fair warning of what it was like to study with Archie. I was to learn by osmosis: through listening, sifting, discussing, reading. "Do you have any hobbies?" he continued. Things were moving right along. I mumbled something about devoting all my free time to writing and began to wish I'd taken that bellydancing course at the Y last year. Archie talked a little about how much his painting had come to mean to him. When people began to leave for their morning classes, he rose and moved off slowly, inviting me to call him at home if I had any questions. His form of motion recalled Carlyle's description of Coleridge: "He hung loosely on his limbs, with knees bent, and stooping attitude; in walking, he rather shuffled than decisively stept."

I left with an impression of him as gracious, modest, playful, unpretentious, and kind. This was correct, as far as it went. His mild, meandering way of speaking made him seem easygoing and approachable. Usually one assumes a new acquaintance will seem foreign and that time will clarify his or her personality. Conversely, Archie appeared understandable at first and became more complicated over time, until one realized that a significant portion of his psyche was utterly private.

Though elusive in spirit, it was easy enough to locate Archie in body. His schedule was regular, and he seemed to relish the comfortable routine he'd established. He disliked holidays because they upset this pleasing order of events. On weekdays, he rose early and often went for a walk around his neighborhood. He arrived at Cornell at 8:00 a.m. and had coffee in Zeus soon thereafter. He drove home around 10:00 and returned at noon to teach or hold what amounted to daylong office hours. Students were encouraged to wander in and chat whenever he was there. His only request was that such meetings be spontaneous. He didn't enjoy formal appointments or the nervous constraint that might accompany them. For many writing students, Archie's office became the focal point of their studies. In him they found a nonjudgmental, empathetic listener. His gentle attitude made people want to confide in him. Students told of crying in his office over homesickness or divorces, and of how he'd helped them come to terms with their feelings. His respect for others showed in small, telling gestures. I noticed that he always stopped to speak with the cleaning women in the halls, and he was probably the only faculty member who knew them all by name.

Aside from an innate generosity, another explanation for Archie's accessibility lay in his method of composition. He wrote fluently, and in true Wordsworthian fashion might compose while walking, or in between visits from students. My reading of Archie's work had led me to imagine his walks as pastoral rambles across hill and dale. It was surprising to learn that he often walked through his suburban neighborhood and that the Triphammer Bridge of his gorgeous poem was heavily trafficked by cars. Most astounding of all, he said he occasionally ran upstairs in the middle of a TV show to jot down a few lines. I found this admission delightful in its modernity and as an example of his ability to transform the most banal aspects of life into poetry. When I said TV would distract me, he said he felt such "distractions" added a valuable element of chance to the environment. He might hear something that would move his mind in a direction it wouldn't have taken otherwise. And lest anyone think the Ammonsonian TV was tuned to *Nova,* I should mention that his favorite shows were *Merv Griffin* and *Barney Miller.*

To my mind, the mundane sites and occasions that prompted his poems underscore his imaginative achievement. He seemed to absorb life and effortlessly render it into metaphor. In fact, on one occasion he thought he'd absorbed a phrase from one of my own poems. Hearing me read a line referring to "ground speed," he said, "So that's where I found the term! It's in my new poem."

When I first arrived at Cornell, I felt shy about stopping in to see Archie, for fear of imposing. Then one day in September, while sitting in a classroom waiting for a seminar to begin, I became aware of a large presence beside me. A barely conscious thought flickered: This guy next to me takes up a lot of room. And why is he staring at me? I finally turned and was startled to see Archie. I was so nervous that I made him nervous. "Why don't you stop by my office sometime with your poems?" he said. Soon thereafter, clutching a sheaf of rolled-up papers in one hand, I timidly presented myself at his door. "Are those your poems?" he asked. I told him they were official announcements I'd found in my mailbox. "In that case, you can put most of them right there," he said somberly, pointing to the trashcan. So much for bureaucracy. His office had a high ceiling and airy blue walls. Everything there seemed serene, orderly. Archie's desk was neat, as if he'd put all of his Dionysian impulses into poems and paintings. There was a brown recliner lounge by the large window, and he'd often be sitting there, reading anything from

John Greenleaf Whittier to Wallace Stevens, when visitors arrived. He invariably rose and insisted that the guest, whether student or colleague, take the most comfortable chair. He sometimes read poems to visitors, and his sensitivity to the subtleties of language made any verse seem new and immediate. Although large groups made Archie nervous, he enjoyed reading to a few friends. I especially liked to hear him read his own writing. The knottier passages unraveled to lucidity when heard in his casual, musical voice, which still had a trace of North Carolina softness. He said he remembered hearing his father call for help and that with his heavy accent the word sounded like "Hope! hope!" This seemed like a natural metaphor for a poem, but the suggestion surprised Archie. His approach was different. Once I asked if he had a favorite from his own work, and he chose a small poem no one had noticed, called "Then One." I had to admit that its particular charm eluded me. One wall of his office was lined with books, and Archie referred to them often during a conversation. He loved the English Romantic poets, but when it came to modern poetry, his bent was strongly Americanist. His method of teaching was Socratic, with a heavy reliance on individual dialogue. If he felt that I'd be interested in a book, or that a certain writer would help my work, he'd loan me his copy.

There was an innocence about Archie that charmed people. It was as if he came from another planet, and everything here was new to him. I remember him complimenting me on a turtleneck sweater and saying, "What do you call that anyway? Is it some kind of jersey?" Perhaps he believed every object had a common and a Latin name, as with plants and birds. His impromptu personal remarks were too ingenuous to be offensive. He seemed to regard women as a foreign country, and himself as the hapless tourist trying to learn their mysterious nomenclature and customs. Out of the blue he asked questions like "Are you wearing stockings?" or "Won't your bellybutton get cold?"

Occasionally I tried to turn this tactic around with an off-the-wall remark of my own. A friend kept insisting that people would like me better if I were blonde. "Do you think I should dye my hair?" I asked Archie.

He was only momentarily nonplussed. "Maybe you could use a new image," he said.

When I complained that a man in the parking lot had hurled sexual comments my way, Archie carefully explained that such reactions were a kind of compliment, indicating the power women wield over men. This turnaround dumbfounded me. He went on to speak eloquently of how men air their deepest, inarticulate needs and feelings through such means. From his description you'd have thought every catcaller suffered from unrequited love. Dear God, I thought, is he confused! And I could see his opinion of me: My word, she's befuddled! With such disparate world views, it was a wonder we could communicate at all.

I took a heavy courseload during my first term and was constantly struggling with a paper or oral report. I'd totter down the halls of Goldwin Smith, going from water fountain to water fountain as if they offered a restorative elixir, walking close to the walls as if to preserve a sense of location. When Archie saw me in this frazzled state, he'd say, "What can we do to cheer you up?" We'd adjourn to his office and talk until my next class. When I left he'd courteously express regret. "Is it time already? We were having so much fun I didn't notice the hour."

I think he's the only man who ever offered to carry my books. I was standing in the Temple of Zeus with the complete works of Shakespeare nestled in my arms, when he gallantly offered assistance. "If you think you can manage," I replied testily.

Archie had his testy moments, also. Like all writers, he was eager to see what the post might bring. Too often, it contained manuscripts or requests for recommendations from aspiring poets whom he'd never met. Of course, he received his share of tributes and personal letters as well. It was these he hoped for daily around 3:00 p.m. when the mail arrived. If I happened to be lingering in his office at that hour, he might signal my eviction by suddenly standing up. Something in his ironic, courtly approach made me feel that we were operating in accordance with a bygone code. It was as if we'd been transported to an age of conventions and cues unknown to me. I was tempted to depart with style, uttering arch lines from Jane Austen novels, such as, "I have delighted you long enough. I must give the other young ladies a chance to exhibit."

Archie's notions of what might cheer a being could be so eccentric they brought smiles. Once, upon finding me in the *Epoch* office in a glum mood, he hunted up an issue of a small magazine with a black-and-white photo of a rock on the cover. "Just look at that, Alice," he said. "Doesn't that make you feel better?"

"Maybe if it were in color . . ." I sighed.

On the whole, Archie didn't seem to regard photography very highly as an art form. When I suggested that Ansel Adams's prints shared an affinity with his work and might be good choices for his book covers, he seemed displeased. His taste in visual art tended toward expressionism. He valued spontaneity, urgency, and the rawness of primitive emotion. Perhaps photography was too technical a medium for his sensibility. He wasn't very mechanically minded. A mention of bookcases and desks built by friends and relatives brought on attacks of inadequacy. "I wish I could do things like that," he'd say wistfully. "Something practical." On the other hand, his aversion to photography might have been a general Cornellian quirk. When I made the mistake of producing a camera during Jim McConkey's annual picnic everyone hied themselves away, leaving me alone with the apricot-champagne punch and a roll of unexposed Kodachrome.

When Archie learned that my husband, Hank De Leo, was an artist, he wanted to see his work. At the time, Hank was working on a series of nude self-portraits in colored pencil. One day he strolled into Archie's office and began unveiling these large, full-frontal drawings of himself. "Why Hank," Archie

drawled, "I didn't know you were so gifted." Archie took a dev-
ilish pleasure in sexual puns, allusions, and jokes. Though his
comments were sportive, they hinted at a subtext of empower-
ment, capability, and vitality. At times it seemed that sexuality
served as a kind of pan-metaphor for Archie, or the closest thing
we have to a grand unified field theory. His letters often take
advantage of the sexual resonance in figures of speech. "Thank
you for that birthday card. Right on the—pardon me—button,"
he might write. Or, "Hank's energy, growing, gathering strength
(suddenly, poor Hank, that all sounds related to the seminal
vesicle) . . ."

Archie and Hank played pool together occasionally, and the
game afforded Archie with a vocabulary of sexual innuendo
based on sticks, holes, and balls. His style of play was a mixture
of brio and self-mockery. If I arrived, the machismo posturing
increased, as if in tribute. There was an element of parody in his
thrusts of the cue (more vigorous than accurate at times), and in
his manqué mask of aggression. There's nothing to it really, he
seemed to say, when you've got the moves. It cost 95 cents to
play pool for an hour. Since 95 couldn't be divided equally, the
extra nickel became a source of contention. "Let's see, did I pay
it last time or did you?" Archie would begin, and the debate was
on. Hank's attempts to assume the burden of payment were
rebuked.

I think Archie's reaction stemmed both from thrift and from
his need to remain unindebted to anyone. He had known real
poverty as a child, which partly accounted for a frugality that
showed itself in little ways: the well-worn edges of his jackets,
the hole in the floor of his Toyota (though his wife drove a new
Oldsmobile), and those disputes over pennies. He wanted everyone to be comfortable, but he saw no sense in squandering spare
change. I think people sometimes noticed his small economies
and failed to balance them against his generosity in regard to
time, words, and attention. Sometimes, too, it seemed that nig-
gling over nickels was a token gesture he made to prove he was

nobody's fool. The notes he left in our mailboxes were written on tiny scraps cut from outdated department announcements. But the size of the paper could be attributed to Archie's modesty. I think he wanted his notes to appear too slight to save. I noticed, too, that Archie couldn't walk for a block without finding coins on the ground. With his downcast eyes, voluminous overcoat, and wool stocking cap in winter, he made a meditative figure. Yet he must have been awake to every crevice, weed, and gleam in the pavement.

Although Archie didn't want to be beholden to anyone, his friends and students wanted to give him gifts. For my part, I was grateful for the encouragement and advice he gave without stint. I suspected I'd never be able to give him anything of the kind in return, but I (and many others) longed to try. We soon learned that the best gifts were those that cost next to nothing, or at least wouldn't hang around too long. He also appreciated letters or poems. Funny junk or transient beauty seemed to hit the spot. Giant rubber pencils, mugs saying "NUMBER ONE," laurels made of cardboard and gilt—these were some of the profferings, along with flowers and houseplants. He was particularly pleased by anything homemade, and one year I made him a valentine with golden arches on it. In fact, as long as the gift wasn't expensive, Archie sweetly put the best light upon it. From a trip to New York I brought a couple of dime store pens that wrote in several colors and received one of his little notes: "The pens are great! Phyllis will like them, too. Great for pockets where they don't have to be attached." When the gift was more burdensome than beautiful or fun, the notes had a certain forced tone. "What a fancy shell!" he wrote in response to a gift from Cape Cod. "Thank you very much. You don't have to be so generous." Once I dreamed that I gave him the ultimate unwanted gift: a giant economy-sized bottle of shampoo. This seemed to summarize all of my previous attempts to please.

Many people dreamed of Archie, and we began to wonder if he might not wander the astral planes at night, getting into the collective unconscious. I asked him if he had psychic abilities, but he firmly denied any such talents. I don't think he knew his own powers. His moods created a considerable forcefield. He had an ability to lift people's spirits when his own equinimity was intact. And if he were upset, his powers of darkness were just as pervasive. At such times, he reminded me of a giant sunflower hit by frost, droopy and ragged in spirit. One day I peered into his office and saw him reading a paper in the dark. He looked up and scowled. Evidently something he'd read had disturbed him. I beat a hasty retreat. "What a gloomy day it is. I wish it would stop raining. Archie's in there ruining his eyes," I remarked to my husband in the hall. He directed my attention to the window, where sun shone brilliantly. What of the dark fog I'd seen moments before? I could only conclude that it emanated from Archie.

It was natural that Archie's unpredictable charms should attract disciples. Every morning a group of his colleagues, students, and friends met in the Temple of Zeus for the ritual known as Coffee. You could hear the capital C when people said the word. In fact, Archie had been taking part in this morning refreshment when I'd first met him. There was more to Coffee than breakfast, though mercifully, no one had told me this before my indoctrination. Every morning Zeus was the scene of battles of wits, quizzes, mental aerobics, exchanges of great and small ideas, bad jokes, good poetry, and vice versa. Tales of personal injury, trauma, revenge, passion—anything might come up. Someone might produce a new Ashbery poem and brows would furrow in bewilderment or admiration. (Archie respectfully referred to him as "Mr. Ashbery" and invariably expressed wonder and delight at his poems.) Or Archie might read us a "dinky" poem he had scribbled in his appointment book that morning. One day the talk might center on Heidegger, Wittgenstein, Barthes, and Derrida. The following morning, having completed the Evelyn Woods deconstructionist speedreading course, you'd come in to find everyone discussing their root canals. Several of the faculty shared the same dentist. With gothic shivers, they dwelled upon his cool sleight of hand and the beautiful daughters who assisted him in his sinister labors. At such times, all you could do was sit silently, cursing your boring teeth.

My slugabed habits made me an infrequent attendant at these gatherings. I found, too, that the intensity of the discussions (or the complacency with which opinions were given) could deplete my energy for the entire day. Archie, however, seemed to thrive on the morning sessions. He enjoyed a lively discussion, as long as no one became emotional. When I confessed to having had a terrible falling out with friends about poetry, he seemed astonished. "What could you find to fight about? Or is it too personal to say? I thought when young couples got together today they had fun. Why didn't you form daisy chains or something like that?"

The surety with which people stated their convictions surprised him. He said he found himself agreeing with several conflicting ideas during the day, and never knew what he thought until he mulled things over alone. He seemed to dislike arguments about ideals almost as much as he enjoyed arguments about ideas. I think on one level he wanted people to be happy but agreement bored him. So he disagreed, perversely, in order to amuse himself. It was difficult to hold the "pet panther" of his attention, as he admitted in his poem. And if he didn't like the way the conversation was going, he felt no compunction about changing the topic abruptly, even rudely.

There were frequent clashes of opinion during morning coffee, and the atmosphere often resembled a cross between *Family Feud* and an oral defense. I always seemed to get caught in the middle, by the shorthairs, *in flagrante delicto*. One morning before I'd sat down, a professor from the math department said, "Quick! Who was E. M. Forster?"

"He wrote *Passage to India*," I began uncertainly.

"Well, there you are! Before you came, E. was saying how shocked he was that none of the Ph.D. candidates in his seminar had heard of E. M. Forster." I sank into a chair. Was it Passage *to* India or Passage *from* India, after all? Should I have mentioned *Aspects of the Novel?*

I was not the only one who found these intellectual gab fests both wonderful and terrible. Several of the faithful admitted to walking away shaken in body and soul, ready for nothing more taxing than a few recuperative hours in bed. Perhaps the Greek grandeur that preened and flexed above our bagels and blue jeans sapped our vitality. For whatever reason, the parade of bleary-eyed scholars and poets issuing from Zeus at 10:00 a.m. after these "indescribable feuds" resembled a satirical dumb-show of Keats's sonnet on the Elgin Marbles. You could almost hear Phyllis Janowitz murmuring "My spirit is too weak; mortality / Weighs heavily on me like unwilling sleep. . . ."

Along with the forthright debates and vivid personal imagery there was a tactful evasiveness, a tendency to say one thing and mean another, or several others. Much of Archie's meaning was communicated through posture, glance, tone, and even, I thought, a kind of aura. Nothing was to be taken at face value; nothing was unambiguous. Everyone tried to anticipate everyone else's feelings and intentions. When this reading of signs ran amuck, the results could be absurd. For example, during one coffee break, Archie politely patted his lips with a napkin and Phyllis Janowitz followed suit. Archie then picked up his napkin and used it again, meticulously. Phyllis did the same. Archie mimicked her. Finally, she said, "Do I have crumbs on my mouth?"

"No. I thought that's what you were trying to tell me," he said.

Archie was on a restricted diet for reasons of health and showed great self-discipline in sticking to his regimen. He had a certain delicacy in regard to table manners. It wasn't that he wanted proper etiquette. Rather he seemed repelled by what Virginia Woolf called "guzzling." He also seemed to have a fear of contagion. Upon receiving a letter from India, he expressed some worries, only half kidding, I think, about what strange germs might lurk beneath the gummed flap. If he offered me a lick of ice cream, I declined, believing that he spoke from courtesy, despite his fastidiousness. Once, in kissing him goodbye after a dinner party, I awkwardly left lipstick on his collar. Hastily grabbing a dishrag, I tried to repair the damage. Only his chivalrous offer to wear it proudly, as a mark of honor, prevented me from drenching his entire shirt in my zeal.

Once or twice, my husband and I stopped by Archie's office with bagels for breakfast, but his observant gaze made me too self-conscious to eat. Though he knew we were late risers he'd say something like, "Did you see that sunrise this morning? My, it was beautiful." As his readers can guess, Archie truly loved weather and the diurnal cycle. He was the only person I've met who considered weather a topic of real interest, rather than a conversational filler. Maybe his fascination with it had something in common with his fondness for serendipity and expressionism. Climate, after all, is clearly beyond our control. Whether it storms or shines depends upon the convergence of chancy fronts. And sunrise, though dependable, is never repetitious in color or form. At first, I couldn't understand how he saw so much in a sunny day, a passing cloud, a rising stream. It says something for his enthusiasm that by the time I left Cornell, I too had become a watcher of the skies.

During my second term, Archie taught the MFA poetry workshop. He never hid the fact that this was not his favorite line of work. A conscientious teacher, he worried about his students, and the MFAs seemed to require an inordinate amount of concern. I was touched by the way he attended all of our readings, whether they were held at night, off-campus, or in a blizzard. (He wasn't quite as attentive to visiting poets. For them, he sat by the door, ready to make his escape should something unbearable be said.) The workshop was a dangerous place for anyone with hypertension. Archie liked to arrive early, as if to stake out his territory. We slumped on the couches and chairs of the mustard-colored graduate lounge, eyeing one another doubt-fully. After a poem was read, there was a weighty silence as we pondered. Nobody wanted to sound foolish, and Archie hesi-tated to criticize before giving the poem every benefit of the doubt. He had a lovely humility in regard to his students' work. I got into the habit of crossing Triphammer Bridge to the Pan-cake House for a glass of wine before class. Then I'd merrily begin speaking if no one else seemed inclined to. To me, a long silence following a poem was a kind of commentary in itself. Archie, however, never seemed to mind whether or not we had a lively discussion. He had a gentle way of conducting the group, and very seldom said anything harsh. His style was discursive, anecdotal. He sometimes told bawdy jokes, perhaps in the hope of dispelling our moroseness. One of his stories ended with the phrase "she made love like a monkey on a grapevine." He was delighted by this figure. (My poems on sex elicited a different reaction. "I don't get it," he wrote on one of them.) Occasion-ally, he would give a difficult, abstract, theoretical analysis. When his exegesis reached its unforeseeable conclusion, he'd select one of our stunned faces for confirmation. "Don't you think so, David?" "Doesn't it seem that way to you, Alice?" he'd appeal.

Although Archie's comments were usually mild, he could tell people some difficult truths about their work—things everyone else might think but hesitate to say. Once when he did this the student began to cry. Surprisingly, Archie held his ground and finished making his point, despite the tears. And if he thought a poem hadn't received the most generous reading, he took pains to say so. Sometimes after my work was discussed, I'd find notes in my box. "How perverse and heavy our response to your poem must have seemed! It takes a while to get to the right tone—then things feel clearer, more playful and serious." Archie talked quite a bit about the tone and diction of my poems, which seemed a kind of elegant swearing to him, "howls restrained by decorum." He favored a highly stressed line, and always called students' attention to "the little words," as if prepositions and articles were sizing to be shrunk out. I listened hard to everything he said and was rewarded with odd wisdoms that stick. One student wrote poems that showed a considerable debt to John Ashbery. Archie's attitude was it's been done. "There are many orders, but only one disorder," he said. I took this to mean that expressions of order contain the possibility of infinite difference, while expressions of disorder tend toward homogeneity. It also implied that Ashbery had wrapped up disorder once and for all. Years later, however, in a letter on the same topic he wrote, "The veracity with which you pursue your own delights is the only truth you'll ever need. You can't imitate anyone really and the extent to which you can't is enough originality."

Archie's birthday fell on a workshop day that year. We gave him flowers ("What are you trying to do to me anyway?") and he brought in a coconut cake his wife Phyllis had made especially for the class. Archie frequently mentioned his family. We heard about John's triumphs at sports and Phyllis's financial acuity. She played the stock market, and stories of her triumphs made me want to ask for tips. Her culinary skills were also justly praised, as we were to learn at the end of our first year when Archie and Phyllis invited the MFA students to their home for a party. Anyone else would have asked each of us to bring a dish, but Phyllis and Archie insisted on providing the food and drink. There were cold salads, a roast, cheeses, cold cuts, breads, quiche, homemade desserts. The house was decorated in serene neutral colors, enlivened by Archie's jubilant, sophisticated ink paintings on the walls. Whether from intimidation or hunger, we MFAs were at our most reticent that day, putting a strain on our hosts. One of our group picked up a magazine, and I recalled my sisters hiding all reading material before their high school parties, to encourage mixing. Were we regressing? My own stabs at conversation sounded forced, affected.

As a group, the MFAs seemed both shy and judgmental. When I'd wondered at this to Archie, he said that the students, being mostly midwesterners, equated restraint with dignity. (My own experience of living in the Midwest has not borne this out.)

During another visit I had the chance to see more of Archie's painting. He took us up to the little room where he writes and opened a closet. It was full of paintings, unceremoniously stacked like so much laundry. There must have been hundreds of small- to medium-sized works on paper, a testimony to the fertility of his creative genius. Archie's style was nonobjective; the delicious, often surprising use of color and the inventive compositions are what I remember most. His typewriter, a rickety old-fashioned model, stood on a table by a window. It was hard to imagine him typing his long poems on such a sorry-looking thing. On these occasions, Phyllis Ammons was quiet and kind. She took the trouble to make special treats (such as chocolate-covered strawberries she and Archie had picked themselves) and to serve them on fine china.

Before leaving Ithaca, I decided to give my husband an impromptu birthday party. Since most of our possessions were packed away, it was to be a casual get-together, so casual that I didn't tell anyone about it until the day of the party. The Ammonses arrived, nonetheless. I opened the door to find Archie clutching a heart-shaped silver balloon. We lived on the upper story of a low-income housing project, and he remarked that the iron railing made him feel as if he were back in the Navy, on a ship. The food that night was as haphazard as the invitations. At one point Archie noticed my confusion and came into the kitchen to help. After dinner, we coaxed him into playing our piano. It had been in my family for almost thirty years, but since Hank and I moved so often we'd decided it had to be sold. Archie gave us a spirited version of a Scott Joplin rag. He played with verve and didn't worry about missing a note here or there. I was happy to think he was the last person to play the piano while we owned it. Though the party was lively, Archie seemed to be in a thoughtful mood. He told a story in which an artist tried to hang himself, was saved when the rope broke, and went on to do the best work of his career. "Doesn't that just make you want to go on living?" he appealed.

"It makes me want to go out and buy some rope," I said.

Everyone laughed, and Archie seemed surprised, but pleased. In spite of all the people who cared about him, he often complained of loneliness and alienation. He sometimes said he had no friends. I think a part of him wanted to be just folks, one of the gang, while another part needed to be alone and eccentric. When in a melancholy mood, he worried that his life was wasted, that he had contributed nothing of practical value. Around the time of this party he had had a notion to perform some simple service for the needy. He said he wanted to push a broom or dish out soup. One morning he went down to the Salvation Army to offer his services, but the door was locked. Apparently, he took this for a sign and never returned.

There was a strong nurturing side to Archie that showed in his love for babies, and in his sweetness toward people with weaknesses or in need of help. I think he liked people who weren't afraid to show some imperfections, and mistrusted anyone too polished or controlled. Personal elegance and over-articulateness were suspect. (I was guilty of these sins at times.) He also disliked what he perceived as slickness. Given this criterion, I couldn't think why he liked Ronald Reagan, but as Whitman said for all poets, "Do I contradict myself? / Very well then . . . I contradict myself; / I am large . . . I contain multitudes."

We left Ithaca soon after the birthday party, but Archie made us feel we'd be welcome back, if need be. "Well, imagine me not knowing what to say—" he wrote, "except that we're already waiting for you. A crazy daffodil has put up a green tip, the snow is almost gone (for now) and the geese will be going over soon. Hurry on yourselves." When I miss his presence, I turn to the poems as refuge. There his spirit is luxuriously and succinctly expressed. He taught me this much at least about sanctuary, that the "word's sound is the one place to dwell: that's it, just / the sound, and the imagination of the sound—a place."

In the Dumpsters of the Gods

David Burak

ARCHIE AMMONS, who died February 25, 2001, at the age of 75, was one of the key occupants of center stage in the cast of creative people at Cornell and in the larger Ithaca community. At the same time, he struggled to maintain space between himself and others, so that he could effectively pursue his poetry. On occasion, when too many people were encroaching on his time and energy, expecting him to read and comment on their work, he would slip into a distressed mode. Once, right after I completed a collection of poetry to satisfy the requirement for a master of fine arts degree, Ammons, always my advisor, said: "Be careful. Taking someone who loves poetry and having him teach it is like taking someone who loves chocolate and putting him to work in a chocolate factory. Pretty soon he can't even stand the smell of it."

However, Ammons did endure, and part of his staying power was derived, as with most of us, from having a good laugh every now and then. One such moment came when his 1993 book, *Garbage,* was in progress. Helen Vendler, then head of the American Studies Program at Harvard, had invited Ammons to be the keynote speaker at Harvard's Phi Beta Kappa ceremonies.

Ammons sent her a portion of the poetry that would be part of
Garbage, saying that was the only thing he could be moved to
present on such an occasion. One morning, while having coffee
with Phyllis Janowitz and me, Ammons mentioned the exchange
with Vendler, one of America's most respected literary critics.
"And what did she say?" asked Janowitz, also a highly regarded
poet. Archie pulled the letter out of his jacket pocket and read
Vendler's response. I'll quote from memory here, but I believe
it's accurate: "I can think of nothing more fitting and useful for
Harvard's Phi Beta Kappa graduates to hear than the portion of
Garbage which you sent me."

Eventually, that oddly named collection of poetic reflections
garnered Ammons his second National Book Award. Here is a
brief excerpt, which provides an example of the poet's ability to
take dislocating experiences and imbue them with strange beauty:

> sometimes old people snap back into life for a
> streak and start making plans, ridiculous, you know,
>
> when they will suddenly think of death again
> and they will see their coffins plunge upward
>
> like whales out of the refused depths of their
> minds and the change will feel so shockingly
>
> different—from the warm movement of a possibility
> to a cold acknowledgment—they will seem not
>
> to understand for a minute: at other times
> with the expiration of plans and friends and
>
> dreams and with the assaults on all sides of
> relapses and pains, they will feel a
>
> smallish ambition to creep into their boxes
> at last and lid the light out and be gone,

nevermore, nevermore to see again, let alone
see trouble come on anyone again: oh, yes, there

are these moods and transitions, these bolt
recollections and these foolish temptations and

stratagems to distract them from the
course: this is why they and we must keep our

minds on the god-solid, not on the vain silks
and sweets of human dissipation, no, sirree:

(*Garbage* 53)

Though Ammons was concerned with spiritual matters, he wasn't an adherent of any particular religious orthodoxy. For example, he follows the above statement (from *Garbage*) by saying "unless of course god is immanent in which case / he may be to some slight extent part of the / sweets, god being in that case nothing more than or / as much as energy at large. . . ."

In a *New Yorker* article that appeared in mid-February 1988, Vendler predicted that Ammons's "definitive 'Collected Poems,' when it appears, will be one of the influential American books of this century, notable for its forgoing of dogmatism and for its tender, shrewd charting of a way to live responsibly." Recently, Dale Corson, Cornell's president emeritus, concurred: "Archie had a facility with words which was unsurpassed, and he had deeper insight into the human condition than most poets do."

Corson, a neighbor and friend of Ammons, recalled a poem entitled "Epiphany," in which a bee flies into a windowpane and then, in a manner of speaking, shrugs its shoulders and moves on as if nothing happened. "It says two things about the human condition—our need to keep on and our unwillingness to admit our failures," Corson reflected. In a related vein, Gould Colman, Cornell's archivist emeritus, recalled Ammons's ability to see the bright side of things and how it was often

intertwined with a wry sense of humor. "One day, we were having coffee, and Archie mentioned how the profession of being a
poet was looking up. 'More people seem to be able to make a
living being a poet without having to take on any other job,' he
said. 'How many would that be?' I asked. 'Oh, about three,'
he said."

Ammons loved America and the opportunities it offered. He
grew up on a small farm outside of Whiteville, North Carolina,
during the Depression. The only book in the house was the
Bible, which was used more as a place to keep birth certificates
and other documents than for reading. In a remembrance that is
moving and funny, Ammons writes, in *The Snow Poems,* of his
attachment to his pet pig, Sparkle, and even throws in the classic
pig call (sooiee, sooiee) for good measure. But Archie's tradi-
tionalist tendencies were accompanied by a willingness to question authority and, if he deemed it necessary, to challenge it. His
iconoclastic perspectives were reminiscent of Mark Twain, echoing the latter's observation that "loyalty to petrified opinion
never yet broke a chain or freed a human soul."

Ammons's approach to inquiry, in his poetic discourses, was
usually through a rigorous form of self-examination, sometimes
combined with an insightful analysis of our collective soul. This
mode is evident in his borrowing from *The Book of Tao,* in *A
Coast of Trees.* In the title poem, he concludes by saying,

> then, with nothing, we turn
> to the cleared particular, not more
> nor less than itself, and we realize
> that whatever it is it is in the Way and
> the Way in it, as in us, emptied full.
>
> (*A Coast of Trees* 1)

Despite the fact that his approach to life seemed to be Emersonian and shamanic, Archie was not too elevated for a good
scrap every now and then. Once, when Allen Ginsberg was visit-

ing Cornell to give a reading of his work, the icon of beat generation poetry and '60s rebellion accepted an invitation from
Archie to sit in on one of his creative-writing classes. Perhaps
because I'd known Ginsberg for about a decade, Ammons asked
me if I'd like to sit in, also. Naturally, I said yes. During the seminar, a disagreement arose about something related to the interplay of politics and poetry. It's an oversimplification to say
Ginsberg favored the use of poetry to address the problems of
the human condition, while Ammons contended that this generally led to a dilution of aesthetic strength and style that was
prone to broad generalization and a lack of depth. Nonetheless,
that description provides a sense of the parameters of the discourse. Most striking was the fact that neither of them would
budge from his position, and the scene made me think of two
champion Sumo wrestlers embracing each other with bear hugs
as each tried to push the other out of the ring. "Can we agree to
disagree?" I asked meekly. They both consented, though not
without a few more exchanges.

That approach to differences in perspectives characterized
Archie's relationship with a number of people. Ken McClane,
Cornell's W. E. B. Du Bois Professor of Literature, noted that
despite disagreements he had with Ammons, "he was a wonderment—no one fought more vigorously for the idea of the
poet. And in that calling, we were all sacred." Another close
colleague, poet Phyllis Janowitz, described Ammons as a
"singer [who] is a sorcerer who will not reveal the secret of his
clear exuberant tunes." Cornell professor Roald Hoffmann, a
1981 Nobel Prize winner in chemistry, described Archie as "a
true natural philosopher, perhaps the smartest man I have ever
known." During his association with Ammons, Janowitz, and
several others in a semi-regular poetry group, Hoffmann has
produced three books of critically praised poetry. I was a member of that group in its early years and was privileged to participate in its sessions on the four or five occasions each year
when I visited Ithaca. "David has the longest commute of any

of us," Archie once said. I remembered feeling honored to still be considered part of the group, despite the 2,500 miles that separated us.

Now Archie has the longest distance to traverse; depending on your belief system, there is no doubt, or no likelihood, that he will come back. Whenever I go back, I'm pretty sure that I'll see his spirit wandering the corridors of Goldwin Smith Hall. Maybe he'll ask, "Did you bring a poem for us?" I hope I don't disappoint him.

A Love Note:
A. R. Ammons as Teacher

Kenneth McClane

and because whatever is
moves in weeds
　　　and stars and spider webs
and known
　　　　　is loved:
　　　in that love,
　　　each of us knowing it,
　　　I love you,
　　　　　("Identity," *Collected Poems* 115)

FIRST MET A. R. AMMONS at the behest of a woman I was
dating when I was a freshman at Cornell in 1969. As a black
student from Harlem who missed the City, I had begun to
write what I then considered to be poems. To be brutally honest,
I didn't know anything about poetry: to me good intentions and
a fistful of pain were art; my suffering was enough. That my cre-
ations were largely eruptions of my own distress was something
I had yet to learn, and most powerfully. Add to that dreary mix
the Vietnam War, the deaths of Dr. Martin Luther King and
Malcolm X, my lust-ridden body and my proverbial loneliness,
and you now have my mental state. My girlfriend, who understood much more about art and its rigors than I, wanted me to

meet "the famous American poet" who taught at the University. I didn't know who A. R. Ammons was, and the fact that he was a great American writer meant little to me. I simply wanted to be corroborated.

In those days, Mr. Ammons's office was located on the second floor of Lincoln Hall and he was directing the Center for the Creative and the Performing Arts, the last time I believe he ever undertook administration. Later on, Ammons would move to the second floor of Goldwin Smith Hall, where E. B. White, Vladimir Nabokov, and Carl Becker had maintained offices, but that day he was still in Lincoln, sitting behind his unusually large desk, topped with an abundance of scraggly plants and a large ficus angling towards the light, like some paean to survival. Archie tended to love plants that were pot-bound and floundering: he coveted—I think in most things—those things most bedraggled and tossed out.

I can vividly recall handing Mr. Ammons a sheaf of poems, which he gracefully accepted, and his offer to read my poems in a week's time. As a teacher of creative writing, I now understand what a great imposition such requests are; and I know that Ammons—then as always—was besieged with the irrepressible output of a legion of young who felt that they had something essential to say. That day, Ammons ended our meeting by saying in a very slow southern drawl, "I'll see you next week."

I did not return. In truth, I felt there was nothing he, a white man, from North Carolina, could tell me. At the time I didn't know anything about Southerners, and I painted them all with a broad stroke, something of which I am not very proud. To me, Archie was a symbol of that litany of racial violence—beginning in 1619 and moving to Selma—a legacy that had hurt me, in many profound and ill-understood ways. I didn't know much— I was a head full of the transgressive and the transgressed—and I was angry. That Archie would become my greatest champion was something I had yet to learn; that we would spend hours talking, become friends and later colleagues, forging an alliance that was as strong as it was sometimes difficult, this, too, was all in the future.

Little did I know then that Archie and I were beginning that difficult dance which taints all relationships between writers: we had work to do, we had to be self-invested, and the thing which made us care for one another, the art, was as ravenous as a Minotaur.

Later, at times, we would have arguments about what a poem could achieve. Here I would argue for writing needing to be political—what else could I believe?—and he, of course, would challenge the narrowness of my beliefs. In truth, I knew he was right; in truth, I suspect, Archie knew I could argue little else. Sadly, at these moments, we were all too human and all too different: our connection made difficult, I submit, because it was a connection.

But in 1970, as luck would have it, I would sign up for Creative Writing, and lo and behold, the teacher was A. R. Ammons. Mr. Ammons never mentioned our previous meeting; he might not have remembered it, although I doubt if that was the case. He, most probably, had the forbearance to excuse my previous lapse, while I, for my part, remained silent. Let me simply state that the class was a wonderful one, and I am glad to this day that fate brought me beyond my own prejudice.

Ammons ran the seminar in a gentle, non-hierarchical way. He did not assign exercises or demand that students experiment, say, with the villanelle or the sonnet form. What Ammons desired was for students to write as their imaginations dictated. It was the writing (and the need to write) that would offer the impetus for refining and divining craft: it was the writing that would suggest one's own individuality. Here, of course, Archie was listening to his own experience. He had not been taught to write in a writing program; he, in truth, had little respect for them. His poems came from his need to convey his wonderment, to find meaning "in the moon-tossed and the vanquished," to invoke those things "left out."

Ammons's method was uniquely suited to me and to many others. What he affirmed was that for him, you were sacred, in all your dilapidation. And for the multitude of us who were the intellectually unwashed, this was the greatest confirmation. Ammons permitted us to speak from a position of strength; we were not simply the raging, the uncouth, the crazed; we were not, that is, what our parents feared. No, we had something precious to relate if only we could honor it. And our own entanglements, our awkwardness, our incoherence, could create heady music.

Ammons's classes were wonderful for another reason. Although we didn't spend a great deal of time talking about famous poets—we rarely read other poets, we never read Archie's poems—we did sense that poetry was the highest calling. Much of this came from the workshop setting itself—we were convened as a congress of wisdoms, impertinences, and enthusiasms; much of this came, no doubt, from the undeniable brilliance of Ammons himself. When he spoke about poems, one felt as if one were in the presence of this century's Coleridge or Dr. Johnson. And indeed one was.

Crucially, Ammons's sense of the world was so omnipresent that when one listened to Archie, one was, in truth, walking in one of his poems. Quintessentially, when Archie was serious (and not playing around or doing his "I'm just a country boy"/hick routine), one could simply put line breaks in his elegant oratory and it would be an Ammons poem. Disconcertingly, for those of us who wanted to be practitioners, it was as if his poems came from some marvelous, bottomless fount. Archie, seemingly, had only to open his mouth and revelation flowed. This, of course, was not always true. But Archie did appear like a poetic medium, a channeler of the consequential. Writing may have been difficult for him, I know at times it was, but still when it came—and it always came—it spewed torrential and provident. To my knowledge, I can think of only one other contemporary poet so closely attuned, in speech and life, to her verse,

Gwendolyn Brooks, who, incidentally, we lost just a few months before Ammons.

Yet the greatest aspect of Archie as mentor was his absolute belief in human individuality and the poem as the ultimate embodiment of truth. As he instructed me in an unpublished poem, "Improvisations for the Main Man Ken McClane":

> Since poetry declares nothing ever
> even in its fantasies and lies
> but the truth
> I do not
> guide the declarations shallow,
> canalized, into only what
> I would hear or have heard:
> If the truth is
> as it is
> unavoidable
> it need not be pursued
> and cannot be fled:
> But there, profound,
> dissolved,
> it doesn't prick your feet with
> thorns
> but sustains you merely into your
> own endeavor:
> truth that deep is perhaps
> no longer truth.

For many of us who have learned from him, it was Archie's irrepressible restlessness that so made us love him. Archie would not lie, he understood the demolitions in the depths, the danger of a wisdom too highly prized, and he asked that we be willing to risk presence, that we not heed the merely easy, the fatuous, or the pretty. In class, his comments on poems tended to be more general than local. Although he was interested in a word or line—his rich, "that's nice" often declaring his joy—Archie tended to engage in large claims and "constellations" of meaning. His method seemed more an affirmation of our small announcements than the nuts and bolts of the poem as thing. Whenever someone would claim that a poem should do this— say, no poem should be a political tract, or no one should write a "love poem"—Archie, deftly, would find a million ways to prove that poet's criticism ill-considered. There are no boundaries on love or poetry, he would say. As he was wont to remind us, "critics are untanglers, poets tangle": our work as poets "is to work wonders."

Once a colleague in the English Department came up to him and asked him in a group of poets if he had read a new book on Wallace Stevens. Archie looked at this self-satisfied critic who, I guess, thought he was making good conversation, and said, with a twinkle in his eye, but not without a touch of anger, "We do not get paid to read books. We get paid to write them. You read us." Those of us who were writers welcomed that tongue-lashing. In the academy, all too often, we are the whipping boys of the scholars who somehow forget that they write about us— that a dead writer was once living. Archie would not brook this. He knew how fragile we all were; he knew, and intimately, how much one could suffer.

It was wonderful to be taught by an elder who saw us as knowledgeable, sacred, in-process, and gifted. I remember how he would prize something I said or wrote because it was out of the academy, street-wise, extra-ordinary, or simply true. That we at times didn't appreciate all that he committed to us is understandable; that he remained a tireless defender of our rights to our authority shall remain with me as the greatest instruction.

The Whistle

Ingrid Arnesen

IT'S THE ONE MEN MAKE to women walking: the first note rises briefly, the second lengthens as the pitch falls like a smooth slope. It's the one you want to miss but can't. That day in the mid-eighties, it was Archie's wink to me, from the steps of Day Hall, the fortress, near Sage Chapel. I may have been there to check a paystub, or on my way to teach, but it made me laugh. "You got a whistle from the McArthur Fellow!" a friend said later. This whistle was quintessential Archie, genius visionary; far from his celebrity, he was free to whistle, to draw a figure in the air:

> life, life is like a poem: the moment it
> begins, it begins to end: the tension this
>
> establishes makes every move and moment, every
> gap and stumble, every glide and rise significant:
>
> for if life or poem went dribbling endlessly
> on, what identifiable arc or measure could it

clarify: within limits the made thing accepts
its revelation and dissolution, its coming and

going, beginning and ending, being and nonbeing:
the poem moves through the smooth or astonished

beginning, the taking on of engagement and
complication, the gathering up of direction and

possibility, and the falling out and fading
away: this is all so reasonable, we sometimes

wonder why grief tells us so we wanted to cling
to being, the good things, oh, the good things,

but in real life as in real poems clarifying
form,

(Garbage 66)

    I first knew Archie as my teacher in a poetry workshop in 1973. I remember that he came to class somewhat beaming and embarrassed one day; he had won a prize (the National Book Award for his *Collected Poems*). I can see the gold seal on the sepia-tinted cover. Our class met in the A. D. White House; we sat around a large wooden table on nineteenth-century chairs, and Archie walked around lively in the room. Once he asked me the difference between a spondee and an anapest and luckily I happened to know. I remember he told us that "poets have to be ruthless" with their writing. Archie was Zen in his teaching; he never touched a line, he refrained from prescription, from sending a student's poem in another direction, but tried to sense the direction it was going in, urging you to follow it. He never believed poetry could be taught, but he laid out the universals as clearly as a blueprint. In that room I was in awe; I knew I was in the presence of the great.

So it was difficult to live up to his attention. I was incredulous at his approachability, his willingness to meet with me through my undergraduate years and after my graduation. He stood in line at my commencement, a clear, hot day in May, and my friend whispered he was there because of me. I didn't believe that then, and do not know to this day if it is true, but now I like to think it is. He and Phyllis Ammons even acted as my matchmaker once, introducing me to an Italian millionaire count, which, of course, turned out to be a fiasco.

Through the last decades of the century Archie was my mentor and friend. The confluence of these roles is intricate and was not easy; he had a profound influence on my life, perhaps greater than he knew. Today, when I tell my student TAs they can make a lifelong impression on their students, I am thinking of Archie. One of my Chinese students quoted his own professor in China, who said "Teaching is the most important activity" because only your students can carry out your research when you are gone. The week Archie died, when I was in St. Louis at the center of the continent, right along the Mississippi, on a Hollywood star marked for T. S. Eliot, alongside one for Red Skelton and Shelley Winters, I stood in tears and my Missouri friend asked, so what did your Chinese student say?

Knowing Archie changed my life. Not only am I still trying to write poetry, not only did I take an MFA at Davis, California, where I met Ruth Stone, not only did I go to Sweden to translate contemporary women's poetry on a Fulbright, not only this plot; Archie's presence is inextricable from place, from this landscape, from Ithaca. It was one of the forces drawing me back in 1982; it is part of what makes this place sacred, magical, or secularly spectacular. I am one of many. Shinji Watanabe came all the way from Tokyo twice; the second time he confided that he was ostensibly on a faculty leave for literary research, but that he really came to "talk to Archie." With Shinji back, we resumed our poetry meetings at Zeus, or in Archie's office, when the voices were too loud. Many times I came poemless. Once when

I was asked, I said all I could write was garbage, and Archie looked at me strangely, for quite a while. I could not know then that he was writing the real *Garbage*.

Later I had started writing "building" poems, the first after reading *Garbage,* but I didn't have a limit or the double line, so there was no time for breath. Archie was vehement about easy abstraction, in his insistence on the poem having motion. It's the verb not the object, nor the cumbersome adjective; as my dance instructor says, it's not the destination but the journey that counts when we plié. I was struggling with lists, naming, blockages that kept me from the motion of the poem then, as well as the confinements of syntax. When language turned against my drift, I'd lash back with a made-up word, or an ungrammaticality, and try to get away with it. Archie responded empathetically, but with surety that he didn't think I could.

It is impossible to believe that Archie isn't coming back, that there will never be his eloquence at the Temple of Zeus, the matching of wits I listened to, our laughter, and talk of the universe, dentistry, and back pain, our sharing of photographs and grapefruit, or seeing his latest publication. Today when I look at the acrid willow sweep branches through March winter, or yesterday's sunset lacing the neighbor's icicles in series, I know Archie would take note. Now the landscape of foothills and glacial beds is bereft, Archie's presence gone to ash. What we can carry is his awe, his wonder: the universe is flat, yet multidimensional; the couple next to our table is love-blind; and what has led up to this particular squirrel leaping on snow, just now—

Balance and Contradiction:
Remembering Archie

Cynthia Bond

'M NOT SURE IF I EVER told Archie that my first meeting
with him was facilitated by the plumbing at Goldwin Smith
Hall. Like all memories, that one's not entirely accurate: I
undoubtedly first met Archie at some Cornell English Department function when I was admitted as an MFA student in 1984.
But when I finally approached Archie to ask him to be my thesis
advisor, I was so terrified by his prominence, by his national reputation (not knowing his local one), that I would repeatedly
walk past his office door and cower in the ladies' room three or
four doors down trying to get up the courage to ask him to be
on my committee. I'm certain on many of those trips I saw him
seated at his low Steelcase desk pressed against the wall thumb-
ing through some book as I slipped by unnoticed, only to try
again when my nerves allowed. Of course I eventually did make
it to his office, of course he agreed to be my advisor and, over
the next 17 years, he became much more to me.

I found out later that the fear was mutual. In the summer of
1985, Archie asked me to be his teaching assistant for a verse-
writing seminar he was teaching. I was his second choice. I
found out why one day when he and I were walking back to

Goldwin Smith from lunch at the Green Dragon, discussing our students. As an explanation for the students' initial shyness, I offered that perhaps Archie intimidated them. Archie countered that he was sure they were afraid of me. While it is true that in those days I had honed the outer face of my shyness and insecurity into a fierce mask of stark, crew-cut angularity, I was surprised by his remark, probably hurt by it. "Why would they be afraid of me?" I asked. "Because I'm afraid of you," Archie answered, characteristically frank, "afraid that you won't like me." It was the first real meeting between us. For he had precisely articulated my fear about him: that my prickly, confused, mannishly-affected self would alienate this old-school gentleman, son of the South like my father and my father's generation. But I didn't really know him then.

I think Archie's greatest gift as a poetry teacher was his forbearance. Archie was not looking for clones nor did he try to put his mark on any student poet. If you sounded like Ammons (or tried to), you chose it or it chose you. In poetry writing, Archie believed in something like William Blake's dictum: if the fool would persist in his folly he would become wise. He used to encourage writers to do the outrageous more outrageously. If there's something that people find sticks out in your work, do it more: maybe that's where the source is. Of course, it was mightily encouraging as a young poet to have my work read and taken seriously by him. But he let me alone in it to write more fully into myself; his praise was weighty but his touch was light.

While Archie was my poetry teacher, my thesis advisor and my teaching mentor, what I learned most directly from him was extra-literary. The poetry seeped in almost as a by-product of our interactions. While certainly he read and critiqued my work and showed his own on a fairly regular basis over the years, it was the daily talks about daily things that sunk in deepest. Archie taught me about anxiety, not the abstract condition of the thinking mind, but the everyday how to live with it. Archie counseled me on my personal relationships (me: "Will I ever meet someone who's nice to me?" he: "You might, but you might not like him very much"). He shared his insights on living far from one's region and family. Or the appeal of Larry King's interviewing style. Or country music lyrics. Archie was a man of extraordinary contradictions: accessible but guarded, generous and cranky, provocative and restrained, impossibly abnegating and proud. It was watching him maintain those contradictions (and as with all of us, sometimes only partly succeeding) that was fascinating and instructive.

Archie was fond of saying that the good thing about poetry is that it is completely, beautifully useless. To be truly useless in this world, he meant, is a rare and special thing. That statement is a classic example of his particular brand of inversion, displaying while simultaneously covering his uncertainty about his project. What is entirely certain is that his readers would not agree that Archie's poetry is useless. Readers find song, solace, great humor and high reflection in his work. Archie's audience is far-reaching and deep loving. It is unfortunate that Archie didn't always believe that. But here we gather together to say again, this time across the divide: we love you, Archie, we miss you, we will never ever let go of you.

Answering the Phone:
A Reminiscence of A. R. Ammons

John Brehm

As HOLDEN CAULFIELD famously said, sometimes when you finish a great book, you just want to call the author up and talk to him. He was thinking of novelists, and the same probably can't so often be said of poets. But certainly there are some poets you wish you could know off the page as well as on it. Something about the work suggests a presence that makes you curious about what the poet's daily life is like, how he thinks and talks and behaves when he stands up from the desk.

A. R. (Archie) Ammons was such a poet. In fact, I know of someone who got his number from the Ithaca directory assistance and, à la Holden Caulfield, called him up. He'd never met Archie but loved his work. Archie's wife, Phyllis, answered the phone and said that Archie was in the garden trimming roses. He heard her call him in. The screen door opening and closing. The sound of gloves being taken off. And then Archie picked up the phone and talked to a perfect stranger for over an hour.

I met Archie Ammons in the fall of 1979, as I entered Cornell's MFA program, and studied with him, formally and informally, for the next four years. But I really got to know him years later when, after I'd written him a letter complaining about my life in Portland, Oregon, he called up and quite out of the blue offered me a visiting writer position for the spring semester of 1996. That was a characteristically helpful gesture, and I think one of Archie's great secret pleasures—despite his poem that says, "being here to be here / with others is for others"—was his ability to make other people happy. I'm sure there are many who could attest to that.

Archie was an amazing poet and an amazing man, generous with his time, his knowledge, his friendship. What struck me most strongly about him was the way he combined a really odd and original brilliance—and he could absolutely dazzle you with an offhand remark—with a comic and unpretentious appreciation of himself and the height to which he'd risen.

He grew up on a farm in North Carolina during the Depression and in his gait, his way of talking, his way of taking the world, you never forgot that. I remember walking with him past the graduate library at Cornell and Archie saying, in his slow drawl, "They oughta just shut that thing down and sell hot dogs out of it."

He was a great reader, of course, would quote Chaucer to you or Dante or Wordsworth without warning. (And he could be acidic about major poets he didn't like. He'd read a passage from Stevens and point out all the weak verbs, "is, is, is, was, was, was, like a bunch of fuckin' bees buzzin' around in there.") But he always seemed connected to a world larger than academia. "The problem with academia," he once told me, "is that everyone is always explaining everything. Nothing is allowed to go uninterpreted. Nothing is allowed to remain mysterious. There's always this filmy gauze of words between you and the rest of the world." But he loved Cornell and he was, I'm sure, the most beloved teacher on that campus.

He probably wasn't the most beloved host to the poets who came to read at Cornell, however. Archie was famous for not revising much; he told me he'd written "Corsons Inlet," his most anthologized poem, in a single sitting. I remember a well-known

poet reading at Cornell and talking a lot about revision, even
saying at one point that he really only wrote so that he'd have an
excuse to revise. Afterwards, Archie suggested to him that "If
you get it right the first time, you don't have to revise." Then,
after a pause, he added: "But you have to burn at a pretty high
heat to do that."

Archie was generous and forgiving with students but with big
names it was a different story. Ashbery was the only living poet
I heard him praise with much warmth. "Ashbery's the one who's
got us all by the balls," was how he expressed it. Often during
readings he would sit at the back of the auditorium with his
head in his hands, staring at the floor, as if in physical pain.
After Robert Bly gave one of his spectacular performances,
replete with lute-playing, masks, and singing, Archie commented, "That man should have been a preacher."

Archie was a strange mixture of humility and overarching
ambition, if I may be forgiven that Ammonsian word play. During one of the rare readings he gave over the last ten years, he
read an older piece and asked the audience how many of them
owned a copy of his *Collected Poems*. A few hands went up.
"Well," he said, "it's been out of print since God created the
earth—approximately." (This has happily changed, as Norton
recently reissued the *Collected*.) "I wish to God you all had a
copy."

He had a voracious appetite for readers, for praise, for attention, that was never really satisfied, even after all the awards and
honors. He could fall in to sulking over how "neglected" he
was, how nobody ever talked about him, how no one cared
about his work. This, after two National Book Awards, a
MacArthur, a Bollingen, a Frost Medal, and other prizes too
numerous to enumerate.

But he never lost for long his oblique and humorous way of
approaching just about everything. He was a mischievous presence in Cornell's English Department and could take the air out
of a faculty meeting with a single sentence. In the early eighties

Cornell was considering whether to offer a PhD in creative writing. Arguments and counter-arguments were tossed back and forth and no one could build a consensus either way. Archie, who had been silent the entire meeting, finally spoke up: "Doctor of Fine Arts, that's kind of a *wussy* degree, isn't it?" And that was the end of that. No further discussion was necessary.

He hated all forms of pretentiousness and posturing, which is probably one of the reasons he gave so few readings (not that his were pretentious) and hated attending them, especially the ones where the poet is given a windy and hyperbolic introduction, where whole poems are quoted and commented on and every one of the poet's achievements is trotted out to impress the audience into submission.

When I was a visiting writer at Cornell in 1996, I gave a reading and Archie introduced me. I didn't know quite what to expect, though I should have seen what was coming based on the questions he'd asked me the week before. "John Brehm was born in 1955," Archie began, "and a year later he was a one-year-old baby." He then went on to talk about what grade-school I attended, my high-school years in Lincoln, Nebraska, where I was "a football player and a lover of Keats," and so on, ending with, "And we're lucky to have him while he's still pretty." It was a hilarious parody of the standard introduction and I've never faced an audience more warmed-up or receptive than that one.

Archie wasn't perhaps the greatest classroom teacher, or the most meticulous close reader. He was better when you dropped into his office and he asked you to read a poem and he'd say, "I'm glad to see you developing some spit in your poems," or something of that sort. Or when he'd give a piece of general advice: "If someone criticizes you for something in your poems, just do it even more." But his presence was a force I'll never forget. He seemed to live inside of poetry rather than to be talking about it. And his casual observations about poetry and poets have become permanent fixtures in the way I think about writing. We were talking about Emily Dickinson once and he said how much he admired her, what a powerful poet she was: "She's just like a Mack truck comin' down the road." When I said I imagined her as a quiet, even fragile woman, he said, "In her life maybe, but in her poems she just runs right over you." And his description of Wordsworth's *Prelude,* a poem he returned to often: "It's the umbrella we're all still living under."

In "Rapids," a visionary short poem from *A Coast of Trees,* Archie makes a characteristically daring statement:

> though I
> have not been here long, I can
> look up at the sky at night and tell
> how things are likely to go for
> the next hundred million years:
> the universe will probably not find
> a way to vanish nor I
> in all that time reappear.
>
> (*A Coast of Trees* 26)

He was both right and wrong in that final assertion. But I trust he knew, on some level, how often and how luminously he would reappear in the poems he left behind.

Ammons Outside the Dragon

Stephen Gutierrez

IN MEMORY
A. R. AMMONS
1926–2001

ARCHIE AMMONS counseled me outside the Green Dragon Café on my last day at Cornell. Done with the defense of my MFA thesis in Creative Writing, I was willing to listen, considering myself a hot young writer again after a stretch of death. I was hopeful and youthful.

The day was balmy and bright. The quad was captivating. A feeling of solemnity and peace pervaded the stillness before the mad rush of fall and the autumnal onslaught of students and lives. We gazed at the trees.

He gave me the go. He gave me the green light. That's what a writer needs and that's what Archie Ammons gave to me.

He didn't give it without a price. He told me things. "Are you really going to live with that line," he asked, "for the rest of your life?"

I stared down at the line. I read it again.

I read it to myself and then aloud: "He looked at his watch before entering the building."

"Naw," I said, "I guess not."

It was a bad line, a serviceable sentence conveying only information in a medium that demanded more. Life. The character in my story didn't look at his watch with intensity. The moment wasn't lived or recreated, only told. Only blathered.

"Good, 'cause it's a cheap line. You can't write like that. You can't say that anymore. Nobody wants to read a line like that. I don't." He leaned back in his chair and guffawed, a veritable guffaw, one of the few I've witnessed in my life, and I have it on record.

Ammons's guffaw.

He leaned back and guffawed with Southern pleasure at the folly of the world, with the aw-shucks sincerity of a learned man who was truly taken aback by that sentence.

"He looked at his watch before entering the building."

"Naw, I think I'm going to keep it," I said, "I like it."

Then he said: "You do what you want, but it's a bad line."

And I agreed with him. I knew he was right. I hadn't fooled him and he hadn't lied to me. He had told me the truth.

The truth. The truth was absent in those days. Only a few people could tell it, in different ways. Writer/profs Jim McConkey and Lamar Herrin. Writer-in-residence William Kennedy. Students didn't know it. They were too busy learning. That's why they were here. They were here to learn the truth and then go building on it. They would erect grander and grander truths. In the end, we would have one big edifice of truth, kind of like a church built on the principles of reason and nature, intertwined as one.

Archie Ammons's poetry is difficult—a brainy network of assertions that is hard to follow if you're looking for a clear easy read. But it's always beautiful and lithesome and lyrical. It always feels important and is, because the weight of the mind behind it informs every line.

He doesn't write: "He looked at his watch before entering the building."

He enters the building three or four ways without a watch and then leaves you to wonder whether there was a building at all to enter and who was doing the entering anyway, being or not-being. He gets you all confused and tangled in his thoughtful possibilities until you just let go and enjoy the swerves of his meanderings, intelligent and controlled, purposeful and moral.

He doesn't say bad things about human beings. He has a belief in our capabilities, in a line here, a line there, soft and gentle as a baby's butt in the woods. He thinks we can get along better if we tried and to hurt and harm is mean-spirited and against the grain of it all. He upholds human beings even though we're so small in the middle of nature.

But then again, I could be plain wrong about him, because he was such an ornery son of a bitch. He was funny and self-mocking in his orneriness, too, so fair game himself.

He was a real card. He said: "Yeah, I remember the transparent eyeball," when I made reference to Emerson's famous line about wanting to be an eyeball, a transparent eyeball. "I become a transparent eyeball." And we both laughed endlessly.

I'm still chuckling about that now. Every time I remember the incident, I break into laughter, and everything is lightened. Taking the bus up to Cornell, everything was heavy, dark, veiled in awful shadows. I was miserable as a student there, miserably unhappy, horribly depressed and stuck. I couldn't write anything anymore. I had reached the famous neighborhood—writer's block.

I knew what it was to not write, to have no confidence in myself, to believe my talent, such as it was, was washed up before it even started. To be through.

"I am through, I am done, I am dead!" I told myself and believed it. Then I dreamed the worst. I was dead. I was at my own funeral.

My girlfriend woke me up, concerned: "Steve, you were moaning so awfully, what's wrong?"

"I was at my own funeral, Jackie, it was awful." Then I got out of bed and made my way to my study. I closed the door behind me. I cried, on my knees, asking God or whoever was in charge of the Big Writing Program in the Sky why I was such an abysmal failure. Why I couldn't do it anymore.

"God," I said, "I can't do it anymore. I'm fucked, I'm up shit creek." It was all over for me as a writer, and as a writer I had lived and breathed.

"Give me a break," I said. "Get me out of here and I'll get back to my pen."

God cut me a deal. He said: "You, Stephen Gutierrez, are meant to suffer. You are meant to wallow in the pain you feel, because it is real, and it is the first time you have felt really, really bad about yourself consciously. It is the first time you have admitted the depths of your insecurity and fragility. You have become human now. We love you."

"We?"

"Look around you, Stephen, and see."

The gods of the Aztecs favored me. They smiled down on me, standing next to Jehovah. They towered over him.

But they were all bosom buddies. "Boys," I said, too late. The room turned black. On my knees, I saw nothingness, and in that nothingness was the mandate to create.

That was the hardest part, writing out of the complete void. Nothing meant anything in itself. At Cornell, I had been taught to devalue myself, implicitly. The liberal bias had killed me. Too many ethnic expectations messed me up. Nobody was after me. I had just succumbed to America. The outsider will find it hard, anywhere. I had begun questioning myself and the very basis of my writing as somehow inadequate to the liberal vision I was supposed to espouse.

This was deep in my brain. A bias, a misunderstanding of the Mexican-American experience had rocked me out of my own deep-rooted and instinctual acceptance of so many assumptions that underlay my own writing.

"I can't write anymore," I said, "I don't know how!"

There was just the challenge of the blank page, without the cultural approval of an unseen editor representing the people, the country, your people, your country. You had to fashion it yourself, this editor, this consciousness. It didn't exist. There was nothing out there remotely like what you wanted to do, remotely like your sensibility. There was no template to refer to.

The void was absolute.

"Oh, come now, Stephen, don't be so precious, so . . ."

"Writerly?"

"Yes."

"Now we're getting somewhere." Dimly, my consciousness awakened. I understood myself better. I gleaned what I was up against.

"What were you up against?"

There was the fearsome task of writing out of nonwhite middle-class experience if you're trying to write honestly and truly and nonstereotypically. If you're trying to write as it's not been written before, it's hard. It's hard for anybody, but it's harder when you know half the country won't give a shit because your name is not Todd or Jeff or Ramón de la Torres Lopez depicting the Immigrant Experience, the prepackaged version delightful to some.

I sulked and lived and brooded and survived. I endured in my own self-loathingness and managed to finish my coursework. I got out of there without completing my thesis. I came back a year later.

I had my thesis done, in hand, and Ammons sitting across from me at a table, grilling me on it. He was hard. Its arrangement disappointed him. He quoted Aristotle to my everlasting vexation and sent me to the great philosopher to study form and order. They were one and the same. You couldn't mix and match too much, the way I had. Still, I passed the test and claimed my degree. I got the signatures I needed.

Then I saw him in the Dragon. Circumstances get cloudy. Perhaps I just chanced upon him in the haunt that forms some of my best memories of Cornell, some of my redeeming moments there, my time in the winter, with Ammons and crew, a couple of poets among us, with other regulars dropping in, early in the morning, after classes, in one of those unspoken arrangements people come to.

We sat at the weirdly shaped table—kidneyish and gray, bumpy and unstable—and drank coffee and talked.

Ammons said: "I wish somebody would smash that damn thing to bits!" when a pretentious poet stopped by, telling us how lucky he was to be going to Greece this summer to study the Parthenon on a grant.

"All that passion underneath it and this little box to reason." He shook his head, sincerely disgusted, and didn't glance up when the poet left, all stammerings and equivocations.

Ammons hardly noticed him.

We had good times there in the Dragon, and I formed a friendship with him, what could be called a student-teacher-relationship-warmed-by-kinship, for lack of a better word. He had chosen to be on my committee, and for that I am forever grateful. I needed a third member, and everybody else was dead or on sabbatical, so I asked him, in his office, among the booked-lined shelves and the papers dashed on his desk, if he would help me.

"Do what?" he asked. "Write the great American novel?"

"Just get out of here," I said.

I was sullen in my moodiness. I don't like being taken lightly when it comes to writing, and the great American novel is a bad joke to anyone now. Who needs the damn thing and I don't care about it.

I just wanted to get out of Cornell and on my way.

"Okay, but I'm a poet," he said. "I hope you know that."

"That's all right," I said. "I'll bring you stuff."

I wanted to write the great American short story, in truth, which would be unlike anything seen before, it would be Mexican-American. But I couldn't muster the energy, will, or confidence to do a single thing, so I just contented myself with bringing in scraps. I recycled stuff from my undergraduate days, more to keep busy, and brought in some sketches and drafty drafts he glanced over.

He was always encouraging. No matter what else he said, and he could be harsh, he would pick some good out and exclaim at it glowingly. "Look at that!" he might say. "My God! That's good! There's nothing like that!"

And I would always leave his office in a mood of hope, no matter how in-the-dumps the rest of my life was.

I was hopelessly beaten except for him. There were a few other mentors, too, mentioned early on, but Ammons takes his place among them as singular in his stature given to me. Not true. McConkey, and the worthwhile discussions in his office, was as important to me as Ammons and maybe more with a closer affinity I felt for him, personally, but maybe that is untrue, too. Maybe McConkey just heartened the prose writer in me with his lucid descriptions of all that was lacking in modern fiction, namely, believability and freshness, and his laying out of a whole aesthetic in his reasons for turning to personal nonfiction as his way out—to the essay. Maybe his warmth and degree of intelligence drew me to him as an antidote to Ammons's magnetism, colder and harder-seeming but actually as caring of human beings as anybody. Maybe I just liked them both in different ways, and they knew two guys in me in the same way I responded to them differently, each of them feeding a need in me as a young writer, as a human being. I valued them both.

And Herrin calling me at midnight: "I think you should change the ending!"

And Kennedy studying me over his desk, flinging a manuscript back at me, and saying, "Wow, I really like that story! Tell me what you're working on now!" referring to an undergraduate piece I had buffed for him, a tough-guy piece he really dug, because he was tough and from Albany, an Irish rake.

And Ammons telling me goodbye, our last meeting, so fraught with meaning for me, as inconsequential as it seems, no doubt, to you.

"She sure did do it right, didn't she?" he said. He was referring to a writer who had just made a splash in New York with her first book of stories.

"Yup, I guess she did," I said.

"But she won't last," he said. "She's no good."

We were standing outside the Green Dragon after our cup of coffee. The evening sunlight was slanting across the lawns, and the low humming of the insects buzzed in my ears.

"You got to work," he said, "and that's all." He put on his hat to leave, and I knew him to include himself among all those who weren't instant, who were hardworking and honorable, and that he considered me among that company working towards something bigger than us both.

The Missing Teacher: The Early Correspondence Between Josephine Miles and A. R. Ammons

Zofia Burr

TOWARD THE END of my first year at Cornell, a morning or two after Josephine Miles died in May 1985, I looked up from my work at the computer in the *Epoch* office to see Archie Ammons leaning heavily in the doorframe. When I met his eyes, he said, "My teacher died." I have no memory of what I said next, or what more he said, but many times since then I've reflected on what was to me a surprising affirmation in the way he said, "my teacher." Though I knew Miles had in some way been his teacher and remained his friend, I knew as his student that even when Archie was not outright resisting the role of teacher, he questioned the value and possibility of its efficacy. And so I was taken aback by the claim to his own role as a student that "my teacher" contained—a role that in this iteration sounded as fundamental in the present as it had ever been in the past.

Miles had been a regular character in our conversations. Because I'd come to Cornell from the San Francisco Bay Area where her influence was significant, she served as the point of connection on which we built our connection, and through which we negotiated our differences. And to his MFA students more generally, he offered her work as an example of concision not loaded with the weight of unnecessary difficulty that he thought burdened the poetry of our generation. He also spoke warmly about the support she gave him early on, but he was also always quick to say she hadn't actually influenced him, and that, in fact, he thought of their projects as somewhat opposed. On both these points, I initially took him at his word. But when I first came across some of Archie's letters to Miles, I began to read a more complicated and interesting relationship between them. Their correspondence from the 1950s provides an entrance onto the ground that defined the profound connection between these poets, and on which their disagreements about poetry emerged. It also illuminates Ammons's struggle with the concept of a "teacher" in general, and what was ultimately a productive resistance to Miles herself.

In the spring of 1951, when A. R. Ammons was twenty-five and in his second semester of graduate work at U.C. Berkeley, he asked Josephine Miles to read some of his poetry. The winner of the Shelley Award in 1935, author of three volumes of poetry and of three critical studies, Miles was well placed to be a young poet's first contact with the public world of poetry. She was also a generous teacher with extraordinary perspective on the limits and possibilities of that role. And the effect of her response to those first poems was monumental. Writing to Miles three years after that first meeting between them, Ammons referred to that "milestone (forgive me) hour" in which she first offered him both encouragement for the work he had shown her and a "plan" to extend and develop those poems into the "unity" that became Ommateum (August 22, 1954).[1]

1. The bulk of the correspondence between Ammons and Miles is housed in Kroch Library at Cornell University (collection number: 14-12-2665). And the letters I quote here are in that collection. Most of the letters are filed chronologically in Ammons's journals. Some of Ammons's correspondence to Miles is housed with the Josephine Miles Papers at the Bancroft Library, University of California at Berkeley

After Ammons left Berkeley, Miles became a significant inter-locutor. And in the years before he achieved critical recognition, Miles was among the few who stood between him and professional isolation. His contact with her represented the possibility that he would not always be separate from the public world of poetry. Writing Miles late in the spring of 1958 about developments in his own work and about the possibility of editing a little magazine, he signals her role in tempering the isolation: "I'm sitting over here feeling I know what I'm about—but so isolated as to what others are thinking, I guess that's another reason I wanted to be an editor. So glad to know you, so long, and so forth" (May 10, 1958). Not that the companionship provided by her correspondence kept him from writerly isolation, for the sense that no one else could really help him with his writing shaped his early practice. About a month before he first met with Miles, he records in his journal a particularly insistent assertion of writerly autonomy: "A writer must know how to improve his own work; there is no one else to tell him because no one else can know the writer as well as he himself does" (March 29, 1951). Nevertheless, he engaged Miles in reading his poems, and he solicited her advice about publishing, and he shared with her his moody process. In return, Miles offered criticism and praise of specific poems, advice and support about publishing, and a sense of balance and perspective.

Two years into the correspondence, it's clear, however, that all Miles's help had not convinced Ammons that he could be helped by another, yet what he says about what her help "means and has meant" to him suggests the value it had. Writing Miles in the spring of 1953, Ammons reiterates his doubt that anyone else can help him find his "peculiar expression" in the same breath that he indirectly registers the efficacy of the other side of the pedagogical equation: the student's motivation to give some-

---

(collection number: 86/107). A selection of this correspondence was published in *Epoch* 52.3 (Spring 2004).

thing to the teacher, in this case, to "amuse" her: "I am very much lost and not certain that anyone else *can* help me find my peculiar expression, but so long as I can amuse you—I hope I am amusing you—perhaps you won't find the task too hard, though I'm afraid you're on the giving end" (March 26, 1953). What Miles is "giving" Ammons, by this account, is her willingness to play the role of interlocutor and audience as he both solicits her advice and denies its potential efficacy. "Please be ruthless," Ammons asks Miles in a letter about the manuscript of *Hymns & Other Poems,*[2] "I must write at least one good poem in this life" (undated, circa January 1958). In the same letter, he also asks her to write a "critical, explanatory introduction" for the book. But such appeals are circumscribed by the strictures of his solitude. In September 1954, he writes to Miles, "I dream about how much I would like to be in somebody's poetry class or helping get out some publication of poetry—having many, many friends," but this dream was not to come true. As he says in the same letter, "It hath been writ, no matter how much I dislike it, I must keep myself sealed off: the only time I dare express any force is when I'm alone" (September 7, 1954).

And the borders of this solitude, as they defined the ground on which he could express what he understood as his singular poetic "force," came to frame his poetics, a poetics defined by spatial as well as ontological distance from his interlocutors and discursive conventions of address. It was a distance designed to bridge the distance its existence bespoke. Speaking thirty years later, Ammons describes how (ideally) the singularity of the speaker outside conventions of address is, in fact, what makes it possible to convey his presence to an audience, albeit one of "single" persons. "What I try to do is through the work possible in writing the poem, I try to create a poem that will come as close as possible to saying the kind of place I am, where I am

2. This was an early draft of the manuscript that ultimately became *Expressions of Sea Level,* 1964.

and what seems to me to be central, and so one . . . As a single person. And then my highest hope is that some equally single, some other person will find that poem and say, 'Yes, this is true for me as well.'"[3] Building on this idea in 1993, Ammons continues to argue that it's at a distance from discursive conventions of address that communication is most successful: "So I was thinking, isn't that an interesting form of address when you don't address anyone. And I would think that this is an important part of what poetry makes possible. There it seems that all conventional means of addressing someone have been put aside and yet the pressure to communicate a presence is never greater or more successfully done."[4] In maintaining such distance from the idea of address and dialogue, Ammons is at his greatest remove from his "teacher" Miles, who is eminently a poet who incorporates other voices and constructs implicit and explicit dialogues between differing perspectives. Ammons in his solitude and Miles engaged with what she called "the drama of somebody else's thought" might seem like unlikely interlocutors.[5] And yet they read and supported and cherished each other as poets—even while they energetically resisted each other's poetry.

Though Miles's overall response to Ammons's early work was certainly very positive, his early penchant for what he identified as poetic "synthesis" at a distance from the "material plane" was clearly not to her taste. Writing in response to a version of what became "Five Praying Poets" (then called "Seven

3. Jim Stahl, "The Unassimilable Fact Leads Us On . . ." *Pembroke Magazine* 18 (1986) 77–85. Reprinted in A. R. Ammons, *Set in Motion: Essays, Interviews, & Dialogues,* edited by Zofia Burr (Ann Arbor: University of Michigan Press, 1996), 41–55, qtd. 51.

4. Zofia Burr, "Perversity, Propaganda, and Poetry," in A. R. Ammons, *Set in Motion,* 73–84, qtd. 73.

5. Josephine Miles, *Poetry, Teaching, and Scholarship. An Interview Conducted by Ruth Teiser and Catherine Harroun in 1977 and 1979.* University History Series (Berkeley: The Bancroft Library, University of California at Berkeley, 1980), 90.

Poets"), she concluded: "You're darn good on infinity, but I'd still like to read you on a glass factory or New Jersey. No?" (August 22, 1955). A few weeks later, he responds to this with an explanation of his position as it was determined by an experience that forever altered his sense of reality and perspective:

> For an instant, about ten years ago, I *felt* the perspective from space to earth. Sick as I may have been, I was *there*. By use of the intelligence, of course, you can work up such perspectives at will, but it's a very different thing from *being* there—in the mixture of joy and of a sort of mad sorrow at the lot of man. What I seemed to see has remained literally the weight of the world. . . . I mean by all this to say that from that position I can't become interested in a glass factory or in describing material objects for their emotive values or in "creating a mood" for the reader, when there is a perfectly cool, adequate, predetermined "mood" inherent in my position, requiring no bamboozling, coloring, or falsification. . . . (September 12, 1955)

As this discussion continues and develops, Ammons identifies a continuum on which both of their projects can be mapped, the ends of which correspond to the traditionally opposed concepts of "concrete" and "abstract." For Ammons, the main difficulty is that in choosing "the small thing" to "illuminate the general," you are on "the material plane with its illimitable diversities," where there may be nothing to "save" you—that is, nothing to lead you toward the "all-comprehending" "synthesis" that he takes as the goal of poetry.

> Really I don't think there is any disagreement between us on the matter of the concrete and the abstract. You say the small things illustrate or illuminate the general, which I wholly accept. My point was that the poet himself must have arrived at the general before he knows what small

thing to select for illustration. Thus, if the poet intends to work from an intellectual stratum, rather than an emotional one (not that one is necessarily superior to *or different from* [written in] the other), he must have made some kind of synthesis that hangs together. The truth is, the only way I can manage such a synthesis is to rise to the fuzzy: to Energy, as the all-comprehending substance, in and out of which all winds. But that is nothing but a word. If you stay on the material plane with its illimitable diversities, what in the devil is there to save you? (November 28, 1955)

But, in a nod to her critique, a few years later he notes the problems with such "syntheses": "I am writing some poems, now and then, but am so tired of doing the same thing, the same type, over and over, and of discovering that every time I try another direction I slump. . . . I suppose I've synthesized myself up so high that there's nothing to talk about and, as in the poems, nothing to do but sit down" (August 8, 1957).

Miles characteristically contextualizes her own advice to Ammons within a play of voices and perspectives, her own and his first of all, but also including editors and readers more generally. Soon after the publication of *Ommateum,* and at the end of an extraordinarily detailed exchange over the draft of the poem "Having carried off the boundary stones,"[6] Miles offers this perspective: "You do ask all the $64 questions, but seriously, I don't think there's any north star for you, but just a lot of complicated navigation. What any editor says individually doesn't matter unless it rings some sort of bell for your own hunches, & if a *lot* of eds agree, why then you might listen, but still maybe yr. just ahead of yr time" (July 4, 1955). She follows this with some specific advice about how to keep himself writing, and then offers an unusually direct evaluation of his poetry as a whole: "You

6. See "Having carried off the boundary stones" with letter of May 20, 1955, in *Epoch* 52.3.

know my own judgment of your poetry is that it's wonderful at times, with a lot of ceremonial and obscure dross, but moments of nonchalant wise & humorous insight. Now who is to say you cd have the one without the other?" Though the comment here about "ceremonial and obscure dross" must have stung,[7] the suggestion that this aspect of his work might, in fact, be necessary to its "insight" likely struck a chord. Perhaps he made use of it as his work loosened up to include the fuller range of modes that his later work explored (and perhaps it was the kernel for the idea that what readers identify as a fault in a piece of work may somehow be key to its realization, which became one of the tenets of his pedagogy). However critical, the impulse guiding Miles's intervention here is an abiding confidence in the possibilities of Ammons's poetry. Though, for instance, when she challenges his determination to assert his "own associations over other people's" in making sense of his poems, she also suggests he may be able to get away with it: "Your letter explaining the puzzle[8] seemed arbitrary to me—you want to assert your own associations over other people's willy-nilly—as in the "Ezra" example.[9] But maybe you can get good enough to get away with it; why should not your Ezra outlast Pound, if you insist. Think about the world you are in and the place you seek in it. Meanwhile, cheers, J" (July 4, 1955). Ammons responds to this letter both with gratitude and with a characteristic admission: "Dear Miss Miles, You turn out wiser than the others: you always stand me back on my own two feet. Actually, I like to stand on my own two feet—in deepest privacy, probably do so, or would

---

7. And a letter he wrote in the context of their disagreement about Miles's *The Poem* makes it clear the comment sticks with him. Refuting her categorization of his poetry, he refers to "what you once called ceremonious dross . . ." (circa February/March 1959).

8. "Having carried off the boundary stones" is something of a "puzzle" to Miles.

9. Ammons explains that "the name Ezra is one of those private associations," not associated with Pound (May 20, 1955).

do so, belligerently. But sometimes it seems so appealingly sweet
to lean, resting on other arms, as on waves" (July 7, 1955). Balancing the autonomy of standing on one's own two feet against
an acknowledgment of the help (often) required to achieve that
stance, an acknowledgment that threatens the autonomy of the
image, Ammons proceeds to construct the connection between
himself and Miles as one in which he remains somewhat
autonomous. He's able to make this work, in part, by responding to Miles's work, demonstrating his ability to provide figura-
tive "arms" on which she might lean.

Early on, Ammons finds great value in Miles's work: "Your
poetry reminds me of a wood-knot: beautiful, suggestive, asym-
metrical (your syntax), uncompromising"(March 8, 1953), but
he resists the more discursive aspects of her project, her poems
that by their particular investments in the "material plane"
(such as "votes and campaigns") can't meet his ideals for synthesis: "Concerning 'The Campaign'¹⁰ I believe I would say at
this premature point that the poetry is certainly better than what
it is *for* . . . if that makes any kind of sense." And in a remarkable claim for a poet who eschews the role of the "teacher" and
insists on the integrity of solitude, he admits that what he wants
her poetry to do is not what she wants. "You have done what
you wanted to do so beautifully, with such counterpoint, tensions between opposite forces. Still, I have to admit, it is not
what I want you to do" (November 28, 1955). The frustration
he most dramatically associates with her work, however, is not
directly associated with either its subject matter or its goals, but
with how her choices bear on the reader's role, and, specifically,
on how he experiences himself as a reader of her work. In
response to *Prefabrications,* he resists her reading of her poems,
her direction for them, and the popular critical reading of her
work, and offers an extended description of his frustration in
reading them:

10. *Hudson Review* 8 (Fall 1955) 386. *Collected Poems,* 118–120.

Here again the jacket has to be endured: "Simple everyday events . . ." Everybody is prepared to say that you strike the concrete, simple, everyday event. Your reverberations however have been neglected. There is one thing you have, even more than the great of the past, above all others: you are a mirror to each reader. Your poems allow him to take his depth: he finds what he brings. He finds a capacity that meets his capacity. So, you can appeal to the least and to the most responsive. . . .

But there is no use to talk of such things. The fact is, I cannot understand your poems. When you sound me, you mark less than twain. Not that I don't get drifts and enjoy them, especially since when you are simplest you are most moving and profound, while when you are difficult you are very often contrived. . . . It is a beautiful book, and it's good the economy won't hear how many man-hours I'll put in reading it to no commercial profit. Long familiarity, which sometimes mitigates my inadequacy, always turns your poems into durable beauty: but at first I am flabbergasted, hurt, and restless. (December 5, 1955)

That the reader finds some of what he brings to the poetry is, of course, somewhat true of reading all poetry, but it's hard to know what to make of his saying that what he finds is that he can't understand the work. What's clear is that he wants to value her poems even as they go against his sense of poetic value. He wants to value her work as the work of his mentor, and to find her work to be like his, like what he wants his work to be. He wants to find in her poetry *what he brings* and is frustrated not to find it easy to do so. At the base of the struggle between them is a disagreement he sums up when he characterizes her work as "your beautiful, mystical verse which you think is so cussed concrete" (October 23, 1959).

This disagreement is connected to a more fundamental divergence in their views on what Ammons called the poet's search

for his or her own "peculiar expression." Miles's literary scholarship argued that poets who are contemporaries share a poetic
idiom, the idiom of the age, more fully than they realize, while
Ammons was equally convinced that the true poet in effect creates his own age. In some contrast to her apparent alignment
with the specificities of the "material plane" in Ammons's
assessment of the differences in their poetries, as a teacher and a
critic, Miles was always interested in categories and generalization, in creating models and producing syntheses, of observing
poets' likenesses and placing them within historical trends. As a
poet in the romantic tradition, Ammons resisted the categorization of poetry within such "neat" structures, or "inadequate
syntheses" in favor of acknowledging the unique complexity
that exceeds models. On these grounds he objected to her mode
of categorizing poems in her textbook, *The Poem: A Critical
Anthology* (1959). In this, she grouped poems by person and
tone, and by way of the traditional distinctions between narrative, dramatic, and lyric poetry. Affronted by Miles's "neat"
structures, Ammons responded with his strongest critique of her,
writing at least three drafts of his initial letter about it.[11] In the
first draft, he criticizes Miles and the audience who will make
use of her book: "You have a fine book. Your finest contribution, though, is in the implicit analysis of the need for ONE
book to do all that! and the way you went about doing it. All the
country professors will love you. But to barge in where there
aren't any docks, . . . it seems to me that your structure is at any
given point infinitely too partial to do justice to any poem
involved in that point of structure" (February 15, 1959). She
responds to his objections coolly—as ever—suggesting that his
poems fit well into the chapter on "Poems in the first person": "I
think the tone & person . . . get down to craft amazingly closely.

11. ARA's initial response to the anthology is extant in two letters
drafted February 15 and 20, marked "not mailed," and one dated the
24th that he has written across. All three contain basically the same
objections.

For example, you are utterly in ch III! No?" (March 4, 1959). This, of course, enrages him. He refutes the generalization both by pointing out that not all of his poems are in the first person, and by claiming a much more complex status for the first person than her model allows. (His poems, he argues, are "lyrical, dramatic, and narrative" at once, the three modes she has distinguished.) In the final letter he sends her on this topic, he suggests that the solution might be to employ such a structure, but then to explicitly defeat it in some instance, to show its partialness. This would be in keeping with his sense of the poem as always driven by the individual and unassimilable, but it would also, perhaps, be a challenge to the idea of synthesis.

Despite such apparently fundamental differences of approach to poetry, what is striking is the extent to which Ammons resisted Miles not to distance himself from her, but in order to draw her closer as one like him. Years of correspondence with Miles in which she offered much that Ammons considered "helpful" would not dislodge the sense that a writer really couldn't be helped to find the "expression" that was exceptionally his. Nor would Miles have expected it to, as she says to him when he asks if she would accept the dedication of *Ommateum*: "the poems are wholly yours" (August 27, 1954). In the discipline of his solitude, Ammons found company in the conversation through which he articulated his difference from Miles. Miles clearly had an aesthetic to which much of Ammons's work did not conform, but because of the kind of teacher she was, eclectic to the root, responsive to the project in front of her whether it was a project she would have sympathy for or not, she was the right partner in correspondence—a correspondence colored throughout by resistance, but punctuated occasionally by moments of convergence.

The early correspondence between Ammons and Miles testifies if not to Miles's influence on Ammons's poetry per se, then to the use he made of what she offered him to make himself as a poet. Repeatedly, he uses her suggestions as the occasion to articulate his own poetics; in resisting her aesthetic preferences, he articulates and defends his own. And it testifies to the example she provided him as a teacher, a model of teaching that was in keeping with his sense of the solitude of the writer. Following this model, he taught his students that it was our job to sift through the comments that are offered, and to embrace as peculiarly our own the "fault" as it was pointed out by another. He would say if people are telling you that something they're noticing about your poems is bothering them, really sticking out, then this is the aspect to pursue because it may be the new or unassimilable element that defines your particular project as your own. By this account, the teacher can only help you see your own work insofar as her observations of it help you see what separates your vision from others. It would not emerge as a point of connection, but could become a connection if fully pursued. This was a model in keeping with his sense of a speaker who is so fully present in his solitude that he has the potential to be present to offer his "reality" to another.

In the first draft of the letter Ammons wrote Miles in response to *The Poem,* he qualifies his objections to her book by describing his perspective as limited as a result of his teacherless state: "But you are a great woman and a great mind and know very many things while I have never been able to know anything except what gave birth inside myself. Not trusting the inner process, I go around begging the spaces of South Jersey to materialize a teacher for me" (February 15, 1959). In the next draft, he is more direct: "Plow into me for my criticisms but consider my stupidity. I don't have you for a teacher" (February 20, 1959). In both these passages we see Ammons's characteristic stance in this period: as he reaches out for mentoring from Miles, he suggests that looking outside himself involves a betrayal of "the inner process." For Ammons, the teacher is always absent even as he calls on her presence. Though the connection between Ammons and Miles endured and took many forms, Ammons's voicing of it never relinquished this double gesture, even, perhaps especially, when he said, "My teacher died."

NOTES ON THE CONTRIBUTORS

INGRID ARNESEN is a senior lecturer in the Intensive English Program at Cornell University. A poet and translator, her work has appeared in *Concourse, The Bookpress,* and in the *1993 Nordic Poetry Festival Anthology.*

JOHN ASHBERY is the author of numerous books of poetry, most recently *Chinese Whispers* and *Where Shall I Wander.* His *Selected Prose* was published in 2004 by the University of Michigan Press. He is Charles P. Stevenson Jr. Professor of Language and Literature at Bard College.

HAROLD BLOOM is the author of twenty-five books of criticism, most recently *Hamlet: Poem Unlimited* and *Where Shall Wisdom Be Found?* His anthology *The Best Poems of the English Language, From Chaucer Through Frost* was published in 2004 by HarperCollins. He is Sterling Professor of Humanities at Yale University.

CYNTHIA BOND received her MFA in poetry from Cornell University in 1987. Her work has appeared in *Ascent, Epoch,* and *Best American Poetry 1994,* among other places. She currently lives in Chicago where she teaches courses in legal writing and law and film.

JOHN BREHM is the author of *Sea of Faith,* which won The University of Wisconsin Press Brittingham Prize in 2004, and a chapbook, *The Way Water Moves,* published by Flume Press in 2002. He is the associate editor of *The Oxford Book of American Poetry,* forthcoming in 2005. A graduate of Cornell's MFA program, he lives in Brooklyn, New York, and works as a freelance writer.

FREDERICK BUELL is professor of English at Queens College. An expert on globalization, environment, and culture, his most recent books are *National Culture and the New Global System* and *From Apocalypse to Way of Life: Environmental Crisis in the American Century.*

DAVID BURAK is the author of three chapbooks of poetry, including *Celebration After the Discovery of a Premature Burial* and *The Dualist*, for which Archie Ammons provided the cover art. He is also the coordinator of The Theater of Ideas, through which he has helped arrange lectures and has conducted local-access television interviews with a broad range of scholars, writers, and public figures, from Jorge Luis Borges and Wole Soyinka to Daniel Ellsberg and M. H. Abrams. He teaches English at Santa Monica College.

ZOFIA BURR is the author of *Of Women, Poetry, and Power: Strategies of Address in the Poetry of Dickinson, Miles, Brooks, Lorde, and Angelou*, and is the editor of *Set in Motion: Essays, Interviews & Dialogues*, by A. R. Ammons. Her poetry has most recently appeared in *Delmar, So to Speak*, and a number of collaborative installations shown and performed in various venues, including Mobius Gallery in Boston, Artemisia in Chicago, and Soho 20 Chelsea in New York. She teaches English at George Mason University.

BONNIE COSTELLO is the author of several books on modern poetry, most recently *Shifting Ground: Reinventing Landscape in Modern American Poetry.* She is professor of English at Boston University.

DANIEL MARK FOGEL studied with A. R. Ammons as an undergraduate and graduate student at Cornell University in the 1960s and 1970s. A poet and literary scholar, he has published on Henry James, James Joyce, Virginia Woolf, English Romanticism, and twentieth-century American poetry, including, in addition to the essay in the present volume, pieces on Ammons in *Diacritics* and in *Contemporary Poetry*. He founded, and for sixteen years edited, the *Henry James Review* at Louisiana State University, where he was a professor of English and executive vice Chancellor and provost before his appointment in 2002 as president of the University of Vermont, where he is also a professor of English.

ALICE FULTON's *Cascade Experiment: Selected Poems* recently appeared from W. W. Norton. Her previous book, *Felt*, received the 2002 Bobbitt Award from the Library of Congress. She is the Anne S. Bowers Professor of English at Cornell University.

ROGER GILBERT is the author of *Walks in the World: Representation and Experience in Modern American Poetry*. He recently edited a special issue of the literary magazine *Epoch* devoted entirely to the life and work of A. R. Ammons. He is currently writing a critical biography of Ammons, for which he has been awarded a Guggenheim fellowship. He is professor of English at Cornell University.

STEPHEN D. GUTIERREZ is the author of *Elements*, which won the Charles H. and N. Mildred Nilon Excellence in Minority Fiction Award. He teaches in the Creative Writing Department at California State University, Hayward.

ROALD HOFFMANN came to Cornell University at about the same time as Archie Ammons, where they became friends. He has published five collections of poetry, most recently *Soliton*. A Nobel Laureate in Chemistry, he is Frank H. T. Rhodes Professor of Humane Letters at Cornell.

RICHARD HOWARD is the author of twelve volumes of poetry, most recently *Inner Voices: Selected Poems, 1963–2003*, and has published more than one hundred fifty translations from the

French. He is also the author of *Alone with America: Essays on the Art of Poetry in the United States since 1950*, first published in 1969 and expanded in 1980. He is currently poetry editor for *The Paris Review*. He teaches literature in the School of the Arts (Writing Division) at Columbia University.

JOSEPHINE JACOBSEN published eight books of poetry, including *In the Crevice of Time: New and Collected Poems*. She was also the author of three short-story collections and three books of criticism, most recently *The Instant of Knowing: Lectures, Criticism, and Occasional Pieces*, edited by Elizabeth Spires. She died in 2004.

DAVID KALSTONE was the author of three books of criticism, including *Becoming a Poet: Elizabeth Bishop with Marianne Moore and Robert Lowell*, published posthumously in 1989. At the time of his death in 1986, he was professor of English at Rutgers University.

DAVID LEHMAN is the author of six books of poetry, most recently *When a Woman Loves a Man*. Since 1987 he has been series editor of the annual *Best American Poetry* anthology. He is also the editor of *The Oxford Book of American Poetry*, forthcoming in 2005. He interviewed A. R. Ammons for *The Paris Review* and has published several essays on his work. He teaches in the Creative Writing program at New School University.

KENNETH MCCLANE is the author of eight books of poems, including *Take Five: Collected Poems, 1971–1986*, and a volume of personal essays, *Walls*. As a sophomore at Cornell University, he was privileged to have been taught by A. R. Ammons, who made him understand that poetry was as essential as air. He is W. E. B. Dubois Professor of English at Cornell.

JAMES MCCONKEY is the author of, most recently, *The Telescope in the Parlor*. His other books include *Court of Memory*,

Stories from my Life with the Other Animals, and *To a Distant Island*. He is Goldwin Smith Professor of English Literature Emeritus at Cornell University.

JOSEPHINE MILES was the author of eleven books of poetry, including *Collected Poems, 1930–83*. Her books of criticism include *Eras and Modes in English Poetry* and *Poetry and Change: Donne, Milton, Wordsworth, and the Equilibrium of the Present*. At the time of her death in 1985 she was University Professor of English Emerita at the University of California, Berkeley.

HELEN VENDLER is the author of sixteen books of criticism, most recently *Coming of Age as a Poet: Milton, Keats, Eliot, Plath* and *Poets Thinking: Pope, Whitman, Dickinson, Yeats*. She is the Arthur Kingsley Porter University Professor at Harvard.

PERMISSIONS

cuse Herald American (March 11, 2001). Copyright © 2001 by David Burak. Reprinted by permission of the author.

"Answering the Phone: A Reminiscence of A. R. Ammons" by John Brehm. From *The Manhattan Review* 10:2 (Winter 2003). Copyright © 2003 by John Brehm. Reprinted by permission of the author.

"Ammons Outside the Dragon" by Stephen Gutierrez. Previously unpublished. Copyright © 2004 by Stephen Gutierrez. Printed by permission of the author.

"The Missing Teacher: The Early Correspondence of A. R. Ammons and Josephine Miles" by Zofia Burr. Previously unpublished. Copyright © 2004 by Zofia Burr. Printed by permission of the author.

"Birthday Poem to My Wife" by A. R. Ammons. From *The New Yorker* 73:32 (October 20–27, 1997). Copyright © 1997 by A. R. Ammons. Reprinted by permission of the author's estate.

CPSIA information can be obtained at www.ICGtesting.com
Printed in the USA
LVOW08*2020010616

490809LV00001B/7/P